Volatile States in International Politics

Volatile States
in International Politics

ELEONORA MATTIACCI

OXFORD
UNIVERSITY PRESS

OXFORD
UNIVERSITY PRESS

Oxford University Press is a department of the University of Oxford. It furthers the University's objective of excellence in research, scholarship, and education by publishing worldwide. Oxford is a registered trade mark of Oxford University Press in the UK and certain other countries.

Published in the United States of America by Oxford University Press
198 Madison Avenue, New York, NY 10016, United States of America.

© Oxford University Press 2023

Library of Congress Control Number: 2022913247
ISBN 978–0–19–763868–2 (pbk.)
ISBN 978–0–19–763867–5 (hbk.)

DOI: 10.1093/oso/9780197638675.001.0001

Omnia mutantur, nihil interit.
Everything changes, nothing perishes.

Ovid, Metamorphoses, Book XV, line 165

Contents

Acknowledgments

This book is the product of many conversations over the course of more than a decade. I am thrilled to have a chance to thank all those people who have helped me along the way.

This project started as a dissertation at The Ohio State University. There, as a student, I had the pleasure to work with a great group of scholars: Janet Box-Steffensmeier, Ted Hopf, Luke Keele, and Irfan Nooruddin. Each of them provided important inspiration for the project and were extremely generous with their time. I will strive to pay forward what I cannot possibly pay back. Bear Braumoeller has been the best dissertation advisor I could hope for. Reading his work or discussing International Relations with him feels like taking a peek into a kaleidoscope: brand new puzzles and captivating perspectives emerge anew. He always makes things sound worthy of exploring further, inspiring his students to push forward with their research. The fundamental idea behind this book owes a lot to our conversations.

At Ohio State, I found a fun and engaged community of students who looked at the field of International Relations from different perspectives and was not afraid to argue about it. It was a pleasure to bounce back and forth ideas in various workshops on the material that would then become this book. My biggest thanks go to Bentley Allan, Zoltán Búzás, Austin Carson, Aldous Cheung, Eunbin Chun, Kevin Duska Jr., Matt Hitt, Fernando Nunez-Mietz, Srdjan Vucetic, and Joshua Wu.

My senior colleagues in the Political Science Department at Amherst College have been crucial in both providing me with time to write this book and instilling in me the desire to do so. I am very grateful to Amrita Basu, Kristin Bumiller, Javier Corrales, Tom Dumm, Pavel Machala, and Austin Sarat for all their support. My junior colleagues Kerry Ratigan and Ruxandra Paul have provided me with great peer support, commenting on different parts of the manuscript. Theresa and Steve Laizer have helped immensely with the book conference, among other things. Provost and Dean of Faculty Catherine Epstein and Associate Provosts Janet Tobin and Jack Cheney have been extremely helpful with the logistics and monetary aspects associated with my research for this book.

In 2019, Benjamin O. Fordham, Jeffrey Friedman, Joshua D. Kertzer, Michaela Mattes, and Sara McLaughlin Mitchell agreed to come to Amherst to discuss an earlier draft of this book. They were very generous with their time and their insights. It was an engaging, productive, and fun book conference—one of my most cherished memories. Thank you.

Several colleagues at other institutions generously provided comments on various segments of this manuscript. I would like to thank in particular Mlada Bukovanski, Charlie Carpenter, Jeff Carter, Adam Dean, Brent Durbin, Vinnie Ferraro, Stacey Goddard, Joe Grieco, Kyle Haynes, Marcus Holmes, Johannes Karreth, Danielle Lupton, Emy Matesan, Rupal N. Mehta, Alexander Montgomery, Paul Musgrave, Bryan Nakayama, Mark David Nieman, Brian Rathbun, Dominic Tierney, David Traven, Greg White, Rachel Elisabeth Whitlark, and Amy Yuen.

The fantastic Erin R. Graham has shared her thoughts on key parts of the book and put up with a lot of angst over the phone as I wrote. The wonderful Benjamin T. Jones commented on various parts of the book, cheered, and helped meet our projects' deadlines while I was working on the book. The peerless Joshua D. Kertzer has been (thankfully and very generously!) involved with various parts and stages of this project, while his creative and rigorous book on resolve in international politics has provided an inspiration. The late and much-beloved Nuno P. Monteiro guided me through the publishing maze with his usual combo of competence and flair: I miss him a lot. The remarkable Kathleen E. Powers has lovingly yet sternly kept me accountable through many years, every day, asking, "Are you working on your book?" while writing her own great book on nationalism. She's also commented on key parts of the book. There are no words to express my admiration and gratitude to these people.

At Oxford University Press (OUP), I was very fortunate to work with David McBride, who, not surprisingly, came highly recommended from fellow authors. Emily Benitez and Jubilee James on the OUP production team were wonderful in guiding me through the process. Two anonymous reviewers read the book: they were both very thorough and very encouraging. I am grateful for their time and their engagement with the manuscript. Elena Abbot edited key areas of the book, providing me with much-needed guidance on how to write more effectively. Mary Elizabeth Strunk at Amherst College kindly read and re-read (and re-re-read) various versions of the Introduction. Hsiu-Ann Tom and Carrie Tallichet Smith helped me research the archives at, respectively, the JFK and the LBJ Libraries.

At Amherst College, I had the pleasure to work with several under-graduate research assistants through the Gregory Call Internship Fund first and then the IR Lab. Their help and their enthusiasm have proved key to finishing the book. Some of my most cherished memories of this book are of working with them. I am quite proud of all they went on to accomplish. I would like to thank in particular Carl Cate, Claire Dennis, Andrew Drinkwater, Richard Figueroa, Dakota C. Foster, Gabrielle Francois, Victoria Gallastegui, Conner Glynn, Olivia Henrikson, Pauline Herbert-Whiting, Ian Husler Matute, David Lee, Spencer Michaels, Taylor Pelletier, Andrew Smith, Jeremy N. Thomas, Jessica Valbrum, Alexander (Gib) Versfeld, and Rebecca Wistreich.

As with every project stretching over the course of many years, good friends have been crucial: Alessandra, Emanuela, and Sara; Adam and Elana; Audrey and Nuno; Ben and Erica; Caroline and Josh; Carrie, Julia, Kiara, and Vanessa; Catherine and Jose; Davide and Pier; Devin and Sara; Francesco, Gaspare, and Lucia; Hannah and Robin; Harris and Marcy; Jeff and Kathryn; Josh and Nick; and Kevin and Kirsten. Thank you for all the cheering, the listening, and the encouragement.

My father, Marco Mattiacci, has read many, many books. He made immense sacrifices to allow both his kids to graduate from college, and then more sacrifices to help with the completion of this book. He never complained about anything. My sister, Valeria Mattiacci, who has been the most loving of all cheerleaders, never asked if I was done with the book (thank you!). And my grandmother Maria Antonietta Albanesi, the rock of the family, has been an inspiration for many things, including this book. This book wouldn't have been possible without their unwavering support—nor would it have been as meaningful to me.

A huge thank you also goes to my family of destination: my son, Cosmo, who made it very hard to justify time spent away from his lovely, opinionated, funny self, and my beloved husband, Jonathan Obert. Throughout several very, very volatile years, he kept his faith in this project, even when I had lost it. He stood by my side on the very good days, the very bad ones, and all the days in between. He listened, read, discussed, advised, and cheered, all with great generosity. I am proud of and very grateful for all his love, wisdom, humor, intellectual curiosity, and good looks. I admire him deeply for his original and rigorous scholarly work. His opinion about the book was always the one that mattered the most to me. Thank you both: this book is for you.

As I was finishing my book, two very important people suddenly passed away: my mother, Lucia Senigagliesi, who was very supportive of the project and never got tired of hearing about it, and my baby son, Wally, who passed away just a few hours before being born. Both of them experienced lots of volatility before passing. Their experience inspired me to think harder about why I wanted to write a book on volatility—about what we can really gain from understanding volatility. I miss them a lot. *Sit vobis terra levis.*

Amherst, MA

January 2022

List of Abbreviations

ARIMA	Autoregressive integrated moving average
ATOP	Alliance Treaty Obligations and Provision
BTA	bilateral trade agreements
CAMEO	Conflict and Mediation Event Observations
CHISOLS	Change in Source of Leader Support
CIMMSS	Cross-National Indices of Multi-Dimensional Measures of Social Structure
CINC	Composite Index of National Capabilities
COPDAB	Conflict and Peace Data Bank
COW	Correlates of War
ECSC	European Coal and Steel Community
EDC	European Defense Community
EEC	European Economic Community
FDI	foreign direct investments
FRUS	Foreign Relations of the United States
GDP	gross domestic product
ICB	International Crisis Behavior
ICPSR	Inter-university Consortium for Political and Social Research
ICEWS	Integrated Crisis Early Warning System
IMF	International Monetary Fund
IR	International Relations
JFKPL	John Fitzgerald Kennedy Presidential Library
LEAD	Leader Experience and Attribute Descriptions
LBJPL	Lyndon B. Johnson Presidential Library
MFN	Most Favored Nation
MID	Militarized Inter-state Disputes
MLF	Multilateral Force
NATO	North Atlantic Treaty Organization
NSF	National Security Files
SARMA	seasonal, autoregressive moving average
SEATO	Southeast Asia Treaty Organization
SMART	State Messaging and Archive Retrieval Toolkit
UN	United Nations
UNGA	United Nations General Assembly
UNSC	United Nations Security Council
WEIS	World Events/Interactions Survey
WTO	World Trade Organization

1

Introduction

On paper, India and Cuba are very different countries. Sitting more than 9,000 miles from one another, they boast different histories, political regimes, leaders, and economies. Yet, in 2015, they shared the spotlight on the international stage as each became part of a momentous reconciliation.

The so-called Cuban thaw between the United States and Cuba was first announced in December 2014 and unfolded over the following year. The rapprochement catalyzed several policy changes that would have seemed unthinkable in the previous five decades.[1] Many observers heralded it as historic and potentially highly consequential.[2] President Barack Obama himself presented the rapprochement as "one of the most significant changes in our policy in more than 50 years."[3] In March 2016, he became the first sitting US president in almost a century to visit Cuba. Meanwhile, on the other side of the world, another important rapprochement was commencing. In December 2015, Indian Prime Minister Narendra Modi traveled to Pakistan and met with Pakistani Prime Minister Nawaz Sharif. The meeting was deemed historic: it was the first time an Indian prime minister had visited Pakistan in more than a decade.[4] Commentators welcomed the event as a sign of easing tensions between the two countries and possibly even a harbinger of deeper cooperation.[5]

Both of these rapprochements came on the heels of decades of conflictual relations among what scholars deem to be historic rivals and were widely considered momentous.[6] Yet, they had quite different outcomes.[7] In the case of Cuba, even suspicions of a sonic attack on the US embassy that sickened numerous American diplomats failed to set relations between the two countries back to previous levels of conflict.[8] By contrast, change did not stick in the case of India's rapprochement with Pakistan. Instead, relations quickly reverted to business as usual, with exchanges of accusations even escalating to border skirmishes in 2016.

It is tempting to dismiss these different outcomes as being the result of idiosyncratic circumstances—for example, different leadership. But, at the very same time, under the very same leader, India behaved quite differently

Volatile States in International Politics. Eleonora Mattiacci, Oxford University Press. © Oxford University Press 2023.
DOI: 10.1093/oso/9780197638675.003.0001

toward another of its historic rivals, China. Just one month before traveling to Pakistan in 2015, Indian Prime Minister Narendra Modi traveled to China for what experts considered a remarkably friendly meeting with Chinese President Xi Jinping.[9] Just a few months prior, skirmishes at the border had served as a powerful reminder of India's numerous points of conflict with China.[10] After the meeting, however, India's behavior toward China was more consistently friendly than its behavior toward Pakistan.[11]

The different outcomes of these 2015 rapprochements might appear surprising and even perhaps downright inexplicable if we, as many scholars do, group together Cuba's behavior toward the US and India's behavior toward Pakistan as rivalrous by focusing exclusively on their conflictual behavior. Instead, when we look beyond this tight focus on the countries' histories and episodes of conflict, the different outcomes start making more sense.

We start to see that Cuba's and India's behaviors are, in fact, not very similar at all. Both have, to be sure, displayed higher-than-average levels of conflict when compared to other countries in the international system. Yet the reoccurrence of conflict within their relations is only part of the story. Upon closer look, Cuba's behavior toward the US has been much more consistent and less volatile over the past fifty years than India's behavior has been toward Pakistan. Before the 2015 Cuban thaw, relations had mostly been reduced to hostile banter, while formal diplomatic contact had remained consistently sparse and unfriendly.[12] By contrast, India's behaviors toward Pakistan have been more volatile, meaning that they have fluctuated in a much more inconsistent manner. In some moments, India has engaged in cooperative overtures (bilateral talks, enhanced cultural and military exchanges, etc.). At other times, it has moved toward more conflictual behaviors (accusations, military exercises at the border, etc.). The first few months of the year 2011, for example, perfectly represent this fluctuating dynamic. In January 2011, India forcibly accused Pakistan of supporting terrorist attacks on Indian soil. Shortly afterward, India agreed to resume conversations about outstanding military and economic bilateral issues. After long and agonizing negotiations, the two countries instituted a joint working group in April of that year to enhance trade ties. Yet, at the beginning of May, India started conducting military exercises at the border with Pakistan, catalyzing violent protests from Pakistan and essentially bringing those painfully achieved bilateral negotiations to an end. By contrast, India's behavior toward China in the years preceding Modi's 2015 meeting with Xi was less volatile than its behavior toward Pakistan.[13]

As the examples above illustrate, looking at conflict alone only gives us part of the picture. Significantly, these states' behaviors toward their counterparts, even though often categorized by scholars as similarly conflictual, clearly differ in terms of volatility. While rapprochements are complex phenomena with many moving parts,[14] volatile behavior tends to generate the type of uncertainty that makes it harder to move past conflict and establish cooperation between actors. Volatility, as I explain in this book, can have serious consequences.

The Puzzle

What increases volatility in states' behaviors toward other states? This is the question at the center of this book. Here, I define volatile behavior as behavior that shifts toward more cooperation and more conflict in a way that looks inconsistent to observers—that is, volatile change is change that appears to follow no clear pattern.[15] A state's behavior becomes progressively more volatile when it increasingly switches toward more cooperation or more conflict in an inconsistent manner. The greater the incidence of inconsistent shifts in a state's behavior and the bigger these shifts are (i.e., the more each shift at time t pushes the country away from its behavior at time $t - 1$), the greater the volatility displayed by that country at a given point in time. In this sense, volatility in states' behaviors is continuous and varies: some countries might display more volatility in their behaviors than other countries, and they might do so at some times but not others. Indeed, the purpose of this book is to understand what prompts certain countries to act in a more volatile manner toward their counterparts in certain moments but not in others.

So far, International Relations (IR) studies have almost exclusively investigated consistent forms of change, studying, for example, how actors become consistently more conflictual toward others (escalation) or less conflictual (reconciliation). But the payoff of explaining the origins of inconsistencies—that is, increases in volatility—is notable.

Some of this payoff has to do with the way scholars and practitioners understand international politics. The study of inconsistent shifts between cooperation and conflict prevents us from reading all the change that we observe as following a specific pattern. This, in turn, will stave off the risk of making false analogies—of mistakenly equating some current events with past ones. Analogies are quite potent in international politics.[16] Providing both policymakers and pundits with crucial information on the expected results of their future actions, analogies can affect what these actors perceive to be their best options. Yet perhaps precisely as a function of their apparent ability to predict the future, analogies have proven to be quite misleading at times. Recognizing the existence of inconsistent change challenges analogical thinking, because it forces us to understand that the present is not simply some version of the past. Rather, we might be observing something new, something that is not congruous with what was there before and that should therefore be explored anew.

In addition, studying volatility pushes IR scholars to embrace a more nuanced view of states' relations. For example, while traditional classifications like rivalries and alliances are useful at capturing key features in international politics, they also conceal a lot of diversity within each classification. There are costs associated with embracing too tightly what are often analytically very useful dichotomizations of states' relations as either conflictual or cooperative. Similarly, understanding states' relations as either stable or unstable tells us quite little regarding what states' activities really look like in these types of relations. For example, the concept of instability does not provide much information on how much cooperation states in conflict with one another actually engage in.

Other benefits associated with a better understanding of volatility deal instead with its broad implications in international politics. Volatility is at the root of many international phenomena we care about, including trust and uncertainty. Understanding where it originates can therefore shed light on these fundamental processes within global politics—perhaps, as this book suggests, even staving off volatility's worse consequences as a result.

Leveraging both statistical analysis and archival data, this book argues that volatility emerges from states' relative power and the competition among domestic groups for the definition of states' behaviors in the international system.

The next section will shed light on how volatility differs from other, well-studied forms of change in states' behaviors, including instability, cycles, and so on. Then, the following sections will delve deeper into, respectively, the value of understanding volatility, how the field of IR ended up lagging behind in the study of volatility in states' behaviors, and why this matters for what we know about the international system.

Making Sense of States' Behaviors

This book's focus on volatility in states' behaviors, as opposed to other (subnational or international) actors' behaviors, positions it in a long tradition of IR studies. States' powers and reach in the international system have secured them their role as crucial players in a global arena populated by different types of actors.[17] Indeed, as I demonstrate in the book's conclusions, the exploration of volatility in states' behaviors can constitute a useful stepping stone to a broader debate on what volatility in other actors' behaviors looks like in the international arena.

In order to understand what sets volatility apart from other forms of change in states' international behaviors, however, it is first necessary to understand how IR scholars have understood change to begin with.

To make sense of the diverse set of behaviors that characterize International Relations, scholars often proceed in two steps. First, they categorize events unfolding in the international arena as being more or less "cooperative" or "conflictual." Cooperative acts usually include instances of countries working together with other countries toward an objective. For example, countries might propose joining forces to carry out initiatives that will be mutually beneficial (signing substantive agreements, declaring a truce, etc.) or responding favorably to such offers (agreeing to meet with them, joining an alliance, changing their claims, etc.). Conversely, conflictual acts tend to encompass any kind of initiative taken by a country to oppose their counterpart (such as turning down a proposal, halting negotiations, or cutting aid) or that displays a violent reaction to it (such as threatening to use force against the opponent or engaging in military confrontations).[18]

Notably, cooperative and conflictual initiatives can be both material (e.g., sending aid) and verbal (e.g., offering an apology). Threatening to attack a country can be just as much a conflictual behavior as actually attacking the country, for example, but the latter entails greater material and ideational resources than the former. For this reason, material conflict is considered more intense than verbal conflict.

After ascertaining whether behaviors are cooperative or conflictual and whether they are material or verbal, scholars often investigate how events unfold through time. In other words, do conflictual actions spur more conflictual actions? Does verbal conflict soon transform into material conflict? Studies of conflict reoccurrence, for example, shed light on when and why conflictual acts are followed by more conflictual acts.[19]

Using this conflict–cooperation continuum framework over time, Figure 1.1 represents the US policy toward South Korea in the summer of 2017. The horizontal axis represents time. The vertical axis represents a conflict–cooperation continuum. On this continuum, countries' actions are ranked based on how cooperative and how conflictual they are.[20] The joint military exercises in which the US participated in August 2017 sit higher and further to the right than the joint statement on cooperation that US President Trump and South Korean President Moon Jae-in released in June of the same year. A line connecting these two events would have a positive slope.[21]

Where, then, does volatility fit in the broader study of states' behaviors? And how does it differ from other forms of change?

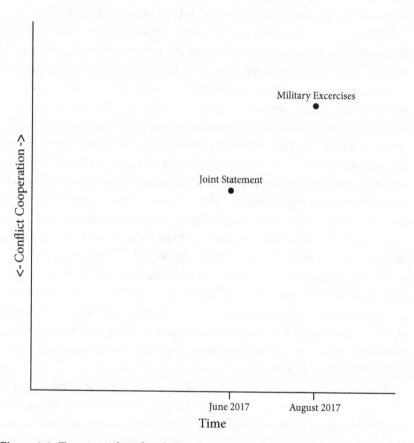

Figure 1.1 Two examples of US behaviors toward South Korea in the summer of 2017. NOTE: *Time is on the x-axis, while the y-axis displays a measure of how cooperative or conflictual behavior is.*

Volatility vs. Other Forms of Change in States' Behaviors

Volatility can provide an important missing piece of the puzzle when it comes to current explanations of states' behaviors. It captures important nuances in behaviors within the international arena that are not well explored in present conceptualizations.

In particular, there are two core attributes that set volatile behavior apart from other foreign policy dynamics: change and inconsistency. Change refers to the fact that volatile behavior in the international arena entails transitioning toward more cooperative or more conflictual acts. Inconsistency, by contrast, refers to the type of change that volatility entails. When change is inconsistent, it cannot be easily predicted (e.g., by the occurrence of cyclical events such as elections). It also does not follow a specific trajectory, such as toward more conflict (as in the case of escalation processes) or more cooperation (as in the case of easing tensions and beginning rapprochement processes).

Thus, if there is no change in a state's behavior toward another country, then their behavior does not appear to display volatility. If there is a change in behavior, then the behavior displays volatility only if the change is inconsistent. Figure 1.2 illustrates volatility in the context of other concepts we use to understand change over time.

To show how volatility differs from other foreign policy dynamics, Figure 1.3 compares different dynamics characterizing states' behaviors. As in Figure 1.1, the horizontal axis represents time, while the vertical axis

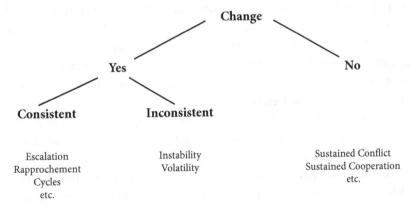

Figure 1.2 Schema of the relative position of volatility compared to other forms of change between states.

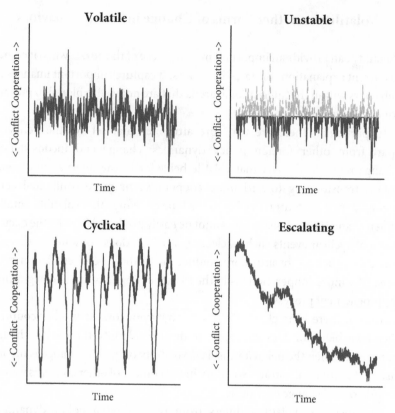

Figure 1.3 Ideal-typical illustrations of how scholars have conceptualized patterns of change in states' behaviors.

represents a conflict–cooperation continuum. The lines within each graph connect the different cooperative and conflictual states' behaviors that have taken place at different points in time, thus visualizing the way in which a country's behavior toward another country unfolds and changes over time. As it emerges from Figure 1.3, behaviors that are primarily volatile experience shifts between cooperation and conflict that appear quite inconsistent— behaviors that, in other words, do not tend to happen exclusively or even mostly during certain pre-established and easily recognizable periods of time or following a specific trend.

The inconsistency of change sets volatility apart from other forms of change in states' behaviors. Behaviors that are cyclical, for example, also experience change between cooperation and conflict. However, these shifts take place at specific, recurring intervals rather than being inconsistent. Cyclical patterns of change make it possible to anticipate when change will happen. For example, studies have found a cyclical component in the behavior of the US toward the Soviet Union.[22] Right before elections, US presidents systematically overreacted to perceived Soviet threats, so that hawkish statements of resolve became more frequent than in other periods of time.[23]

When countries escalate or de-escalate conflict, they change their behavior, becoming more conflictual or more cooperative, respectively. Unlike volatile change, however, such change is not inconsistent. Instead, it follows a specific trajectory toward, respectively, more conflictual or more cooperative acts. Studies of escalation have focused on how, for example, some countries sharing a long history of hostilities may be more prone to crises that become increasingly violent.[24] Other studies have focused on the opposite process, investigating foreign policy normalization or de-escalation to analyze when and why countries' relations become systematically more cooperative over time.[25]

Another way existing studies explore change is through the concept of instability.[26] In these studies, states' behaviors are labeled as "unstable" when they are interspersed with frequent episodes of conflict. When states display instability traits in their behaviors toward their counterparts, they are likely to repeatedly engage in conflictual behavior. While capturing an important facet of states' behaviors (their propensity to engage over and over again in conflict), the concept of instability only focuses on the occurrence or reoccurrence of conflict. This focus comes at a clear inferential cost, as it leaves observers unable to capture important variations in the international system. For some countries, periods of no conflict are at times characterized by cooperation, as in the case of India's relations with Pakistan. For others, like Cuba and the US, periods of no conflict are characterized by far fewer episodes of cooperation.

Stability, similarly, has been used to describe the lack of severe conflict between states. Yet this concept specifies nothing regarding the degree of cooperation experienced by "stable" countries and their counterparts.[27] The concept of "stable peace," for example, refers to a condition where the probability of conflict is minimal, but it stays silent regarding what activities are involved.[28] In the upper right plot on Figure 1.3, then, using stability as a conceptual category to explain states' behaviors would entail only focusing on the light gray portion of the line, disregarding the dark gray one.

Therefore, the concept of stability can be misleading. Quite intuitively, for example, there is a difference between the behaviors of states engaged in a security community and those of countries that neither engage in conflict nor are part of a security community. Take, for example, South Korea's behaviors toward Japan (and vice versa) in the 2000s. Relations between these two countries, albeit not entailing the use of force,[29] have never reached a point of "shared meanings, constituted by interaction, engender[ed] collective identities,"[30] as would be the case for states in a security community. Yet, both relations between South Korea and Japan and relations between members of a security community would be labeled as "stable," according to the current definition of the term. Thus, using the concept of stability risks concealing consequential nuances.[31]

In this sense, the concepts of "instability" and "stability" in studies of International Relations only capture a subset of important phenomena. They largely ignore whether episodes of, respectively, cooperation or conflict occur and, when they do, what shape they take. By contrast, studying volatility requires a more encompassing view of states' relations. Volatility considers whether the conflict we observe is intertwined with episodes of cooperation, and, if so, whether moving toward cooperation and conflict entails inconsistent shifts in policy.

Ultimately, Figure 1.3 presents the ideal types of foreign policy dynamics. In other words, each panel in the figure represents dynamics that are mostly volatile, mostly unstable, and so on. In practice, however, states' behaviors can unfold through time by combining different types of dynamic change. For example, states' behaviors could be increasingly volatile while still showing signs of steady improvement toward greater cooperation, as in the case of US behaviors toward Russia (and vice versa) after the end of the Cold War.[32]

Yet the overlap is not complete. Relations that are improving or deteriorating, for example, are not necessarily volatile. For instance, China's behavior toward Taiwan after China's nuclear explosion in 1964 was not volatile. Instead, it was rather consistently conflictual.[33] Conversely, behaviors that are volatile do not necessarily improve or deteriorate, as was the case for India's behavior toward Pakistan after the 1998 nuclear tests.[34]

In sum, arguably, no one dynamic of change in states' behaviors subsumes the others, even though each might manifest itself in conjunction with others. Since volatility is a unique manifestation of change, understanding volatility can offer unique insights into how International Relations unfold. For one, exploring volatility helps us avoid conflating behaviors that are similarly conflictual (or cooperative) but that vary in how inconsistently they transition toward more cooperation (or conflict). Shedding light on what increases volatility will also help us better understand why states act the way they do. In short, understanding volatility makes scholars' grasp of International Relations firmer.

But there is yet another reason why volatility matters. It has to do with the unique role it plays in international politics, as illustrated in the next section.

Why Volatility Matters

Volatility in states' behaviors can have profound effects on the international arena because it catalyzes uncertainty.[35]

Volatility catalyzes uncertainty because the inconsistent and unexpected nature of change it entails makes it hard to accurately predict future events. When faced with cycles of behavior, by contrast, policymakers can use the past as a predictor of what comes next. This is the case because they can gauge what kinds of reoccurrences will prompt change and in which directions change will go. Soviets, as the example above suggests, could expect the Americans to become more assertive right before elections. When behavior is volatile, however, change cannot be predicted by using past behavior or major events as guidelines.

In the classic Knightian distinction, people facing a risky situation can accurately measure or estimate the risk of a particular event taking place by attaching a number bound between 0 and 1 to it. With uncertainty, estimating such probabilities with any accuracy is not possible.[36] In other words, "parameters are too unstable to quantify the prospects for events that may or may not happen in the future."[37]

Given that accurate probability estimations are not possible, individuals facing uncertainty are likely to be surprised by future events. In turn, this feeling of surprise makes it so that people do not react to uncertainty as they would to risk—that is, they do not weigh the costs and benefits of their actions in relation to future events. Instead, since "the brain abhors surprises," as neuroscientific findings show, uncertainty catalyzes such visceral reactions among individuals that it often leads to irrational behaviors.[38]

In particular, by forcing individuals to face surprise and uncertainty, volatility creates fear. Fear, in turn, generates incentives in favor of risk-averse behavior, which often leads to self-defeating behavior.[39] Perhaps the most classic example of self-defeating behavior is the phenomenon of ambiguity aversion captured by the *Ellsberg paradox*.[40] American economist David Ellsberg demonstrated that individuals systematically prefer dealing with risk to dealing with uncertainty, even when it comes at a real cost. When given a choice, actors prefer bets where the probability of winning is known but low to bets where the probabilities are high but unknown.

Examples of fear-catalyzed, counterproductive behavior abound and are investigated in multiple fields of inquiry.[41] Stock market volatility has been found to be the top concern for investors, so much so that it trumps concerns for gains.[42] In finance, the index of market volatility (VIX) is aptly called the "investors' fear gauge."[43] Similarly, laypeople grow fearful in the face of international markets' volatility and make counterproductive decisions.[44] Volatility in presidential approval, by the same token, has been shown to be so concerning for decision makers that US presidents aggressively try to minimize it—even at the expense of policies that might appeal to the "median voter" and thus prove key to shoring up electoral support.[45]

In international politics, the type of fear that uncertainty generates shapes how states read each other's intentions—and therefore how they interact.[46] Given that it catalyzes fear, volatility can have important reverberations within the international arena, in several ways.

Fear, for instance, can be a powerful catalyst for the spiral model of conflict, wherein countries systematically inch closer to escalating conflict even though neither of them has any intention of doing so.[47] A country displaying volatile behavior often leaves its counterpart at a loss when trying to predict its future behavior. Facing such unpredictability, in turn, can often push countries to embrace a more defensive stance toward volatile counterparts. Disputes initiated against a country displaying volatile foreign policy behavior are significantly more likely to escalate to higher levels of violence than disputes initiated against nonvolatile states.[48] And escalation, as a dynamic process, often hampers attempts at mediation.[49]

In addition to fueling violence, volatility can also stymie the possibility of long-term cooperation by increasing the perceived dangers of trusting the volatile counterpart. By undermining trust, volatility can fundamentally alter the face of international politics, as trust is a crucial component of the very fabric of International Relations. For example, trust has been found to be essential for the process of rivals overcoming their suspicions of one another, including in the case of historical rivals such as Germany and France and Israel and Palestine.[50] When trust is eroded, evidence from the Cold War further suggests, policymakers systematically miss crucial opportunities for cooperation because they are more prone to dismiss their counterparts' cooperative proposals.[51] Trust has also proven crucial for promoting intelligence sharing within alliances, which, in turn, has been key for alliance commitments to endure.[52] Forming clear expectations as to how a country's counterpart will behave is a fundamental component of establishing trust.[53] Yet the presence of inconsistent shifts in a counterpart's past behavior hampers countries' capabilities to form such expectations on future behavior. Volatile behavior can therefore discourage countries from trusting their counterparts because it leaves them unable to predict what will happen if they do.

Augmenting uncertainty and fueling fear, volatility also complicates efforts to plan for the future by posing a fundamental challenge to decision makers' ability and willingness to elaborate strategies.[54] At their core, strategies must plan for the future and deal with uncertainty. In particular, strategies work by balancing two priorities: "be[ing] robust across multiple alternative future events" and "still [being] tailored to meet the challenges of the most likely future events."[55] By increasing uncertainty, volatility undercuts efforts to produce sound strategies, including by increasing the number of plausible "alternative future events" that strategies need to account for. However, according to their proponents, strategies matter greatly in order to keep countries safe because they constitute an antidote to decision makers' propensity to base national security on "what the purveyor prefers rather than what the situation demands."[56] Given the wide-ranging benefits of elaborating strategies, the obstacles that volatility poses to such exercise can be quite consequential for international politics.

Volatility's effects on crucial phenomena in the international arena such as trust, escalation, and strategy suggest that volatility makes international politics more unpredictable. It produces what political scientist Robert Jervis defined as "system effects," thus augmenting the complexity and interdependence of the international system.[57] For example, because actors responding to a volatile counterpart will react not only to the counterpart's specific actions but also to the inconsistency or change they witness in such behavior (nonlinearity), volatility adds an extra layer of complexity to states' interactions that can potentially generate unintended consequences.[58] System effects matter greatly because they "limit both the control that political decision-makers exercise over the outcomes of their actions and the explanatory power of the theories that scholars develop to explain those outcomes."[59] In this sense, volatility complicates interactions in the international system as well as the way we understand them.

In sum, since volatility is a peculiar type of change in states' behaviors that entails inconsistency, it can easily generate uncertainty and fear. Uncertainty and fear, in turn, push actors to engage in counterproductive behaviors, as studies ranging from economics to psychology to political science have shown. In international politics, volatility in states' behaviors therefore has the potential to fuel escalation, stymie trust, and fundamentally hamper decision makers' capability to formulate strategies, thus increasing the occurrence of systems effects.

For all these reasons, understanding where volatility in states' behaviors originates is important. How, then, have scholars made sense of this so far?

Two Ways to (Wrongly) Dismiss Volatility

Volatility is the undisputed protagonist of numerous studies of politics and economics, including explorations of electoral volatility, trade volatility, economic performance volatility, party volatility, and exchange rate volatility, just to cite a few examples.[60]

While we are presumably just as likely to observe volatility in the study of International Relations as we are in the study of other political and economic processes, scholars of international politics have yet to explain when and why it develops.[61]

When faced with volatility in states' behaviors, scholars often just implicitly dismiss it, discounting its complexity in one of two ways. Some have suggested that states are inconsistent in their foreign policy behavior simply because they almost cannot not be. According to this perspective, volatility is the natural byproduct of making politics: as long as countries conduct international politics, volatility will always be there, simply as background noise. Scholars exploring the impact of bureaucracy, for example, explain inconsistencies in a country's foreign policy by emphasizing that actual foreign policy is often (and perhaps inevitably) colored by bureaucrats' activities.[62] Within bureaucracies, individuals involved in making decisions that affect foreign policy are likely to have different preferences that depend on their position. Since these individuals are fundamental to the everyday implementation of international politics, the noise their actions produce will never go away. For instance, according to former US secretary of state Henry Kissinger, inconsistency in foreign policy is almost innate:

There is not such a thing as an American foreign policy. [There is only] a series of moves that have produced a certain result [that they] may not have been planned to produce.[63]

In other words, inconsistencies and unsteady changes are the inevitable "noise" that is generated when sending a "signal" in the international arena. Thus, to correctly gauge international politics, it would be advisable to dismiss the inevitable, uninformative noise and focus instead on the signal. Volatility, this approach seems to suggest, is something we should tune out.

But if international politics cannot help but be volatile, why does volatility in countries' behaviors vary? In the 2010s, for example, India's behavior toward China was far less volatile, on average, than its behavior toward Pakistan. Stated differently, if volatility is the constant of international policy, why does it fluctuate? By dismissing volatility as the natural fallout of the process of policymaking, this approach fails to explain its variation through time and across cases.

Another way that scholars have implicitly dismissed volatility is by taking the opposite approach and arguing that, instead of being a constant, volatility does not exist. They suggest that as long as we divide interactions between states into specific "issues"—meaning important, well-defined topics over which political actors can negotiate[64]—we can see that countries consistently cooperate or fight in the context of those specific issues. Thus, even though it might look as though countries have inconsistent shifts between cooperation or conflict when looking at their actions in the aggregate, such inconsistent shifts are simply the product of looking at their policies across different issues.

Given what we know about how issues emerge, however, this approach to explaining volatility is not satisfying. As research shows, the creation of issues is itself endogenous to a state's decision to behave in a cooperative or conflictual manner. For example, responding to pressures from domestic interests, decision makers generate contentious issues a posteriori as "what states *choose* to fight over."[65] In other words, first, countries decide whether to fight, and then they transform a feature of their interaction into a contentious issue. The reason territories such as Jerusalem and Northern Ireland have been perceived as "indivisible" and thus more likely to catalyze conflict, for example, is not that they stand out in terms of their physical characteristics or history. Rather, domestic interests leveraging political rhetoric opt to represent these territories as "indivisible," so as to stoke and protract conflict when such conflict serves their agenda.[66] Decision makers, responding to domestic interests, might also decide to make some issues more salient at specific points in time—for example, by attaching more tangible or intangible value to them.[67] When seeking out opportunities for cooperation, similarly, states often link together areas that are quite separate on paper, including areas with different individuals, interests, and procedures involved, such as military alliances and trade.[68]

Indeed, the fact that issues emerge as a consequence of the decision to fight or cooperate as opposed to the other way around helps explain several important empirical findings. For example, the very same feature, such as an outstanding territory claim, might become an issue of contention in some relations but fail to do so in others, depending on decision makers' preferences.[69]

So, if volatility waxes and wanes, unlike constant noise, and if issues are better explained as emerging from shifts toward more cooperation or conflict than the other way around, then what explains volatility?

The Argument in Brief

Volatility in states' behaviors, this book posits, emerges from the combination of two distinct processes. Each process unfolds, respectively, at the domestic and international level: the unbridled competition among domestic groups and a state's growing relative power.

Power vis-à-vis a counterpart, when it increases, acts as a permissive condition for volatility: it expands the policies at a state's disposal to include more cooperative and combative options. Power increases the policies available to a country because it makes more options available to them, both cooperative and conflictual. For example, a country that has acquired nuclear weapons has more foreign policy options vis-à-vis their counterpart than does a nonnuclear weapon state. Researchers have found that after China exploded its first nuclear weapon in October 1964, its material and ideational power increased, leaving the country with more cooperative and conflictual options at its disposal to deal with other states.[70] Indeed, nuclear weapon states can rely on more conflictual options to achieve their objectives than nonnuclear weapon states can. In particular, they become more likely to prevail in crises, more comfortable with possibly increasing the level of violence used in each crisis (i.e., escalating the crisis), and even more likely to engage in low-level violence with other nuclear weapon states.[71]

Increasing relative power also increases the cooperative options at a state's disposal, both by providing it with more "bargaining chips" to use in cooperative overtures and by encouraging the state to take on the risks involved in cooperating with others. For example, within five years of acquiring nuclear weapons, Great Britain bolstered its ties with fellow Southeast Asia Treaty Organization (SEATO) and Baghdad Pact members through renewed offers of cooperation and commitments of support. Before acquiring nuclear weapons, Britain lacked the resources and the willingness necessary to contribute substantial conventional forces to those alliances.[72] Making such contributions only became an option when its relative power increased.

If greater power allows countries to embrace volatility, it does not per se explain when and why countries' behaviors will be volatile. While more relative power increases the options at a country's disposal, it does not provide the country with a specific reason to embrace volatile behavior. Just because a country has more options at its disposal to achieve its preferred outcome does not mean it will use all of those options.

The precipitant cause of volatility is actually the clash, at the domestic level, between diverging interests seeking to influence the course of foreign policy. Domestic groups often compete to impose their preferred behaviors within the international arena, as such behaviors can often have important consequences for these groups' preferences. When those domestic groups have interests that do not overlap, they will each prefer distinct states' behaviors on the international arena. Those groups will compete to establish their favorite course of action. If those groups have a say on what countries can do, some groups might prevail at certain points in time, while others might prevail later on. In the 2010s, for example, Japan shifted between offers to trade and demands for official apologies when dealing with China, exemplifying the government's attempt to satisfy two vociferous, opposing groups: those in favor of free trade and those with protectionist and nationalist preferences.

Power and interests work together to produce unruly behavior in the global arena. The further apart domestic groups' preferences are, the more diverse their preferred behaviors, on average. And the greater a country's relative power, the more likely it is that these opposing behavior preferences will be put in practice. The outcome of the interaction between interests and power, therefore, is increased volatility in states' behaviors toward their counterparts.

The Goals of This Book

The aim of this book is twofold. First, in offering the first systematic account of volatility in states' behaviors toward other states, this book seeks to spark an in-depth conversation about volatility in international politics. Scholars have so far remained silent on the origins of volatility. This reticence has multiple, concatenated causes.

To start, there are several cognitive obstacles to studying volatility. Individuals have a natural aversion toward the surprises that characterize volatility, to a degree that suggests that "human decision-making is better explained by surprise minimization compared to utility maximization."[73] Individuals' innate aversion to surprise has often translated into "creeping determinism" or "hindsight bias," wherein surprising events are dismissed ex post facto as having been more predictable than they actually were. Dismissing surprises ex post makes volatility hard to study because it makes surprising, inconsistent behaviors hard to register to begin with.[74]

These tendencies regarding how to process surprises are likely at the core of a central feature of international politics studies. Perhaps in an innate attempt to find patterns, even studies addressing change in the international arena tend to focus on change that takes place in consistent ways. Many focus, for example, on change that follows a clear direction, such as conflict that entails greater and greater violence, or relations that systematically improve.

Yet, as I discussed above, albeit subject to similar aversion to surprises as scholars in international politics, scholars in other social science fields and subfields have investigated volatility in depth. So, in order to understand the lack of studies related to volatility in international politics, it is important to reflect on other factors as well. First is the widespread tendency to embrace a mean-centric approach, therefore asking: which relations see, on average, the occurrence of greater episodes of conflict or cooperation?[75] This almost exclusive focus on central tendencies has led scholars to downplay behavior that deviates from the norm. Thus, this mean-centric approach may have contributed to the prevalence of accounts that dichotomize states' behaviors toward specific other states as being either, on average, mostly conflictual or mostly cooperative.[76] Such dichotomization, in turn, is very useful. But it must be understood for what it is: a simplification of reality. Otherwise, it can bias our representation of the international arena. For example, as Robert Jervis argued, political scientists have historically studied conflict as separate from cooperation, which is a problem for how we understand international politics.[77] In addition, even when we study peace, we too often oversimplify it as just the absence of conflict—a choice that limits our ability to capture the multifaceted nature of peace.[78]

By exclusively embracing mean-centric approaches, we leave out crucial information: what explains the full range of cooperative and conflictual behaviors states engage in with their counterparts? Why is that range bigger when confronting some states but not others? And what pushes states to explore the extremes on this conflict–cooperation continuum? Answering these questions can help us produce a more realistic picture of the international system, one that fully captures the diversity of states' behaviors we actually observe in the international arena.[79]

The need to capture a broad range of states' behaviors and the dynamics that characterize this range seems particularly pressing in the current international context. Possibly as a consequence of the expanding regulation of conflict, states increasingly refrain from engaging in overt forms of conflict, such as wars. Instead, they still seek to coerce other states, but they do so in a variety of ways, each displaying varying degrees of hostility.[80] Studying their behaviors as being on a continuum between cooperation and conflict is therefore paramount.

The second goal of the book is to show ways in which it is possible to change the impact of volatility on international politics. To the extent that volatility emerges from an interaction between interests and power, as this book argues, volatility provides a considerably less noisy signal of intentions than casual observers may think. Indeed, observing behavior that is inconsistent can produce a much higher informational content than observing consistent behavior, as per mathematician Claude Shannon's definition of information.[81] This is the case because when an actor sends a variety of signals by engaging in a diverse set of behaviors, their counterparts become better able to understand the possible range of behaviors that that actor can engage in.

But for volatility to provide useful information to observers and thus to reduce its negative implications, it is crucial for observers to understand where it comes from. This book's argument is that volatility is rooted in power and interests. If a counterpart knows that volatile behavior emerges from power and interests, then volatile behavior will speak volumes about states' preferences and capabilities. Even if it would still be hard to know where volatile actors will go next, observers could better understand where they are coming from.

Moreover, this book invites us to challenge the way IR has often imagined the role of consistency in behavior. A pervasive assumption too often left unquestioned is that consistent behavior is key to cooperation, while ambiguity is a crucial contributor to conflict.[82] For realists, inconsistent behavior is seen as likely to bring about war, while for liberal institutionalists, the ability to form consistent expectations about what happens next is crucial to sustain cooperation.[83] Further, constructivists emphasize the importance of all actors consistently abiding by the same norms of behavior to achieve successful collaboration.[84] This book proposes that we question this pervasive assumption about the prerequisites for cooperation. Understanding the origins of volatility can change the ways states gauge volatile countries' intentions. What if inconsistent behavior, when properly contextualized, can inspire durable understanding and cooperation among states?

Research Design

To provide empirical support for my argument and test it against alternative explanations, this book leverages a diverse set of sources and methods.

First, it proposes a new measure of volatility in states' behaviors, so as to move from the abstract concept of volatility to its concrete manifestations. The measure seeks to capture volatility in different contexts while parsing it out from different forms of change in states' behaviors. To do this, I leverage statistical concepts and techniques, such as simulations, as well as visualization tools. The measure of volatility that emerges is fundamental to capturing when volatility ebbs and flows, which is, in turn, a fundamental first step to understanding why it does so. I further illustrate the procedure by applying it to several recent cases.

The book then performs a comprehensive analysis of when and why countries behave in a more volatile manner. To this end, I propose a multipronged approach. First, a large-N analysis allows me to test the validity of my theoretical construct across time and space, while also systematically controlling for the potential effect of alternative explanations. I focus in particular on data regarding states' behaviors toward their rivals.

Then, to complement the insights that emerge from this large-*N* analysis, the book also leverages an in-depth case study of how relations between France and the US became increasingly more volatile in the years leading up to France's decision to leave the North Atlantic Treaty Organization (NATO), in 1966. This in-depth case study is crucial for expanding our understanding of volatility to encompass relations between allies, as these are some of the most complex relations in the international system. This approach allows me to "zoom in" to show how volatility in a state's behavior increases, tracing the relative impact of my explanatory variables as well as alternative explanations. Moreover, focusing on a historical case facilitates the perusal of declassified official documents and ex-post memoirs and assessments. Such sources reveal crucial information on actors' perceptions of volatile behavior both while volatile behavior unfolds and in its aftermath.

While the argument put forward in this book is likely to apply to states' behaviors toward different counterparts, the richness of evidence documenting behaviors toward allies and rivals makes these types of relations particularly interesting and productive for studying volatility.

Book Outline

This introduction has taken the first essential step toward understanding volatility in states' behaviors. It has defined volatile states' behaviors as behaviors that shift toward more cooperation and conflict in ways that appear inconsistent to observers. Leveraging data simulations and historical examples, this chapter has explained how its inconsistent nature makes volatility differ from other well-studied ideas of change in states' behaviors (such as cycles, escalation, or instability).[85] Scholars have so far dismissed volatility in states' behaviors. But, this chapter has explained, volatility can ignite conflict and hamper conflict by spurring fear. Given the wide-ranging consequences of states' volatile behaviors, explaining where such behaviors come from is important for understanding international politics. This chapter has also discussed how the prevalent mean-centric approach in IR studies has kept scholars from studying a salient concept that has received much attention in other fields of inquiry. After briefly explaining why volatility emerges from the interaction of power and domestic interests, this chapter has also presented the book's mixed-method research design.

Chapter 2 explores the role of power and interests in increasing volatility in states' behaviors toward their counterparts. It argues that growing relative power acts a permissive condition, thus making volatile behavior possible. The presence of a heterogeneous set of domestic interests with access to power, in contrast, catalyzes volatility.

The chapter also explains why alternative explanations (mixed signals, leaders' type, and contentious issues) are not sufficient to account for volatility. In addition to putting forward a theory of variance, this chapter rejects an episodic understanding of international politics in favor of looking at dynamics. It also explains what we gain when we embrace a variance-centric approach to explaining international politics.

Since volatility is but one type of change that states' behaviors can display, current measurements of volatility employed in other areas of study are inadequate for this task. The third chapter presents the basic intuition behind a new way of measuring volatility: using the residuals of a Box-Jenkins procedure applied to the time series of a state's behavior toward its counterpart. It explains why this measure is both valid and reliable. The chapter then compares volatility in the behaviors of countries such as India, Cuba, Pakistan, Iran, Japan, and South Korea toward both allies and rivals. The chapter demonstrates that volatility cannot be reduced to other forms of change in states' behaviors; that it greatly varies across time and cases; and that, by abandoning useful but at times overly restrictive dichotomizations such as those suggested by the concepts of "alliances" and "rivalries," it can help us achieve a richer, more satisfying understanding of the international arena.

The fourth chapter deepens the book's inquiry into volatility in states' behaviors by providing a systematic assessment of the theory presented in Chapter 2. It leverages a large-N analysis of countries involved in both a strategic and enduring rivalry over the period from 1948 to 1992. Though the theory generalizes to all states, this chapter focuses on this specific group of countries to improve the quality of the test. Volatility in these states' behaviors is retraced using data from news services. Rivals are often in the news and thus their interactions are more likely to appear in the data than those of less salient countries. The chapter finds that the interaction of power and interests is a powerful predictor of increases in volatility—specifically, volatility increases as a function of both power and interests increasing. This result holds, the chapter finds, even when controlling for plausible alternative explanations, including mixed signals, leaders' traits and transitions, and the presence of contentious issues.

The fifth chapter explores the occurrence of volatility in an unexpected context: between countries committed to defend one another in case of a military attack. This chapter leverages primary sources in both French and English to trace how, just a few years into the 1950s, France's behavior toward the US started fluctuating, often inconsistently, between cooperative events (e.g., bilateral talks, military and economic aid, etc.) and conflictual ones (e.g., public accusations, refusals to cooperate on crucial issues, etc.). These shifts culminated with France's decision to leave NATO in 1966. The chapter finds that increases in France's volatility toward the United States can be explained by an interaction of domestic interests and relative power.

The concluding chapter puts this book's argument and theory into conversation with current understandings of international politics. In particular, it elaborates on the following question: what is, in practice, the value added of studying volatility in states' behaviors? The chapter is divided into three parts. The first part illuminates how understanding the root causes of volatility can stave off its worse consequences in international politics. It focuses in particular on volatility's implications for crucial phenomena like trust and escalation, among others. The second section explains how this book's findings on the connection between power and interests on the one hand and volatility on the other can illuminate different paths of research to address some of the mixed findings in the field of IR on key issues such as compliance, reputation, credible commitments, and even audience costs. Finally, the chapter explores the value added of further exploring volatility in international politics. It thus charts out future directions for research, outlining the ways in which the theory and findings in this book can help extend the study of volatility in International Relations beyond volatility in states' behaviors. In particular, it points toward the study of nonstate actors and of the international system itself.

2

Theory

When Does Volatility Increase?

Volatility in states' behaviors, as the previous chapter explained, refers to inconsistent shifts toward more conflict or more cooperation. As such, it differs from other forms of change in states' behaviors that scholars have more closely investigated. But what makes volatility in states' behaviors increase?

This chapter advances a three-step argument. In the first step, the theory specifies the permissive condition for volatile behavior—that is, the circumstances that make volatility possible to begin with. Such permissive condition, I argue, is a country's relative power vis-à-vis its counterpart. As their relative power increases, states will gain more cooperative and conflictual options to deal with their counterparts. Having more options to choose from, in turn, is key to being better able to shift between more options. Therefore, as their relative power increases, states become better able, if they so choose, to act inconsistently toward their counterpart. The mechanism at play here is one of resource availability. In other words, growing relative power can increase volatility by augmenting the resources available to countries in the pursuit of their goals in the international arena. The more resources available to deal with their counterpart, the easier for a country to employ a diverse set of tools that includes cooperation and conflict.

Knowing what makes volatile behavior possible, however, is not sufficient per se to explain when and why volatility occurs. Thus, the second step of the argument entails specifying the catalyzing condition for volatile behavior: the presence of a heterogeneous set of domestic interests competing for the definition of foreign policy. The mechanism at play here is one of diverging preferences. Domestic actors can differ in their preferences regarding states' behaviors and thus compete to assert their favorite option. Yet, the outcomes of such competition will depend on what those interests look like. When the interests' preferences overlap very little, those interests will ask for very different policies. In such circumstances, countries will be more likely to shift inconsistently between cooperation and conflict—that is, to act in a volatile

Volatile States in International Politics. Eleonora Mattiacci, Oxford University Press. © Oxford University Press 2023.
DOI: 10.1093/oso/9780197638675.003.0002

manner. Thus, the presence of a heterogeneous set of interests can catalyze volatility by giving rise to competing pulls that might steer foreign policy in opposite directions.

Finally, the argument's third step consists of connecting the first two steps together. In this third step, relative power and the presence of a heterogeneous set of interests in the domestic sphere interact to produce volatility. In a context of increasing relative power (permissive condition), access to the definition of foreign policy by a competing and nonoverlapping set of interests (catalyzing condition) will augment the volatility of one state toward its counterpart. As its relative power increases, so do a state's options available for volatile behavior. The greater the diversity of interests being represented, the stronger a state's incentive to engage in a diverse set of behaviors.

The rest of this chapter proceeds as follows. The next section explains the role of relative power. It clarifies which resources contribute to increase relative power and when and how relative power can shape volatility. Then, I dedicate a section to parsing out the impact of domestic interests, illustrating when and why their competition can result in volatile behavior. Finally, the third section explains how power and interests interact together to produce volatility and why both factors matter for the final outcome. The fourth section presents plausible alternative hypotheses. In the conclusion, I reflect on what the value added of this theory is for our understanding of international politics.

Step One: Relative Power

Power can take many different forms—for example, power can be, to a different degree, material, ideational, resource based, relation based, and so on.[1] But it is material, relative power that is particularly important, I argue in this section, to explain increases in states' volatile behaviors. This is the case because when relative, material power increases, it tends to equip countries with more options, both conflictual and cooperative.[2]

US President Barack Obama effectively captured the essence of the role of relative material power on countries' behavior when speaking to *New York Times* journalist Thomas Friedman in 2015. The international political context could have hardly been more momentous for the US. Just four months earlier, President Obama had announced a process of normalization of relations with one of the US historic rivals, Cuba. Such process, known informally as the "Cuban thaw," sought to end more than half a century of distrust and conflict between the two countries. It boasted bold cooperative moves, including the reopening of the Cuban and American embassies, each closed since 1961. At the time of President Obama's interview with Friedman, Americans were just starting to learn about the Cuban thaw. Meanwhile, in the Middle East, the US was busy negotiating a historic nuclear deal, dubbed the Joint Comprehensive Plan of Action, with Iran, the P5+1 (the five permanent members of the United Nations Security Council plus Germany), and the European Union. Just a few days after the interview took place, on April 12, negotiators announced that they had reached an agreement on a general framework and were aiming to finalize the deal within two months.[3] The deal was going to be a hard sell domestically. In the years 2006–2012, Iran topped the Gallup list of the greatest US enemies according to public opinion.[4] In 2015, only 11% of Americans saw Iran favorably.[5] Battling opposition from numerous members of Congress and faced with a lack of enthusiasm on the part of the American public, the president had to explain why the US was undertaking what could have struck observers as an unusually cooperative route to deal with a rival's nuclear plans.

It was in this deeply uncertain context that President Obama met with Friedman. During the interview, he clearly highlighted the role of US power in explaining which options were available to the US for dealing with Iran and Cuba, arguing:

> Take a country like Cuba. For us to test the possibility that engagement leads to a better outcome for the Cuban people, there aren't that many risks for us. It's a tiny little country. [. . .] And if it turns out that it doesn't lead to better outcomes, we can adjust our policies. The same is true with respect to Iran, a larger country, a dangerous country, one that has engaged in activities that resulted in the death of U.S. citizens, but the truth of the matter is: Iran's defense budget is $30 billion. Our defense budget is closer to $600 billion.[6]

As the quote makes clear, a country's material capabilities in reference to those of its counterparts—that is, its relative, as opposed to absolute, power—shapes the options, both cooperative and conflictual, that such country has vis-à-vis its counterparts.

Growing material, relative power grants countries more ways in which to engage in conflictual actions. On average, the more military capabilities one state has relative to another country, the more conflictual options a country acquires toward that country.[7] Indeed, direct, positive correlations between a country's capabilities and its military options have been explored at length—for example, in the context of the debate on the advantages and disadvantages of offensive and defensive weapons and postures.[8] A state that possesses nuclear weapons, for instance, can more credibly threaten a nuclear attack than a state that does not have nuclear weapons. For example, China's acquisition of nuclear weapons in October 1964 and of several delivery systems shortly thereafter enabled the country to launch a nuclear attack on another country, something it could not have done before.[9] And, research shows, a nuclear attack is an even more credible option for nuclear states depending on what the nuclear status of the counterpart is.[10] Such an understanding of the importance of relative power also emerges in President Obama's quote. There, to make sense of which options are available to the US to deal with Iran, the president takes into account the US power relative to Iran's by comparing the US military budget to the budget of Iran.

Perhaps more counterintuitively, relative material capabilities can also expand the set of cooperative options available to each country when dealing with other countries, in multiple ways. First, expanding relative material capabilities often provides new opportunities for cooperation. Studies of hegemonic power demonstrate, for example, that hegemons can leverage their increasing relative material power to offer more cooperative overtures in various realms of international politics—for example, by providing military or economic aid, offering military or diplomatic protection, increasing trade flows, and so on.[11]

In addition to providing more opportunities to cooperate, increasing relative power makes it so that seizing those opportunities also becomes more appealing, in two ways. First, cooperation can feel "safer." As President Obama's quote reveals, the US relative material capabilities with respect to Iran and Cuba made it so that "there [weren't] many risks" for the US to invest in a more cooperative course of action with those countries. Second, cooperation can also seem more "appropriate" for a state whose power is increasing, as a way to project such power. Since 2000, for example, as its relative capabilities increased, China has sought to project its soft power by expanding its cooperation with other countries, including by offering more loans to other governments.[12] By the same token, evidence suggests that increasing relative power has encouraged countries to take on new avenues of cooperation with others, even with countries that remain more powerful.[13] For their part, others become more open to reciprocating cooperative overtures extended by those countries whose relative power is increasing, in part because the prestige of those countries also increases. For example, diplomatic exchanges are a reflection of a country's prestige in the international system.[14] In the fifty years after the end of the Second World War, countries going from the top 25th to the top 10th percentile in terms of relative power have witnessed a 24% increase in the relative number of diplomatic exchanges received from other countries.[15]

It is also important to note that for a state's relative material capabilities to increase their cooperative and conflictual options vis-à-vis their counterpart, there does not need to be power preponderance. As a state's relative material capabilities increase, so do their options. For example, North Korea's nuclear weapons acquisition has provided the country with an important bargaining chip that it did not have before in its negotiations with the US, even though such program did not give North Korea power preponderance with respect to the US. North Korea has offered, at different points in time, to cooperate with the US in exchange for stopping or slowing its nuclear weapons program.[16] The expansion of North Korea's relative power with respect to the US brought about by its nuclear program also made North Korea more open to seeking cooperation, and not just conflict, with the US.[17]

Which Mechanism?

Increasing relative material capabilities can augment volatility via a mechanism of "resource availability." Specifically, relative power increases volatility in states' behaviors by equipping them with more options, both cooperative and conflictual. A country with more options at its disposal has more opportunities to act in a more volatile manner than a country with fewer options.

In expanding the options at a country's disposal, relative power acts as a permissive condition. It makes it possible for a country to engage in volatile behavior but does not necessarily trigger such behavior. In other words, power increases the opportunity for (i.e., permits) shifts toward more cooperative and conflictual actions, but it does not systematically trigger such shifts.

In stating the role of relative power in allowing for volatile behavior, my argument directly builds on findings on foreign policy portfolios by positing that relative power increases the options available to states to achieve their goals.[18] My argument also builds on the role of relative power that some theories of foreign policy hedging seem to suggest (see the next section in this chapter).[19] However, the theory moves both debates forward by arguing that, as a permissive condition for volatility, power is insufficient per se to understand why states switch inconsistently between different options.

Step Two: Interest Heterogeneity

While relative power provides the permissive condition for volatility, thus explaining the conditions under which volatile behavior is possible to begin with, it is domestic factors that have the potential to spur an increase in volatility toward other states. In particular, I argue that the presence of a heterogeneous set of domestic interests competing for the definition of foreign policy behavior can catalyze foreign policy volatility. The mechanism operating at the domestic level is one of diverging preferences. I explain my claim in this section.

Countries have often at their disposal multiple, different policies when interacting with other countries. If a country decides to increase its security in the international system, for instance, it could do so by increasing its defense spending ("internal balancing") or by joining a defensive alliance with a more powerful state ("external balancing").[20]

Each of the possible alternatives often presents very different implications for domestic groups, given their preferences. If, for instance, the US decides to increase ita security via internal balancing, thus expanding its military budget, certain constituencies—namely those living in states where the defense industry employs a lot of people or those that prefer self-reliant security policies—will gain from this choice. In 2011, for example, military cuts following the Great Recession in the US threatened to reshape the economy of the state of Virginia, given the state's dependence on military contracts.

Because each foreign policy has the potential to affect the distribution of material and symbolic resources among domestic groups, each policy, on average, can go against the preferences of some groups.[21] The decision to pursue one policy over another is, at least in part, a decision to redistribute symbolic and material resources within the domestic realm. Arguably, for example, by reducing defense spending, the 2011 military cuts in the US reshuffled resources. Namely, it brought material and symbolic resources away from individuals working in the defense industry in Virginia and from those preferring self-reliant security policies toward other domestic groups such as taxpayers in the other states and those in favor of multilateral international policies.[22]

Since different groups stand to gain or lose depending on the policy chosen, each group will likely prefer, and thus support, one policy over another. Those domestic interests that benefit from access to global markets, such as export-oriented firms, for example, will likely oppose the decision of states whose nuclear status is not recognized under the Treaty on the Non-proliferation of Nuclear Weapons (NPT) to invest in their existing nuclear programs. This is because the presence of nuclear programs that have not been recognized under the NPT might entail reduced access to global markets. Similarly, more dovish audiences that are against weapons acquisition will also oppose this investment decision. By contrast, hawkish groups and those groups that stand to benefit from the presence of nuclear programs (such as engineers and defense contractors as well as more hawkish members of the public) will support a non-NPT country's decision to invest in a nuclear program.[23] Indeed, India's decision to invest in a nuclear program and to authorize its second nuclear explosion in Pokhran affected the Indian population differently, boosting investments in some (geographic and social) sectors of society while subjecting most of the population to the negative consequences originating from the economic sanctions that ensued.[24]

Thus, given different domestic groups' diverging preferences, when a state chooses one foreign policy option over another, it will likely create, domestically, winners and losers. These individuals will, respectively, support or oppose such policies.[25] Research has shown this to be the case in all realms of foreign policy, from trade to security policies. Consider, for example, evidence on trade deals and aid packages. Domestic groups' preferences have been found to affect not just public perceptions of foreign countries involved in these processes[26] but also how their representatives will vote on such deals[27] and thus, ultimately, whether such international commitments are carried through.[28] Similarly, considerations on how strategies such as conflict escalation and diversionary conflict affect domestic preferences have been shown to affect states' decisions regarding whether to implement such strategies.[29] Conflicting domestic groups' preferences also shape how countries' grand strategies are being pursued[30] and whether states use force abroad.[31] Competition between different interest groups can also determine a country's decisions in realms as salient and diverse as nuclear weapons ambitions,[32] international interventions,[33] United Nations (UN) voting,[34] alliance formation and reliability,[35] and sanction effectiveness,[36] just to name a few.

Policies in the international arena, therefore, are likely to divide domestic groups between winners and losers depending on each group's preferences. But the specific divisions among domestic interests in each country will be different because they emerge from each country's social cleavage configuration. If cleavages in society tend to be more reinforcing and less cross-cutting, domestic groups' preferences will be more heterogeneous, in the aggregate, and therefore divisions among interests will be sharper.[37]

To elaborate, each cleavage consists of a "division on the basis of some criteria of individuals, groups, or organizations [between] whom conflict may arise."[38] Examples of such criteria include race, language, religion, income, and region. Cleavages, in other words, by pointing to what divides domestic populations into different groups, can suggest where differences between groups' preferences lie. Cleavages might tell us, for example, that religion is a salient division within a specific country and that therefore there might be groups of individuals whose diverging policy preferences reflect divisions in terms of religion. In Belgium, for example, there exist prominent cleavages based on both language and religion, as domestic groups differ significantly in terms of the language they speak and the religion they practice. In Sweden, by contrast, where the population is religiously more homogeneous, the religious cleavage has not been traditionally as salient as it has been in Belgium.

Yet, cleavages per se do not tell us how distant in terms of preferences those groups are—in other words, they do not tell us how marked the differences identified by the cleavages are. It could be, for example, that certain individuals within a group, divided in terms of religion, have instead a lot in common when it comes to their income. This is the case, for example, in Belgium, and, consequently, individuals belonging to different religious groups share income-based preferences with others who belong to different religious groups.[39] In Northern Ireland, instead, religious and economic cleavages coincide, so that Catholics also tend to be much poorer than Protestants. Thus, in both Northern Ireland and Belgium, religion is a cleavage that identifies different groups. But in Belgium, domestic preferences among religious groups are likely not to be as distant, on average, as they are in Northern Ireland, where religious differences are reinforced by income differences. In Northern Ireland, the cleavage configuration forms two groups where creed differences overlap with income differences, thus driving the groups even further apart in terms of preferences.[40] In cases such as the Northern Irish one, cleavages are defined as reinforcing.

Cleavages are considered to be reinforcing (and not cross-cutting) when knowing where one individual stands on religion can help us predict their income, for example. In the presence of reinforcing cleavages, domestic groups' interests differ on multiple accounts—in the previous example, both in terms of religion and in terms of income. When cleavages are cross-cutting, by contrast, knowing an individual's religious beliefs does not tell us anything about where they stand on the income ladder.[41] On average, the set of domestic interests within a country tends to be more heterogeneous when domestic cleavages are reinforcing than when they are cross-cutting, because individuals within each group tend to differ from individuals within other groups on multiple dimensions. Thus, in a society with reinforcing cleavages, each domestic group is, on average, even more likely to support policies that other groups oppose, compared to a society with cross-cutting cleavages.

Thus, in the reinforcing cleavages domestic configuration, some states' behaviors in the international arena are likely to generate an even sharper division between winners and losers than in cross-cutting social settings, because the policy will appeal or fail to appeal to certain groups based on multiple grounds.[42]

Thus, I argue, when cleavages are reinforcing, countries will tend to engage more often in policies that shift inconsistently between cooperation and conflict. This is the case because when a policy is implemented, such policy is likely to advantage one group more than the other. The other group will therefore ask to be compensated via the adoption of other policies. Such policies will tend to be quite different from the one previously implemented, precisely because their interests do not overlap much. For example, if a country where cleavages are reinforcing imposes a tariff on goods from another country, those individuals who are protectionist and nationalist will benefit from it, but those who are both internationalist and pro-trade will oppose it. If a tariff is imposed, this latter group will require some sort of foreign policy redress to offset the tariff's negative implications.

Although, of course, it does not have to take the form of a foreign policy action, there are several reasons that repayment will be, on average, more likely to be in the form of foreign policies.[43]

First, other, more fungible forms of compensation outside the realm of foreign policy, such as wealth redistribution, can often prove unfeasible. This is the case because there are challenges to systematically quantifying and translating what counts as proper compensation across foreign policy categories.[44] For instance, consider states' decisions to conclude bilateral trade agreements (BTAs) that open the way to foreign direct investments (FDIs) on the part of multinationals. When citizens in those states incur a loss due to the BTAs, it might be possible to estimate, albeit imperfectly, such loss and compensate those individuals economically.[45] However, in addition to the difficulties associated with assessing the correct amount of wealth redistribution needed for compensation, how should we quantify the toll that such liberalizing policies take on those individuals opposing such FDIs as odious forms of neocolonialism?[46] Given how complex it is to quantitatively measure how much a group loses from a certain policy, compensation tends to be more successful when it happens in the very "currency of issues linked to the bargain question," and thus it is more likely to take place in the form of other foreign policy actions.[47]

Second, compensation in the form of foreign policy behavior often meets the requests of the "wronged" group more directly. In 2005, for example, when Japanese business leaders successfully advocated for increasing trade ties with China, nationalist groups asked for compensation for this foreign policy shift in the form of the prime minister promptly engaging in a diplomatic act with a deeply hostile symbolic meaning in the relation between China and Japan: a visit to the Yasukuni Shrine. These groups saw the visit as an effective way to compensate them for their perceived losses associated with a change of behavior toward China because the gesture directly and powerfully evoked the memory of the military confrontations between China and Japan.[48]

Finally, domestic groups often show a genuine interest not just in any type of resources, but rather those that descend specifically from the control of the course of foreign policy.[49] In other words, compensation is often requested in terms of foreign policy because it is the conduct of foreign policy that these actors want to control. This feature, therefore, makes it harder for policymakers to substitute for the perceived loss in foreign policy by providing alternative forms of compensation in the form of domestic policies. Take, for instance, the relation between the US and China. While numerous groups in the US had interests in freely trading with that country, other groups, concerned by China's poor human rights record, sought to control how the US behaved toward China. This tension influenced US behaviors toward China in the 1990s, which was characterized at the same time by protestations on issues of human rights as well as increasing trade flows.[50]

A special form that compensation can take is logrolling, defined as the exchange of favors between small groups, each with the aim of imposing their favorite foreign policy options. In perhaps the most famous discussion of logrolling in international politics, political scientist Jack Snyder investigates why countries across the globe and over time embrace a policy of overexpansion, even though it proves to be a counterproductive policy for the great majority of individuals in each country.[51] Snyder argues that overexpansion is the unintended consequence of small interest groups within a country forming a coalition where each group will support the other group's preferences in exchange for support for their own agenda.[52]

Logrolling, therefore, is a special type of compensation because it seeks to explain how an outcome that is only optimal for a small number of domestic groups can manifest itself. As with compensation, logrolling is a way in which different domestic groups get the policy they prefer to be implemented. However, unlike logrolling, arguing that compensation is likely to emerge from certain interest configurations does not make assumptions on the size of the interests to be "bought off." It also avoids assuming that policies supported by (logrolling) groups should be compatible.[53]

Which Mechanism?

The presence of a heterogeneous set of domestic interests can increase volatility via a diverging preferences mechanism. The presence of reinforcing cleavages divides a country's society into groups with very little in common with other groups in terms of preferences. Such opposing preferences push and pull states' behaviors in different directions. These pushes and pulls tend to increase, on average, the occurrence of inconsistent changes toward more cooperation and conflict in how states behave toward other states—that is, it tends to increase, potentially, volatility.

In order for the presence of a heterogeneous set of interests to impact volatility, however, such competing interests have to have access to the definition of a state's foreign policy actions. Interest configuration, obviously, matters less to understand foreign policy if interests cannot compete to define policy, as "wronged" groups will be less likely to find a way to ask for a compensation in foreign policy.

The ability of groups with diverging preferences to compete, therefore, plays an important role in the theory. In singling out one specific facet of domestic institutions and highlighting its role in explaining how states behave, this argument echoes recent advancements in research on domestic institutions. Specifically, scholars have increasingly recognized the importance of opening the black box of regime type in order to understand the complex impact of domestic institutions on policy choices.[54] In particular, focusing on specific features of the institutions can prove especially helpful, this literature suggests, to avoid making inaccurate generalizations on how group preferences find representation.[55]

Focusing on how domestic preferences diverge and compete, moreover, is crucial to explain volatility. To clarify why this is the case, it is helpful to employ a comparison with other ways in which the impact of domestic interests in foreign policy is understood in the literature.

Selectorate theory, for example, recognizes the role that different domestic groups play but ignores their preferences. Therefore, selectorate theory leads to only generic predictions regarding future states' behaviors, but it leaves us unable to forecast what type of cooperation and conflict states will actually engage in. And because understanding the degree to which cooperative and conflictual behavior occurs is important to understand how states' behaviors are shifting inconsistently, this approach cannot quite explain volatility.

An example can help clarify the shortcomings of using selectorate theory to explain volatility: the theory's approach to explaining national security. The theory identifies national security as a typical example of a public good, a good that benefits all members of society.[56] But states can enhance national security through different policies and each has consequences for domestic groups. The theory cannot predict which policies will be more likely to be put in place. Will they be consistently conflictual? Will they fluctuate instead toward greater cooperation? In order to understand which behaviors will be chosen, it is crucial to understand the configuration of domestic preferences. For example, as discussed above, if a leader decides to pursue national security by increasing the defense budget and investing in the navy rather than by joining defensive alliances or investing in other sectors of defense, some sectors of the population (such as those with hawkish preferences or those invested in the production of those goods) will benefit more than others (such as taxpayers or those with strong preferences for multilateral solutions to security).[57] By claiming that national security is a public good that benefits everyone, the theory masks the consequences that each specific policy designed to achieve national security has on different domestic groups.[58] Thus, selectorate theory cannot predict which policies each state will put in place in order to achieve national security. But understanding specific policies is crucial to understand how cooperatively and conflictually states behave, and thus whether they shift inconsistently toward more cooperation or conflict.

Another approach to explaining how domestic interests can shape states' behaviors is the one proposed by theories of veto players. Veto player theory focuses on those institutional or partisan actors whose agreement is necessary for a new policy to be adopted, and therefore to change the legislative status quo.[59] Specifically, the higher the number of veto players and the more diverse their preferences, the smaller the win-set—that is, the set of outcomes that can replace the status quo. Thus, the higher the number of veto players is, the smaller the probability of changes in the status quo becomes. Higher numbers of veto players with diverse preferences increase the probability of stability in policies precisely in this fashion.

Veto player theory cannot explain volatility because the presence of a larger win-set simply sets more possibility for change, without explaining if or when change will take place, nor what form change will take (i.e., Will it be volatile? Will it be cyclical?).[60] In other words, the lack of constraints to stability does not systematically imply volatility. Other forms of change could take place (cycles, trends, etc.), or stability could continue. In sum, veto player theory is poorly suited to explain volatility, because it theorizes the conditions for the endurance of stability, and the absence of those conditions cannot be taken to explain the occurrence of change, let alone a specific kind of change such as volatility.[61] Instead of relying on veto player and selectorate theories, I argue that the best way to understand the impact of domestic preferences on volatility is to focus on whether a diverse set of interests can compete for the definition of states' behaviors in the international arena.

Step Three: The Interaction

Given this theoretical framework, a country will behave with greater volatility toward another country when two conditions are present: in the domestic sphere, the presence of a heterogeneous set of domestic interests having access to the definition of states' behaviors and, in the international sphere, an increase in its relative power vis-à-vis itscounterparts. The presence of both factors together increases volatility.[62]

While both of these factors are crucial conditions for the outcome of interest, the roles that each factor plays in increasing volatility are different. Relative power sets a permissive condition for volatility in that it expands the range of possible options available to states. Relative power therefore influences volatility by increasing the resources available to a country to deal with its counterpart. The greater the number of options at a country's disposal, the more volatile a country can be in its behavior. But relative power alone does not explain why states engage in volatile behavior: it could well be that states with increasing relative power become more consistent in their behavior, for example, becoming more cooperative or more conflictual. The precipitant (or catalyzing) cause for volatility stems from the fact that domestically each decision will impact domestic groups differently, and therefore the presence of a set of multiple actors with heterogeneous preferences will translate into inconsistent shifts between cooperation and conflict. Because each foreign policy decision affects groups differently given their preferences, advantaging some and disadvantaging others, these groups will try to advance their own agenda on the definition of foreign policy. When that fails, the losing constituencies will ask for compensation in foreign policy from the other groups. On average, clashing domestic interests, when represented, will translate into more volatile behavior for a country when that country's relative power increases. This is the case because the greater the power, the more options at a country's disposal to satisfy those interests in the realm of foreign policy. Thus, resource availability and preference divergence tend to make states' behaviors more volatile.[63]

To further clarify how the different mechanisms connect, Figure 2.1 represents the interactive effect between the international and the domestic realm. The x-axis represents time and the y-axis represents a scale of foreign policy action from less to more cooperative. Inside the graph, the line simulates the foreign policy behaviors of a hypothetical country.

Relative power with respect to the counterpart will determine the range of options available to one country. The bracket illustrates this function that power plays: the greater the relative power, the wider the bracket, and the further up or down on the y-axis the black line can shift. By contrast, arrows in the figure represent the role of the presence of multiple and heterogeneous interests controlling the definition of the foreign policy: to catalyze movement within the bracket. Each component of the theory, the figure suggests, plays a distinct and complementary role in explaining volatility.

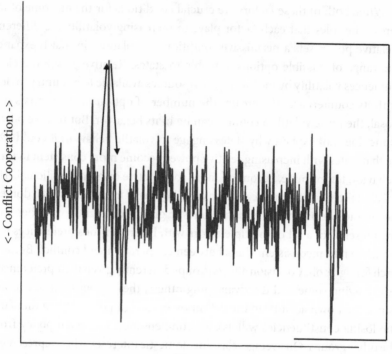

Figure 2.1 The sources of volatility. The bracket depicts the role of relative power: establishing the range of behaviors available to states. Arrows, on the other hand, depict the role of domestic interests: to shift behaviors toward greater cooperation and conflict.

Another way to think about the interaction between the two factors is through the opportunity-willingness framework.[64] In this sense, relative power provides the opportunity to pursue a volatile foreign policy, but the willingness to do so resides at the domestic level, and in particular in what the domestic interests configuration looks like.

> Hypothesis 1: Volatility in a state's behavior toward another state increases as a function of an increase in its relative power and the presence of a heterogeneous set of domestic interests with access to decision-making.

The idea that the determinants of countries' behavior in the international arena rest on both the domestic and foreign sphere of interaction has deep roots in the study of international politics. Hans Morgenthau, for example, claimed: "domestic and international politics are but two different manifestations of the same phenomenon."[65] More recently, scholars in the so-called neoclassical realist tradition have argued that a country's behavior in the international arena depends on the interaction between domestic and international stimuli.[66] Domestic politics, for example, might explain why countries might fail to balance, even though their position in the international system prescribes them to, and why they decide instead to bandwagon.[67]

My argument sits at the intersection of neoclassical approaches and Innerpolitik perspectives.[68] Like Neoclassical Realists, the argument recognizes the importance of modeling the interaction between domestic and international factors. Yet, as Innerpolitik approaches do, I theorize the domestic environment as the catalyst for foreign policy action. Specifically, in neoclassical accounts, the relative power position of a country in the international arena drives its actions, albeit the effect is mediated by leaders' perceptions of that power.[69] In my theory, by contrast, relative power positions set a permissive condition for volatile foreign policy behavior.[70]

The argument further builds on a key insight from the literature on foreign policy substitutability: that states can pursue similar foreign policy objectives through different foreign policies.[71] My argument, however, departs from this literature because, as others have done, it relaxes the assumption that states are unitary actors.[72] This assumption masks the fact that each of the possible alternatives presents very different implications for domestic groups with different preferences, and therefore that those groups will compete for their favorite option, thus explaining why countries opt for one versus another option.

The argument proposed here also expands on the literature on coalition governments. This approach has pointed to the importance of investigating the effects of multiple and heterogenous interests controlling foreign policy.[73] But studies in this tradition have mostly focused on investigations of the impact of domestic interests on the choice of one option over the other. Instead, my argument points to how the presence of a heterogeneous set of interests, combined with increasing relative power, can also explain the overall trajectory of a state's behavior toward another state—and, in particular, if it is characterized by volatile change or not.[74]

Alternative Explanations

To assess the validity of my argument in an empirical setting, it is essential to test it against alternative accounts. As I argued in the previous chapter, current studies of International Relations have yet to produce an explanation of what prompts states to act in a volatile manner—and this lack of a systematic account of volatility in states' behaviors is indeed what motivates this book's inquiry to begin with.

There are, however, approaches that seek to illuminate states' behaviors that combine cooperation and conflict. For example, "mixed signal" explanations refer to mixing cooperation and conflict together, though nothing is said about whether such mixing needs to be inconsistent. Even though they do not exactly seek to predict volatility but rather, more broadly, change between cooperation and conflict, each of these approaches provides a potentially interesting perspective through which to explore volatility in states' behaviors. I explore three such approaches below: explanations of "mixed signals," explanations of leaders' impact, and issue-based explanations.

Mixed Signals

Volatility could emerge from countries' decisions to mix their foreign policy signals toward a counterpart. In this sense, volatility could constitute the foreign policy manifestation of a state's commitment to embrace a hedging strategy. Such strategy consists of pursuing states' goals by combining both cooperative and conflictual initiatives at once vis-à-vis their counterpart. For example, a country hedging against another might seek to strengthen its economic ties with said country while at the same time preparing itself to fight against it.[75]

Some scholars have argued, for instance, that starting in the 1990s till about the mid-2000s, Japan embraced a hedging strategy toward China by deepening economic ties with the country while also developing stronger security ties with China's rival, the US.

In this sense, states embracing a strategy of hedging send mixed signals, by employing both cooperation and conflict. "Hedging, in short, is a strategic behavior that works for the best and prepares for the worst."[76]

According to theories of foreign policy hedging, mixing signals is particularly useful because it allows states to hedge their bets, thus lessening the probability of being on the losing side of an interaction.[77] If states commit to sending only cooperative signals, they risk appeasing aggressive opponents. If they commit to sending only conflictual signals, they might fuel escalation and propel a security dilemma.[78] Relying on both cooperative and conflictual signals together amounts to diversifying their policy portfolio, thus spreading the risks involved in each foreign policy option by investing in multiple foreign policy options.[79]

For most of these hedging accounts, the determinants of states' decisions to embrace hedging and send mixed signals reside in states' relative power positions.[80] Accounts differ on whether relative power superiority or inferiority is the force behind states' decisions to embrace this strategy. On the one hand, as relative power vis-à-vis a counterpart decreases, the impetus to hedge increases. This is the case because such power differentials increase uncertainty over intentions, so that resorting to hedging strategies helps states decrease the risks involved with the interaction. On the other hand, as relative power increases, so does the number of options that states can use in order to hedge. In this scenario, it is not so much the impetus for hedging that increases, but rather the opportunity. Thus:

> Hypothesis 2a. Increases in relative power increase volatility in states' behaviors toward other states.
>
> Hypothesis 2b. Increases in relative power decrease volatility in states' behaviors toward other states.

Polarity can also function as an important predictor of hedging. While hedging, some scholars have argued, is less likely in a bipolar world, it becomes an important strategy in a unipolar or multipolar world.[81] For example, scholars have employed the foreign policy hedging framing to explain China's decision to adopt a conflictual posture on the Taiwanese affair while also expanding their cultural and economic trade with the US during the early 2000s.[82]

> Hypothesis 3: Volatility in states' behaviors toward other states increases in a nonbipolar international system.

Hedging theories provide rich accounts of countries' strategies in the international system that challenge the traditional dichotomy between balancing and bandwagoning. However, these approaches cannot successfully explain volatility in states' behaviors. While able to generally predict when states will engage in both cooperation and conflict, these approaches cannot produce educated guesses regarding what, in practice, that will look like—in other words, regarding the specific type of behaviors chosen.

This is the case because hedging studies, building on the tradition of defensive realism, assume that states are unitary actors. Thus, they discount the different repercussions that each state's behavior can have on that state's domestic groups. Yet understanding these repercussions, I argue, is essential to shed light on when and why one option is preferred over others. Domestic interests are likely to mobilize in favor of or against specific states' behaviors, and their reactions will then guide states' behaviors in the international arena.

Japan, for example, represents for many an instance of a country adopting a hedging strategy. In the 2010s, it would trade with China while also tightening its alliance with China's rival, the US. Yet, what explains a change in the type of hedging policies chosen? Specifically, Japan decided to first hedge its bets by tightening its relations with the US. In 2015, however, it switched to doing so by investing more heavily in its security and by removing the ban on self-defense, thus allowing Japan's military to mobilize overseas. Both behaviors (investing in national security vs. investing in existing alliances) are consistent with the idea of hedging. But hedging accounts are not able to explain why Japan decided to hedge with external balancing for a long time and then switch to internal balancing.

The timing of this shift is instead consistent with the increased prominence of domestic nationalist groups that preferred to see more investing in the Japanese military.[83] In fact, studies have demonstrated the impact of domestic interests in influencing Japan's actions, arguing that, at times, "Japan has been unable to hedge in its strategy toward China largely because of domestic interests."[84] In other words, domestic politics is likely to have shaped the way in which Japan has responded to its changing relative power vis-à-vis China. Since understanding the choice of one behavior over another and the timing of this choice is important to explain shifts between cooperation and conflict and thus shed light on volatility, this hedging theoretical approach is ill-suited to do just that.

Leaders

An increase in the volatility in a state's behavior toward its counterpart could be instead due to that state's leader. Specifically, the literature on leadership has identified two pathways through which the specifics of a leader can impact political outcomes: leaders' transitions and leaders' traits.

The first pathway highlights the importance of changes in leadership. Transitions could either increase or decrease volatility. New leaders, some accounts argue, are likely to bring new, different beliefs, and such beliefs can change a country's international agenda.[85] This change can take the form of volatile behavior as leaders experiment with different ways to interact with their counterparts. But, other studies have found, new leaders' reputations are also much less established, so they might seek to behave in a less volatile way.[86] A change in leadership could therefore entail behavior that is more consistently conflictual instead of being more volatile.

Hypothesis 4a. A change in leadership increases volatility in states' behaviors toward its counterparts.

Hypothesis 4b. A change in leadership decreases volatility in states' behaviors toward its counterparts.

Leaders can also affect foreign policy outcomes through their own idiosyncrasies, whether they are rooted in their socializing experiences or in their ascriptive traits.[87] Socializing experiences such as military service can affect leaders' willingness to cooperate or fight.[88] In particular, leaders with military service but no combat experience initiate disputes more often,[89] suggesting that this characteristic might have important implications for volatility. Ascriptive characteristics such as leaders' gender can also predict their propensity to use conflictual tools in crises, and thus could be predictive of whether they shift inconsistently toward more cooperation or conflict.[90] Female leaders, for example, are found to be more prone to conflict to gain credibility in environments usually populated by male leaders.[91]

Hypothesis 5a. Leaders' military experiences increase volatility in states' behaviors toward its counterparts.

Hypothesis 5b. Leaders' gender increases volatility in states' behaviors toward its counterparts.

Approaches that look at leaders' characteristics are less well suited to predict volatility than other approaches, for two reasons. First, the type of new leader that is selected is likely to be endogenous to the configuration of domestic interests. For example, if such domestic groups fear a potential conflict in the future, they may choose a leader with military experience. Thus, we might observe a correlation between a leader's military experience and conflict occurrence. But concluding that such military experience is what leads to more conflict would be erroneous. Similarly, it could be the case that the incumbent fails to get re-elected because the country is involved in a difficult situation abroad. If so, again, we would observe the transition to a new leader correlate with more turmoil in a country's foreign policy, but in reality such connection would be spurious.[92] In other words, to the extent to which leaders' selection is not random but instead influenced by their biographical traits, focusing on leaders' characteristics might mask the real engines of change.

Second, leaders do not operate in a vacuum, but rather within the constraints posed by states' capabilities. This is crucial for explaining volatility, for two reasons. First, states with greater capabilities, research shows, are more prone to select female leaders.[93] Second, greater capabilities act as a permissive condition for volatility, as I argue here.

Given this complex relation between leaders' gender and their countries' capabilities and volatile behaviors, it becomes easy to mistakenly attribute volatility to gender, ignoring the link between capabilities and leaders' gender (attribution error). Even setting this attribution error aside, only focusing on leaders' characteristics and ignoring power makes it hard to gauge how volatile a leader is compared to other leaders who display the same traits or socializing experiences. This is the case because, given different levels of relative power, similar leaders might have different ranges of options at their disposal in the international arena.

Leaders' Coalitions

Another possible explanation for changes between cooperation and conflict in states' behaviors resides not so much in leaders' personalities or socializing experiences as in the coalition that supports them.[94] When a new leader takes office, they may rely on a domestic coalition of support that differs from the one on which their predecessor relies. These coalitions emerge from social cleavages and therefore tend to have different preferences in matters of foreign policy. Thus, whenever a new leader comes to power, and whenever that leader relies on a different coalition of support compared to their predecessor, change in foreign policy becomes possible, because the new leadership has to cater to different preferences. After the end of the Second World

War, for example, countries' voting patterns at the UN General Assembly were found to significantly shift whenever a new leader relying on a different domestic coalition of interests came to power in that country.[95]

> Hypothesis 6: Changes in the coalition that supports a state's leader increase volatility in that state's behaviors toward its counterparts.

This approach takes on the endogeneity challenge posed by studies of leadership by explicitly accounting for the selection process that leaders undergo. However, this approach is less well suited to explain volatility, for two reasons. First, knowing whether the preferences of the supporting coalitions have changed tells us neither the direction nor the intensity of such change. To keep with the example, countries could consistently move further away in their voting patterns from US voting patterns when the coalition of support changes. Conversely, they could shift inconsistently between cooperation and conflict in their voting patterns vis-à-vis the US, and thus act in a volatile manner toward the US. Simply looking at coalition changes does not allow us to narrow down which of these different types of change would take place.

Second, approaches focusing exclusively on domestic configurations are insufficient to predict volatile behavior toward another state because they focus on what catalyzes change while ignoring what makes change possible to begin with. But countries might differ profoundly when it comes to their capabilities. Since capabilities provide states with different options that might satisfy different domestic constituencies, states with similarly heterogeneous sets of domestic interests can differ profoundly in terms of what they can do to satisfy such domestic interests. Increasing relative capabilities will likely augment the probability of volatility across countries with similar switches in support coalitions.

Contentious Issues

Volatility could instead be the outcome of certain features of states' relations with their counterparts and, in particular, of the issues that are present in the relation.

For example, countries might behave with greater volatility toward other countries when there are more outstanding contentious issues with those countries. The presence of such issues, for example, could increase the frequency of interactions, and thus, ceteris paribus, the probability of experiencing volatile behavior would also increase. Conversely, the key to volatility might not be the number of contentious issues present, but rather their salience. When contentious issues become salient, they might also catalyze more conflictual behaviors. But salient contentious issues might at times attract more cooperative behavior, with the latter developing as an attempt to defuse the increase in conflict.

> Hypothesis 7a. The greater the number of issues present in the relation, the greater the volatility in a state's behavior toward its counterpart.
>
> Hypothesis 7b. The more salient the issues present in the relation, the greater the volatility in a state's behavior toward its counterpart.

Issue-based explanations of international politics provide foundational insights on states' behaviors and motives. Per se, however, these approaches cannot shed light on volatility. First, the process through which issues become salient or contentious is not exogenous to states' relations. Contentious issues emerge a posteriori as "what states choose to fight over."[96]

Domestic interests also make some issues more salient by attaching more value to them, either tangible or intangible.[97] Similarly, it is contending domestic interests, research shows, that make territorial issues such as Jerusalem or Northern Ireland conflictual to begin with.[98]

Second, even if issues are present and they do lead to change, it is not clear that they would lead to volatile change. In some cases, conflict might steadily escalate; in others, conflict might inconsistently alternate with cooperation. A simple t-test on the difference in mean volatility in dyads where issues are present and ones without outstanding issues fails to reject the null of no difference ($p = 0.459$).[99]

Conclusions

This chapter has proposed a new explanation for why volatility in states' behaviors toward other states increases. Volatility, this chapter has argued, is the outcome of the interaction between relative power and a heterogeneous set of domestic groups that compete to influence a state's behavior toward its counterpart.

More broadly, this argument seeks to make three contributions to the way we understand international politics. First, the argument seeks to explain a facet of international politics that current approaches to the study of international politics have so far not explained: states' behaviors becoming more diverse—that is, increasingly encompassing different, opposing behaviors, both cooperative and conflictual. In other words, this theoretical approach seeks to explain the variance in the distribution of behaviors as opposed to the average or most recurrent behavior, as mean-centric approaches tend to do.[100] Such theories of variance encourage scholars and practitioners to consider the nuances of international politics more closely.[101] For example, by exploring when and why relations among countries become volatile, we become better able to understand the differences in relations such as rivalries that are considered to be, on average, more conflictual than the modal international interaction in the international arena but that might vary considerably in terms of how cooperative they are.

Second, this book offers an argument to make sense of dynamics in international politics. In other words, the book offers an explanation for how relations unfold through time to understand when such relations might become more or less volatile and why. In this sense, this argument is an important complement to other theories in International Relations that adopt instead an episodic notion of foreign policy, whereupon relations unfolding in the international arena are conceptualized as a set of discrete and distinguishable events—such as the outbreak of a war, the escalation of a crisis, the signing of an agreement, and so on.[102] In this conceptualization of states' behaviors as a set of discrete episodes, it is important to clarify what propels states to engage in a certain kind of behavior. For instance, in order to understand whether democracies are less likely to wage wars against each other, it is crucial to conceptualize, isolate, and compare different instances of war, both temporally and cross-sectionally. However, this episodic approach necessarily ignores the specific dynamics linking together these different episodes, which might be quite different. For example, distinct instances of conflict between two countries can be separated by periods of no interactions at all or by stages of increasing cooperation. Ignoring the dynamics that connect all the instances of the foreign policy behavior of interest amounts to ignoring important differences in relations between countries. Studying only separate events forces us to disregard the context in which they take place, thus severely limiting our inference abilities.[103]

A third way in which my argument adds to current arguments in the literature is by identifying a process. A process is a compound of mechanisms interacting at different levels.[104] Processes are fundamental components of the study of International Relations because, especially to explain change, it is important to understand both what states can do (and why) and when they decide to do it (and why). To explain change, we need to be able to explain what makes it possible and what catalyzes it. Similarly, in order to explain when and how states' foreign policy interactions shift inconsistently between cooperation and conflict, it is crucial to understand how mechanisms making shifts possible and mechanisms catalyzing such shifts interact to create a dynamic process.

After presenting the main argument put forward by the book, this chapter has also presented plausible alternatives: mixed signals, leaders, coalitions, and issue-based explanations. These alternatives descend from approaches that seek to understand the mixing of cooperation and conflict, if not explicitly volatility. The chapter then explained why these accounts, while providing important perspectives on the states' decisions to combine cooperation and conflict, are ultimately insufficient to provide an exhaustive explanation of volatility.

The next section of the book explores the empirical manifestations of volatility in states' behaviors. After proposing a new measurement of volatility and applying it to several cases (Chapter 3), the book tests the validity of the argument proposed in this chapter through both a large-N approach (Chapter 4) and a case study (Chapter 5).

3

Measuring Volatility

Chapter 1 explained the value added of understanding volatility in states' behaviors toward other states. It also provided a conceptualization of volatility. Chapter 2 proposed instead an explanation of when states' behaviors become increasingly volatile. A logical question follows: what does volatility in states' behaviors look like in the real world? This chapter addresses precisely this question, proposing a new measurement of volatility.

In doing so, this chapter serves three functions. First, it provides researchers with tools to recognize volatility as it occurs in the international arena and to distinguish it from other forms of change in states' behaviors. This distinction, this book has argued, can shed light on important dynamics in International Relations. Second, since measurement constitutes "a linkage operation, an act of translation" between theoretical concepts and empirical events, the chapter takes a fundamental first step toward testing my theoretical account of volatility against possible alternative explanations by elaborating a measurement of volatility in states' behaviors.[1] Measurement, by closely representing the concept that generates it, plays an essential role in achieving construct validity in the empirical analysis.[2] Third, this chapter puts the concept and measurement of volatility presented to work by using it to shed light on the behaviors of various states. In so doing, it provides empirical evidence for how volatility varies across states and time while also significantly differing from other dynamics in states' behaviors that bring about change.

Thus, this chapter demonstrates the value added of volatility in achieving a richer, more satisfying understanding of the international arena. Specifically, countries whose behavior we traditionally characterize as mostly hostile toward certain countries and mostly friendly toward others show at times great volatility. At times, states shift inconsistently toward cooperation and conflict toward their allies just as much as they do toward their rivals. This finding, in turn, raises the question: what do useful dichotomizations such as those suggested in the concepts of "alliances" and "rivalries" belie?

Volatile States in International Politics. Eleonora Mattiacci, Oxford University Press. © Oxford University Press 2023.
DOI: 10.1093/oso/9780197638675.003.0003

This chapter therefore illustrates the multipronged approach to the study of volatility that this book employs in order to produce a valid and reliable measures of volatility in states' behaviors. In other words, a sound measure of volatility will identify instances of volatility in a way that, respectively, both accurately captures what the concept of volatility entails and does so consistently across different empirical cases.[3] Doing so entails facing two distinct yet interrelated challenges. First, such measurement needs to correctly capture inconsistent change toward more cooperation and conflict, without conflating it with other forms of change. Not all types of change are volatile, Chapter 1 argued. Avoiding confusion with other concepts is particularly important, as the book seeks to establish the study of volatility in international politics as an important area that complements existing accounts of change in the international arena. Second, the measurement must also be able to consistently capture volatility in different contexts, through both time and space. This feature will allow the measure to exactly compare instances of greater or less volatile behavior, so as to assess whether the theory can explain those different instances.

The chapter proceeds as follows. The next section explains how to gather data that gives a realistic representation to the diverse set of behaviors states engage in. It then explores how to go from a collection of states' behaviors to an orderly sequence of events (or time series). Then, a new section sheds light on why current approaches to measuring volatility are insufficient to capture volatility in states' behaviors. It also shows why applying the Box-Jenkins procedure constitutes instead a more fruitful strategy. Then, the chapter presents some examples of the procedure. The sections that follow put the procedure just described in the broader context of the book's empirical analysis. In particular, these sections explain how the measure scales up in the context of a large-N study and how it can be complemented with data from different sources. Conclusions follow, explaining the value added of the measurement that I propose for how we understand international politics and previewing the content of the next chapters.

Capturing Cooperation and Conflict

Countries' behaviors in the international system are multifaceted, encompassing myriad activities—from wars to rapprochements, to diplomatic visits, to aid, to sanctions, to threats, to promises, to apologies, etc., just to name a few. When seeking to understand where inconsistent shifts toward more cooperative or more conflictual behaviors come from, therefore, it is important to, first, be able to capture such diversity of behaviors in the measure, and second, avoid conflating different instances of behavior.

To reliably capture all the different instances of countries' behaviors in the international arena, I use event data—that is, extensive, systematic records of states' behaviors. Event data leverage news accounts of international politics. From these reports, event data extracts information on multiple facets of foreign policy actions—namely, which action is carried on, which country is engaging in a specific foreign policy activity ("source"), toward which country ("target") that activity is directed, and when.[4] For example, when US President Donald Trump threatened North Korea with retaliation in case of a nuclear attack, the event would be coded as the US president (source) threatening (action) the North Korean leader (target) on January 2, 2018.[5]

Event data present particularly rich accounts of states' everyday activities, because they rely on a very thorough and diverse schema or ontology. An ontology is a set of categories of events that records and parses out over 100 types of countries' behaviors.[6] Ontologies allow scholars to both capture and record actions as disparate as amassing troops at the border, thanking another state for their aid in times of emergency, threatening to withdraw from an alliance, praising the activities of other countries, asking for military aid, and so on.

Using a comprehensive ontology to record countries' behaviors presents important advantages. First, unlike datasets that only report specific instances of countries' behaviors, event data can be leveraged to paint a more comprehensive picture of states' activities because they include more categories of behavior. To understand this, it is important to compare event data to other, widely used datasets, such as the International Crisis Behavior Project (ICB) or the Correlates of War Project's Militarized Interstate Disputes (MID).[7] Each of these datasets specializes in identifying one type of behavior (respectively, crises and disputes) and reporting all instances of such behavior occurring. This procedure is crucial to increase the replicability of scholarly analyses of countries' behaviors. Yet the picture of the relations between countries emerging from such sources is limited to when and whether those two countries had, respectively, crises or militarized disputes.

For instance, during the 1990s, the ICB dataset describes the India-Pakistan relation by only reporting emergency situations taking place between them and involving various degrees of military escalation or mediation (such as the 2001 Indian Parliament attack).[8] The MID dataset only reports the threat, show, and use of force between India and Pakistan occurring during those periods (such as the Kashmir war). During the same period of time, by contrast, event data report both crises and disputes between the two states, as the ICB and MID data sources do, and also include cooperative events like the non-nuclear aggression agreement signed in 1988 and entered into force in 1991, various diplomatic statements between the two countries, and so on.

The inclusive and diverse nature of event data is particularly relevant to capture volatility, for two reasons. First, to capture switches toward more cooperation or conflict, it is important that both types of behaviors be present in the data. Second, comprehensive data is also important to accurately capture which dynamics characterize states' behaviors. For example, we could witness recurrent conflict between states. But without information on whether episodes of conflict are interspersed with episodes of cooperation, and how they are interspersed, it would be impossible to parse out cases when such recurrent conflict is also accompanied by volatility and cases when it is not. Thus, registering what happens in the international system in a comprehensive way, event data help capture volatility as distinct from other forms of change.[9]

While event data can help build comprehensive data on states' behaviors, it is also important to avoid conflating such behaviors. Scaling event data consist of going one step forward in categorizing these events. It entails actually putting events on a continuum of cooperation and conflict and assessing how cooperative or conflictual each event is. Therefore, precisely because event data systematically store and measure a wide array of behaviors, I follow common practice and weigh them using the widely used Goldstein scale.[10]

The scale is the product of a survey of international politics experts and scholars who shared their informed opinion on how cooperative or conflictual each event in the international system is. It ranges between −10 (conflict) and 10 (cooperation). It answers questions such as: In states' interactions, how salient are episodes of material, military conflict (such as a military attack on another state) compared to episodes of material, economic conflict (such as the imposition of sanctions)? Or, how much should verbal, diplomatic cooperation (such as praising the other state's behavior) weigh compared to material, diplomatic cooperation (such as recognizing another state or releasing prisoners of war)?

The scale therefore allows researchers to capitalize on the diversity of data available on countries' behaviors without grouping together instances of apples and oranges.[11] For example, threats to use force against another country represent examples of conflictual behavior, whereas offers of military aid represent cooperation between countries. Not only does this expert-based scale distinguish between cooperative and conflictual episodes, attaching to the former positive weights and to the latter negative ones, but also the scale allows researchers to capture the different intensities of each action. It does so by giving greater weight to material actions than to verbal actions. By weighing different events on the basis of how salient they are, the scale makes it possible to avoid assuming that, for example, fishing disputes have the same salience in the interaction between India and Pakistan as the 1971 war does—or that routine diplomatic visits have the same salience as the 1988 Indo-Pakistani nonattack agreement. This feature is important when seeking to combine different events in states' behaviors without confusing them.

Capturing Dynamics

Once I obtain a comprehensive and weighted list of episodes of cooperation and conflict, I use these event data to build a time series of the interactions of one state ("source") toward another ("target"). A time series is a sequence of data points. Each data point constitutes the behavior of one state toward another at time t, organized in a temporal sequence.

A time series represents interactions between states as interconnected sequences of cooperative and conflictual events unfolding through time, rather than as separate episodes of conflict or cooperation. Studying interactions as interconnected sequences, in turn, is a crucial preliminary step to understand volatility. This is the case because, as I explain in the next section, once events are organized diachronically, it becomes possible to track movement between cooperation and conflict in states' behaviors, so as to detect which type of change is taking place in states' behaviors and whether the change that is taking place is volatile or not.

Figure 3.1 displays the end product of this data-gathering process. It represents Pakistan's behavior toward India, reconstructed via event data. The x-axis represents time, and the y-axis represents the conflict–cooperation continuum.[12] Each data point captures an event taking place in the behavior

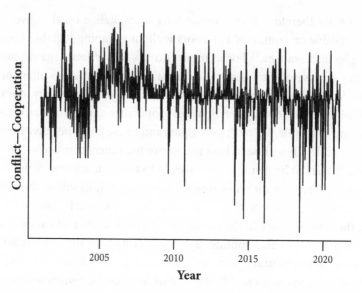

Figure 3.1 The behavior of Pakistan toward India, reconstructed via event data. *Source:* Integrated Crisis Early Warning System (ICEWS).

of one country toward another, coded as an instance of cooperation or conflict, according to the CAMEO ontology or schema, and weighted based on its salience, according to the Goldstein (1992) scale. The line connecting all those data points represents the time series of the actions of one country toward another throughout that period of time.

Figure 3.1 displays a crucial advantage emerging from measuring volatility using time series. Building individual time series allows researchers to examine volatility in each country's behavior toward another country separately. In this case, it is possible to study when volatility appears in Pakistan's behavior toward India and vice versa. Looking at each time series separately is important to avoid assuming that, for example, Pakistan's behavior toward India changes in response to the same stimuli as India's behavior toward Pakistan.

These time series therefore offer an important starting point to parse out volatile change. The next section explores how to then leverage these time series to identify volatile behavior.

Isolating Volatility

When explored in other contexts, volatility has been measured in one of two ways. In some cases, volatility has been measured as the standard deviation of a specific phenomenon of interest. This procedure entails recording how different each manifestation of such a phenomenon is from its usual manifestations. Scholars have measured growth-rate volatility, for example, by measuring the standard deviation in the gross domestic product annual growth rate, therefore measuring how far from the mean each annual growth rate was.[13] The volatility of external powers' support in civil wars, similarly, has been captured as the absolute value of the standard deviation of the signals sent to civil war combatants by each external power.[14]

In other cases, volatility has been measured as the absolute change in a quantity between two time periods. Trade volatility, for example, has been measured as the absolute value of the change in the logged value of real exports between $t - 1$ and t.[15]

What these two ways of measuring volatility have in common is that they focus on capturing how different each iteration of a phenomenon is from its other iterations. While such difference is important, these approaches to measuring volatility cannot be directly used to measure volatility in states' behaviors. This is the case because each fails to address two challenges.

First, if we simply measure volatility as the distance from the mean of each observed behavior, as taking the standard deviation of the time series directly would, then we are implicitly assuming that every deviation from the mean behavior entails volatile behavior. In other words, every time a country would change course from its usual behavior, we would label that as amounting to volatile behavior. Yet, as Chapter 1 makes clear, change in states' behaviors can take multiple forms, and volatility is just one of those forms. Countries who often face each other in conflict, for example, present strong path dependency in their behaviors, so that past episodes of conflict beget more episodes of conflict.[16] In other words, in those relations, past actions are likely to predict current ones, possibly manifesting themselves in a progressive deterioration of the relation. Not all changes in states' behaviors can be attributed to volatility. But this is exactly what measuring volatility through the standard deviation of the distribution of behaviors would do, because it would not parse out change that is due to path dependency or cycles from change that takes a volatile form. A similar problem of attribution would also emerge if we measure volatility by looking at the different values of a variable between two time periods.

Moreover, multiple dynamics of change could be present at once. After the end of the Cold War, for instance, relations between the US and Russia denoted traits of volatility but also signs of consistent, systematic improvement or rapprochement.[17] If we simply assumed that all change that we measure is volatile, we would risk conflating different processes at once—volatile processes and positive trends toward rapprochement, in this case. This would risk flattening and oversimplifying our account of change in international politics. In the appendix, I decompose a time series of a state's behavior toward its counterpart, showing the presence of different forms of change in it (see Figure A.1).

The second challenge to using pre-existing approaches to measuring volatility is that the degree to which each dynamic characterizes a country's behavior in international politics might be different. In other words, not every country's policy toward another undergoes phases, trends toward rapprochement, moments of inertia, and so on. Nor should we assume that these dynamics are present for every country at the same point in time. Instead, it becomes crucial to not make a priori assumptions as to which dynamics characterize which relations and when.

Measuring Volatility: A Two-Step Procedure

To address these challenges that I just described, I focus on the time series of each state's behavior toward their counterpart. For each of them, I apply a time series procedure that makes it possible to isolate volatility from other forms of change. I describe this procedure in broad strokes below and in greater detail in the appendix.[18]

Step One: The Box-Jenkins Procedure

First, I seek to understand which dynamics of change are present in each country's behavior toward their counterpart as represented in the time series (Step One). This step entails answering questions such as: How prevalent is cyclical behavior for this state? How strong is the pull of inertia? Will the effect of past events decrease over time, and if so, how quickly? And so on.

Following Box-Steffensmeier et al. (2014), I apply the Box-Jenkins procedure to the univariate time series of each country's behavior toward a specific counterpart.[19] The aim of the procedure is to identify the model specification that best captures the temporal dynamics in the data by triangulating among different tests and model specifications. The procedure itself comprises several stages, each geared toward identifying the model that best represents the dynamics in the data.

In this manner, Step One deductively identifies the specific dynamics characterizing the behavior of each country toward one of their counterparts. In other words, this step answers the question of whether we observe change in states' behaviors and whether the change that we observe is consistent, explained by the presence of trends, cycles, and so on. This step is essential because it enables the analysis to acknowledge that not all change in international politics is a symptom of volatility, and that instead such change can come from sources other than volatility (such as escalation, inertia, etc.).[20]

For example, shifts between cooperation and conflict could depend on specific events that are set to take place during specific times. Every January since 1992, for instance, India and Pakistan have exchanged the list of nuclear installations and facilities, per the Agreement on the Prohibition of Attack against Nuclear Installations signed in 1988. This might constitute a shift toward cooperation, but one that happens just at specific points in time, due to recurring deadlines that make it predictable. Therefore, the Box-Jenkins procedure would identify the cyclical component of such changes in states' behaviors. This would avoid confusing cyclical change with volatile change.

The Box-Jenkins procedure, therefore, presents a reliable tool to measure volatility because it is possible to employ it in a flexible and systematic way across the study of multiple time series, each representing one country's behavior toward a specific counterpart, without making a priori assumptions regarding if and when volatility will be present in such behaviors. Moreover, the procedure described here can also be used to study volatility in the behavior of different, nonstate actors, because it simply parses out and analyzes behavior over time.

Therefore, the Box-Jenkins procedure avoids adopting a "one solution fits all" approach and can help achieve reliability by tailoring the investigation of volatility to reflect and capture the idiosyncratic patterns of behaviors that each country can embrace through time.

Step Two: The Residuals

In the appendix, I provide more details on Step Two. Here, I offer the intuition behind it. Step Two entails subtracting the original time series from the time series estimated through the Box-Jenkins procedure. The residuals that emerge from this operation represent the difference between observed changes and changes that happen in a consistent manner—that is, a manner consistent with the presence of trends, inertia, cycles, and so on. Thus, these residuals represent change between cooperation and conflict that is inconsistent—that is, volatile behavior.

These residuals can then form their own time series. The appendix shows results from 1,000 simulated residuals time series. These simulations reveal two important features of volatility. First, residuals' series displaying greater volatility present greater shifts toward cooperation or conflict than series displaying less volatility. Second, focusing on what happens between contiguous time periods, on average, shifts between more cooperation and more conflict from $t - 1$ to t tend to be both bigger and harder to predict in more volatile series than in less volatile series. In the appendix, I plot these series and discuss these features more at greater length.

Summarizing Volatility

Measuring volatility as the residuals of a Box-Jenkins procedure applied to a weekly or monthly time series is useful to capture the exact timing at which inconsistent shifts take place. However, most of the phenomena we study in international politics, such as political regimes, economic growth, military capabilities, and so on, vary meaningfully on a yearly basis rather than a weekly or monthly basis, so it is important to have a sense for how volatile a year will be. In addition, a measure that can capture the overall volatility in a series is also helpful to compare levels of volatility across cases. It is hard to understand which series display more volatility or less volatility just looking at the time series of the residuals. Therefore, I also estimate the standard deviation of these residuals, squared. In the appendix, I further detail this procedure.

The standard deviation offers a compact measure of how far each observed behavior is with respect to the average observed behavior. The greater the standard deviation, the greater the level of volatility experienced by each country in each year. I square the residuals because what I am interested in is summarizing how big inconsistent shifts toward more cooperation and more conflict are, not so much whether each shift was toward cooperation or conflict. The outcome of these steps is an estimate of how much inconsistent change in the behavior of one state toward another deviated from the mean inconsistent change in a given year.

Such measure can then be used to compare different series in terms of their volatility. The higher the standard deviation, the greater the volatility will be.

Combining the outcome of the Box-Jenkins procedure with a large-N analysis makes it possible to carefully investigate complex questions regarding the origins of volatility. It could be the case that issues dictate whether countries behave in a more volatile manner. For example, states could always cooperate on military matters but also always disagree on economic issues. Would this behavior be counted as volatile by the measure presented here? First, the Box-Jenkins procedure would make it possible to investigate whether this change between conflict and cooperation happens in a consistent manner or not. For instance, relations between countries could deteriorate progressively, and cooperation on military issues could be systematically followed by conflict on economic issues. If so, the Box-Jenkins procedure would identify the presence of a trend and would not confuse these shifts between cooperation and conflict with volatile behavior. By contrast, if countries were to shift inconsistently between cooperating on military issues and disagreeing on economic matters, then that change would indeed amount to volatile behavior according to the procedure. The question would then become: What correlates with whether those shifts will take place? Could it be the presence of contentious issues per se, so that when controlling for that, the effect of power and interests would disappear? The large-N analysis makes it possible to test for this possibility, controlling for the issues at stake as one possible alternative explanation of volatility.

The Measure in Practice

This section explores what we learn about states' behaviors in the international arena when we study volatility. It does so by exploring the application of the measure presented earlier in this chapter to some of the best-studied countries in the past twenty years. Several findings emerge.

First, states' behaviors look more complex (and even perhaps more interesting) when we account for the different levels of volatility that characterize them. Figure 3.2(a) plots Cuban behavior toward the US, while Figure 3.2(b) plots Indian behavior toward Pakistan.[21] The x-axis represents time (in weeks). As discussed in Chapters 1 and 3, the y-axis represents a continuum ranging from material conflict (negative values) to material cooperation (positive values), also including, respectively, verbal conflict and verbal

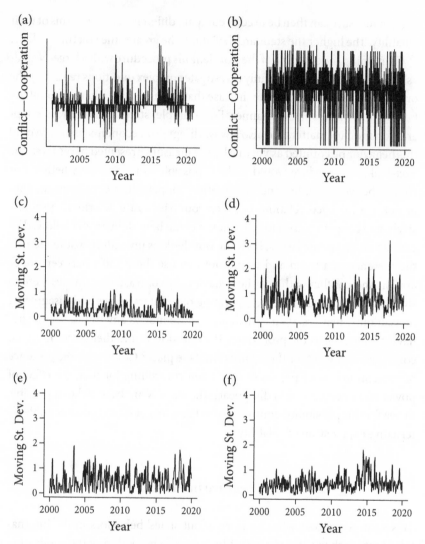

Figure 3.2 A comparison of behaviors and volatility. Cuban behavior toward the US (a), Indian behavior toward Pakistan (b), volatility in Cuba's behavior toward the US (c), volatility in India's behavior toward Pakistan (d), volatility in India's behavior toward China (e), and volatility in Iranian behavior toward the US (f).

cooperation.[22] As Chapter 1 makes clear, Cuba and India were at the center of two momentous rapprochements in 2015, with, respectively, the US and Pakistan. In both cases, such rapprochements came after years of conflict in what scholars have termed "rivalrous relationships." The graphs suggest indeed that both countries engaged in conflictual behavior quite often. Moreover, the scope of behaviors these two countries engaged in during those years is also comparable: the standard deviation of the two time series depicted in Figure 3.2(a) and Figure 3.2(b) are similar at, respectively, 3.80 and 3.99.

However, there is an important difference between Cuba's behavior toward the US and India's behavior toward Pakistan: the degree to which such behaviors display volatility.

Figure 3.2(c) and Figure 3.2(d) plot, respectively, volatility in Cuba's behavior toward the US and volatility in India's behavior toward Pakistan.[23] India's behavior toward Pakistan has tended to display greater volatility over time. So, while conflict has been present in both relations, in the case of India there has been also inconsistent change toward more cooperation or conflict. In this sense, looking at volatility makes it possible to capture further nuances in the relations between states. Relations that seemed quite similar when only looking at their conflictual component display much more complexity when we also consider volatility.

Second, volatility adds nuances to our understanding of key relations in international politics. For example, comparing the volatility registered in Cuban behavior toward the US (Figure 3.2[c]) to the volatility in Iranian behavior toward the US in the period 2000–2019 (Figure 3.2[f]) is instructive. Both countries occupied prominent positions in the US agenda during the years under analysis here, as the quote by President Obama in Chapter 2 suggests. Both relationships have been characterized as rivalrous. Indeed, in both cases, data reveal that the incidence of conflictual behavior as a proportion of total behavior is comparable at, respectively, 69.46% and 72.94%.[24] And yet, as the figures reveal, only focusing on conflict does not tell us the whole story. Iran behaved in a more volatile manner toward the US in the period under analysis. Where did such differences in volatility levels come from?

A similar insight emerges when looking at alliances. Volatility is by no means the exclusive realm of countries with inimical relationships. Figure 3.3(a) and Figure 3.3(b) compare instead volatility in the behavior of two US allies, Japan and Pakistan, respectively, toward the US. In both cases, the modal behavior toward the US corresponds to verbal cooperation, including cooperative overture for further cooperation. As it emerges from the graphs, volatility can be much higher in the behavior of certain allies (in this case, Pakistan) compared to the behavior of other allies (Japan). Indeed, because

(a)

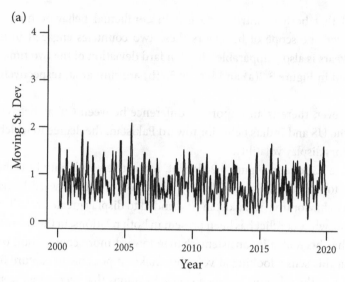

(b)

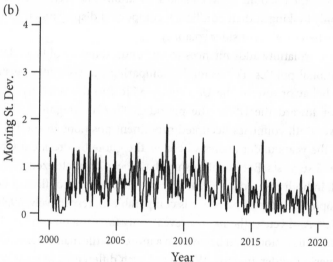

Figure 3.3 Comparing allies' volatile behaviors. Volatility in Japanese behavior toward the US (a) and volatility in Pakistani behavior toward the US (b).

volatility varies over time, it is possible to see that at times allies display more volatility than enemies. In the period under analysis, for instance, Figure 3.3(b) shows that there were moments when the volatility of Pakistan toward the US was higher than the volatility of Cuba toward the US (Figure 3.2(c)). We know that cooperation is not the exclusive realm of allies and conflict is not the exclusive realm of enemies. But the concept of volatility also helps us understand how comparable inconsistent shifts toward more cooperation or more conflict can be present in both interactions. Consistent change is not a given in either interaction, and uncertainty can be quite salient in both.

Third, volatility cannot be reduced to other forms of change. As Chapters 1 and 3 have argued, volatility is not the only dynamic present in states' behaviors. Figure 3.5(a) plots South Korean behavior toward the US (left graph), further isolating its trend and volatile component (see, respectively, middle and left graph). The figure shows how in practice multiple dynamics can be present at the same time and one does not subsume the others. Change responding to trends follows a pattern. Volatile change, in contrast, does not. Both types of change are present in that behavior but are not the same thing. Figure 3.5 (b) (left graph) displays instead South Korean behavior toward Japan, again isolating different dynamics present in the data. A comparison between the two figures reveals an important insight: the incidence of trends or volatile behaviors increases or decreases at different points in time in the behavior of the same country toward different counterparts. This, in turn, emphasizes the importance of not assuming that certain types of change (like volatile change) will happen at specific points in time. Rather, it is best to estimate its occurrence inductively, as the Box-Jenkins procedure does.

Not only is volatility different from other forms of change, and thus should be studied as such, but also it is often more informative than some of the change concepts we usually use. Over the past 20 years, for example, Pakistan's behavior toward India has been defined as unstable, just like Iran's behavior toward Israel.[25] But instability does not tell us much about the incidence of cooperation. Pakistan's behavior has seen a lot more cooperation toward India than Iran's behavior has displayed toward Israel, on average, during this time period. The way behavior shifted between cooperation and conflict was also different between the two countries, as Figure 3.4(a) and Figure 3.4(b) show us. Pakistan's behavior was more volatile than Iran's behavior. The concept of instability does not really capture the degree to which different relations, while all unstable, differ in terms of how many episodes of cooperation they witness. The concept of instability also does not measure whether states that are for the most part unstable shift toward more conflict or cooperation in volatile ways or in consistent ways. Therefore, the concept of instability misses important dynamics taking place on the international arena.

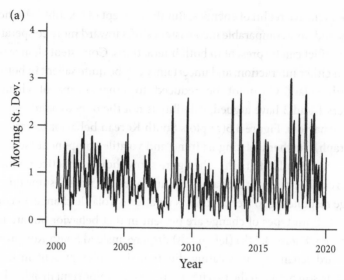

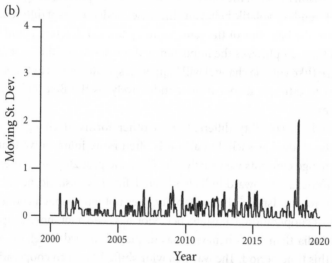

Figure 3.4 Comparing rivals' volatile behaviors. Volatility in Pakistani behavior toward India (a) and volatility in Iranian behavior toward Israel (b).

Finally, volatility is a phenomenon worth explaining in depth. Two findings in particular emerge from all those figures presented so far. First, volatility shifts through time: in each plot, volatility acquires different values over the years, varying considerably. Second, volatility varies across cases: throughout the period under analysis, volatility tended to be higher

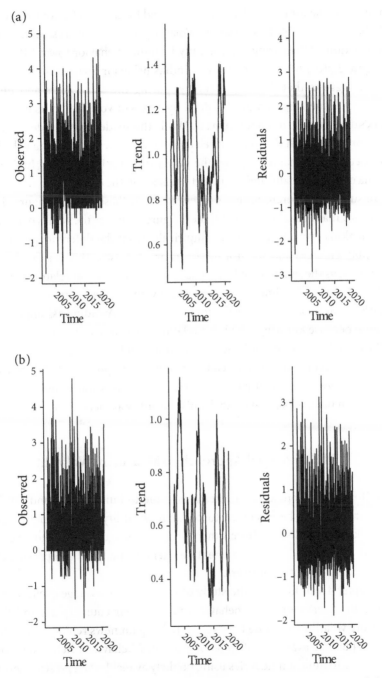

Figure 3.5 Decomposed time series graph. South Korean behavior toward the US (a) and South Korean behavior toward Japan (b).

in India's behavior toward Pakistan compared to Cuba's behavior toward the US. So, what explains this variation? Volatility moreover also eschews simple explanations. Comparing the volatility in India's behavior toward Pakistan (Figure 3.2(d)) with the volatility in India's behavior toward China (Figure 3.2(e))suggests that the same country, during the same years and under the same leadership, can display different levels of volatility in its behavior, depending on who its counterpart is. While this evidence is just descriptive, it is consistent with the role that relative power plays in increasing volatility as discussed in Chapter 2, given the power distribution between India and China on the one hand and India and Pakistan on the other.

In sum, the different findings emerging from these different figures lead us to two main conclusions. First, these figures show us the values of using a Box-Jenkins procedure to derive empirically from the different cases when volatility emerges and when it increases or decreases. This is a flexible in-strument, as the same procedure can be applied to different relations during different points in time. It does not really make assumptions regarding where change will emerge or the form it will take. Avoiding assumptions is helpful because knowing whether a relation is rivalrous or amicable cannot tell us much about how volatile that relation will be. Second, when we take this case-specific approach instead of making assumptions as to where vola-tility emerges, we see that volatility varies across cases and across time. This finding, in turn, makes it hard to dismiss volatility as mere noise.

A Multipronged Approach to Measuring Volatility

The Box-Jenkins procedure makes it possible to build a valid and reliable measure that can be leveraged to compare volatility in different contexts while keeping it distinct from other forms of change. But how to leverage data to measure volatility? Different chapters in the book will provide dif-ferent, complementary answers.

Chapter 4 will focus on the study of rivalries and leverage event data to create time series of states' behaviors toward their counterparts and then measure volatility on those time series. Relying on news reports, event data collect publicly available information on states' behaviors. Retracing states' behaviors to build a time series using publicly available data presents several advantages.

First, research suggests that public events tend to constitute costlier expressions of countries' preferences and intentions than secret events, and that, for this reason, these behaviors possibly represent less noisy manifestations of these countries' intentions than secret events do.[26] Public behaviors systematically stand out as displaying greater "performativity" compared to behaviors kept secret.[27] In other words, since public actions, by definition, happen in front of one or multiple audiences (domestic, international, or both), they might shape a country's reputation in the eyes of other countries, possibly influencing future interactions with such countries. Public behaviors send clearer signals of resolve to which their targets respond more readily, compared to secret behaviors.[28] Indeed, decision makers appear to give greater weight to public behaviors.[29] For these reasons, public events tend to uniquely capture salient instances of states' behaviors—that is, instances in which countries behave in a way that is especially meaningful to them and to others. Given their salience and special meaning, public events constitute an important context in which to study volatility.

Second, retracing states' behaviors to build a time series using exclusively publicly available data is important to avoid adding noise to the measure. The fact that secret and public behaviors differ systematically in their degree of performativity and in their poignancy for decision makers suggests that the data-generating process is different for public and secret events. Thus, mixing the two together when building a time series of states' actions risks creating a noisy account of states' interactions with their counterparts. By avoiding mixing secret and public events, using event data avoids making false analogies between different types of behaviors.

Finally, leveraging data that, like event data, use the same sources for different countries makes it possible to generate less noisy data than choosing ad hoc sources that change for each country. While it is possible that English-language sources will be more receptive to events taking place in English-speaking countries, this is less of a concern for those pairs of states, such as the ones analyzed in this book in Chapters 4 and 5, that are often in the news: major rivals and allies.

Therefore, for the purpose of building a comprehensive time series of states' behaviors, event data outperform archival data. These latter present several disadvantages to this end. First, the completeness of archival data available varies significantly by country because each country can decide which documents they can keep secret and for how long.[30] This means that the amount and quality of information disclosed in declassified documents vary substantively and nonrandomly.

Second, even when documents are declassified, they often still have several parts redacted. Research has shown that "when material is deleted, it is not being sanitized out in a totally random way."[31] Individual decision makers at times get to decide what they put on record. In 2009, for example, the State Department introduced a new system, called the State Messaging and Archive Retrieval Toolkit (SMART), that would allow staff to preserve emails and cables directly. Five years later, reviewing the State Department's email recording practices for the three initial months in 2016, the Office of the Inspector General found that the difference between how many emails were produced and how many emails were kept was staggering: in 2011, for example, just 61,156 emails were recorded out of a billion.[32]

However, archival data produces other, helpful forms of information. For example, archives can at times reveal information on how decision makers perceive the behavior of their counterparts as such behavior unfolds in real time. This is particularly important in the case of volatile behavior, because it makes it possible to understand how volatility can increase uncertainty and thus mistrust. Moreover, archival documents reveal how issues are created and dissolved via processes such as issue linkage, thus illuminating the dynamics underpinning change in the relations between countries. It is possible, for example, that shifts toward more cooperation and conflict appear in an inconsistent way. With archival data, it is at times possible to shed light on when and how decision makers combined or separated issues in a way whose by-product was inconsistent change. Thus, in Chapter 5, I complement event data with archival sources. I choose to do so because the chapter focuses on behavior between allies. Since alliances require often coordinating action on multiple fronts, these relations tend to be quite complex. Thus, leveraging different types of data sources can be particularly fruitful.

In sum, each chapter in this book sheds light on volatility in states' behaviors in a way that complements the other chapters, with the aim of producing a rich empirical account of relations between states. Overall, triangulating across different data and techniques makes it possible to produce a well-rounded measurement of volatility, one that is better able to faithfully translate the theoretical concept presented in Chapter 1 into its proper empirical representation.

Conclusions

This chapter has proposed a measurement of volatility in states' behaviors. It then applied it to the study of a number of states' behaviors toward their counterparts.

The chapter presents five main conclusions. First, while in other fields volatility has been measured directly as the standard deviation of one variable or the difference between past and present values for each variable, these "one solution fits all" approaches do not work to measure volatility in states' behaviors. Doing so risks creating a noisy measure of volatility, possibly inflating its occurrence with the occurrence of other types of change. It is therefore not feasible to simply import the measurement of volatility employed elsewhere.

Second, applying a Box-Jenkins procedure to the time series of states' behaviors toward their counterparts can uniquely mitigate the problem above, consistently isolating volatility even across different cases and time periods. Since this measurement is flexible, deriving patterns of change directly from the empirical records instead of assuming them, it can also be used across different cases and different time periods. In other words, the measure can be generalized and is transportable to capture volatility in a diverse set of countries and time periods. Indeed, this procedure can also be used to study volatility by other international actors, as I explain more in depth in the conclusion to this book. By making it possible to measure volatility in an intuitive way, this chapter hopes to inspire further explorations on this very topic in International Relations.

Third, the Box-Jenkins procedure shows how studying volatility can improve our grasp of international politics. To begin, relations between countries are more diverse than our classic classifications (such as rivalries and alliances) suggest. Even though these classifications are still useful, they also belie a lot of diversity within each type—diversity that will be analyzed directly in the subsequent chapters. Looking at transitions toward more cooperation and more conflict, as opposed to just looking at the incidence of conflict, can reveal important facets of these relationships. States' behaviors look different—richer—when we study volatility. Moreover, volatility varies over time and across cases: explaining this variation becomes all the more important. And, since volatility cannot be reduced to other forms of change, when we miss an explanation of volatility, we are missing an important piece of the puzzle.

Finally, because volatility is a complex, multifaceted phenomenon, it is important to adopt a broader, diverse approach to studying volatility, one that combines different data sources. Doing so matters in particular when testing alternative explanations for why volatility develops. Overall, triangulating across different data and techniques makes it possible to produce a well-rounded measurement of volatility, one that is better able to faithfully translate the theoretical concept presented in Chapter 1 into its proper empirical representation.

Therefore, the rest of the book will employ a multipronged approach to the measurement of volatility. In particular, Chapter 4 employs the standard deviation of the residuals of the Box-Jenkins procedure to build a yearly measure of volatility and perform a panel-data test of my argument, also controlling for alternative explanations. Chapter 5 complements event data with archival and declassified sources.

In both chapters, the analysis will focus on salient dyads that are often in the news— rivalries and alliances. This is so that it is possible to consistently gather significant information from news sources on these states' behavior, in a way that would be less likely if states in less salient dyads were included. While the selection of these cases makes the test of the theory more rigorous, the theory is meant to explain volatility in all states' behaviors, not just in those facing rivals or allies.

4

Volatility and Rivals

Previous chapters have offered a theoretical conceptualization of what volatility in states' behaviors toward other states looks like, proposed an explanation of where it comes from, and described ways to measure this phenomenon. The objective of this chapter is to investigate empirically whether power and interests interact to increase volatility in states' behaviors, as my argument posits. In particular, this chapter focuses on whether the effect of power and interests on volatility holds across time and space while controlling for alternative explanations.

Thus, this chapter focuses on the relations between thirty-six pairs of rivals (countries that have repeatedly raised to the ranks of the most conflict prone in the international arena, according to multiple studies). Gathering data on their behavior in foreign policy, this chapter tracks such behavior over time, identifying the impact of power and interests on surges in volatility. I use time series techniques and statistical models to gain empirical leverage and to systematically assess the relative impact on volatility of different factors— and to rigorously assess whether the theory I propose can help us explain volatility in international politics. Therefore, this chapter deepens the book's inquiry into volatility in international politics by providing a systematic assessment of the theory presented in Chapter 2.

In particular, to show that the theory proposed has purchasing power and that indeed the combination of power and interests spurs increased volatility, I design this empirical analysis with three tasks in mind. First, the analysis will have to show that the effect of interests on volatility depends on power and that the effect of power on volatility depends on interests. Put differently, the analysis would have to demonstrate that greater relative power increases volatility when there exists a set of heterogeneous domestic interests that can influence foreign policy. By the same token, the analysis would also have to demonstrate that the effect of those interests on volatility is greater in the presence of relative power superiority. This is the case because my argument posits that volatility is the outcome of an interaction between these two factors.[1]

Volatile States in International Politics. Eleonora Mattiacci, Oxford University Press. © Oxford University Press 2023.
DOI: 10.1093/oso/9780197638675.003.0004

Second, and relatedly, this analysis will have to show that when countries are in a position of power superiority relative to their counterpart and when a heterogeneous set of domestic interests have access to the definition of foreign policy, countries display greater volatility in their behavior. The presence of both conditions together will have to be shown to increase volatile behavior, as each factor is theorized as producing greater volatility when interacting with the other.

Finally, even if the analysis did find that greater volatility emerges in conditions of relative power superiority and competing domestic interests, it would still have to convincingly exclude the possibility that this observed relationship between the two factors and volatility emerges spuriously. In other words, it is important to exclude the possibility that the positive relation between the interaction of interests and power and volatility depends on other, concomitant factors. If that was the case, we would witness both values for the predictors (interests and power) and the predicted variable (volatility) increase together, but there would be no real relation between those variables. To this end, the analysis will have to control for plausible, alternative explanations between the independent and dependent variables.

This chapter proceeds as follows. The next section will explore the design of the statistical analysis. In that section, I present the unit of analysis, specifying both the geographical and temporal span covered in the analysis and the model I employ. I then discuss how I measure interests and power, the factors that the theory posits as interacting to produce volatility, and how I operationalize possible alternative hypotheses. The next two sections discuss the results of the analysis. Conclusions follow, explaining the value added of this analysis for our understanding of volatility in international politics.

Statistical Analysis Design

Historically, there have been multiple examples of volatile states' behaviors that can be traced back to the interaction between power superiority and domestic interests. India's volatile foreign policy toward Sri Lanka in the 2000s has been catalyzed by the presence of strong, reinforcing geographical and economic cleavages within the country.[2] In the early 1990s, the diverse set of domestic interests that reacted to the Tiananmen Square events pushed the US foreign policy vis-à-vis China through the full range of options that the US material capabilities granted—with inconsistent shifts between episodes such as the imposition of sanctions and bans on arm shipments on one hand and the inauguration of high-level talks and renewals of the most favored nation (MFN) condition on the other.[3] In the 2010s, multiple and heterogeneous domestic interests also propelled the Japanese foreign policy toward China to shift within a broad range of cooperative and conflictual options—renewed economic and security co-operation; disputes over the Senkaku Islands; attempts to revive regional cooperation in the energy, economic, and security sector; and politically charged visits to the Yasukuni Shrine.[4]

While numerous episodes of volatility can be traced back to the interaction between power and interests, it is important to answer the following question: is there a systematic relation between power superiority and domestic interests and volatile behavior?

To address this question, I design a large-N analysis to test the determinants of volatility. First, I select a sample for the analysis. To test when and why volatility in the behavior of one country toward another increases, I focus in particular on volatility in international politics within a set of specific pairs of countries (or dyads): rivals.

Before explaining which rivals I will be analyzing, one question needs to be addressed: why focus on a select number of countries for this analysis? Concentrating on this subset of countries presents several advantages. First, it shows how learning about volatility might challenge what we think we know, even when we analyze some of the best-studied countries in world politics. Rivalries represent a set of dyads that has been at the center of many studies of International Relations because of their frequent involvement in wars.[5] Specifically, with some variation depending on which definition of rivalry is adopted, almost 78% of wars since 1816[6] and over 90% of all wars since World War II[7] have taken place between rivals. My analysis will shed light on important nuances regarding these countries' relations. In particular, because they tend to last for a significant period of time, rivalries have often evoked the image of a static relation between countries, with relations often reaching a point where conflict is the norm and not much cooperation happens.[8] But measuring their volatility paints a different picture, as Chapter 3 illustrates. Showing how rivalries can vary in the extent to which they experience volatility toward more cooperation and conflict can add an important nuance to our understanding of these central and well-studied relations in international politics.

Second, relations between rivals are characterized by strong dyadic dynamics. In other words, the behavior of one country toward its counterpart when both countries are members of a rivalry is often explained in large part by the behavior of the opponent. This characteristic of rivalries sets them apart from other forms of interactions in the international system, such as interactions between allies, which instead have been found to display fewer dyadic tendencies.[9] This characteristic also makes rivalries an especially interesting set of countries for an argument, like the one put forward here, that posits that volatility emerges from factors other than the back-and-forth dynamics of the relation with other countries. Therefore, testing this theory on this subset of countries makes it possible to gauge whether interests and power play a role in generating volatility even in cases where these dyadic dynamics are very strong.

Third, being selective about which relations to study and focusing on these types of relations makes it possible to conduct a focused comparison on the determinants of volatility in international politics.[10] Reducing the sample to more comparable units, as opposed to including every single observation available, enables researchers to reduce the risks of possible confounders—and increase instead the internal validity of the design.[11] Thus, increasing the internal validity of the design improves the trustworthiness of the results. In addition, those results emerging from such analysis will also be easier to interpret, because such matched dataset will have to include fewer controls in the analysis.[12]

In particular, I focus on rivalrous countries that have been identified by existing studies as both "strategic rivalries" and "enduring rivalries." Countries form strategic rivalries if the following conditions hold true: "the actors in question must regard each other as (a) competitors, (b) the source of actual or latent threats that pose some possibility of becoming militarized, (c) enemies."[13] Such a definition of rivalries adopts a so-called "perceptual" approach, focusing on how countries perceive their counterparts. Within those countries that perceive each other as a threat, I further select those that have fought against each other repeatedly in militarized disputes, specifically at least six of them in twenty years or fewer. In other words, I focus on strategic rivalries that also count as "enduring rivalries."[14] So, for example, the US and the Soviet Union are included in the analysis. However, El Salvador and Guatemala are not. While sharing a strategic rivalry, these two countries were not involved in six or more disputes over the course of twenty years. In sum, I select countries that have shared sentiments of hostility toward one another while also facing each other in militarized disputes more often than other pairs of countries in the international system have in a given time interval.

Why use both criteria instead of just one? I triangulate between these two different definitions of rivalries because I want to capture pairs of dyads that are similar to one another in terms of both how they perceive their counterparts and how they behave toward them. In other words, those dyads both have a motive for conflict and have indeed been involved in multiple conflicts. The fact that they need to be both willing and able to fight often (as opposed to only being willing or only being able), in turn, can maximize the precision of the comparison by increasing the number of criteria that the dyad has to meet in order to qualify. These dyads have an expectation of future conflict, as strategic dyads do, while also having a history of conflict, as enduring rivals do. Under what conditions are their activities toward their counterparts steady, and when do they instead shift inconsistently toward cooperation and conflict?[15]

Being selective when choosing a sample is particularly important when using event data. This is the case because event data rely on the newswires to record events. Therefore, event data are better suited to capture episodes of conflict and cooperation that occur between states that are often in the news. Rivals have historically made the news often compared to other states, because they tend to generate newsworthy episodes of conflict or cooperation. Therefore, that set of countries is likely to be more consistently in the news than other sets of countries are, allowing me to avoid missing important events taking place in the dyad.

Table 4.1 lists the dyads included in the analysis. I select those strategic and enduring rivalries that start in or after 1948, the date when event data start. Due to data availability, the analysis therefore extends for the years 1948–1992.[16]

In sum, each observation in my dataset represents a directed dyad-year, meaning that the behavior of each component of the pair of rival states is recorded in the data. The outcome variable captures the yearly level of volatility registered in the behavior of one country in the dyad toward another. Volatility is measured as the standard deviation of the squared residuals emerging from a Box-Jenkins procedure on the time series of the behavior of that country toward its counterpart. Chapter 3 describes the procedure used at length, providing more details on the data. In the appendix, I replicate the analysis using the same procedure but with a monthly unit of analysis instead of a yearly unit of analysis, finding that my results are consistent.[17]

Table 4.1 List of directed dyads included in the analysis.

Rivalries
Afghanistan-Pakistan
Algeria-Morocco
Argentina-Chile
Cambodia-Thailand
China-India
China–South Korea
China-Philippines
China-Japan
China-US
Congo-Zaire
Cuba-US
Cyprus-Turkey
Ecuador-US
Egypt-Israel
Ethiopia-Somalia
Ethiopia-Sudan
Greece-Turkey
India-Pakistan
Iran-Iraq
Iraq-Israel
Iraq-Kuwait
Israel-Jordan
Israel–Saudi Arabia
Iraq-UK
Israel-Syria
Japan–South Korea
Jordan-Syria
Laos-Thailand
Morocco-Spain
North Korea–South Korea
North Korea-US
Norway-Russia
Peru-US
Russia-US
Saudi Arabia–Yemen
Thailand-Vietnam

Measuring Relative Power Superiority

To operationalize the relative power of a state vis-à-vis its counterpart, I rely on the Composite Index of National Capabilities, or CINC, score.[18] The CINC score is calculated as follows. First, the score identifies six indicators of material capabilities: total population, urban population, energy consumption, iron and steel production, military expenditures, and military personnel. Data on each indicator emerge from consistently triangulating across different sources for each country and each year.[19] Taken together, such indicators are meant to capture the three main dimensions of power: demographic capabilities (leveraging data on total population and urban population), industrial capabilities (employing data on energy consumption and iron/steel production), and military capabilities (employing, instead, data on total military expenditures and size of the armed forces).[20] Then, for each indicator, the CINC score generates the ratio of the individual country's value on that indicator and the global value registered. Finally, the index emerges from the average of these ratios for each indicator, to capture the actual and potential capabilities of each country relative to those of other countries. In sum, the CINC score represents the annual average of the individual countries' share of the total, system-wide demographic, industrial, and military capabilities. In particular, for each country in this dataset of directed dyads, I calculate the ratio of their CINC score to that of their counterpart. For directed dyad members i and j, therefore, the relative power of country i vis-à-vis country j will be measured as $CINCi/CINCj$.

It is hard to exhaustively measure the complex dimensions of power in international politics. This CINC score ratio, however, is suitable to capture each country's relative power as conceptualized in my argument, for several reasons. First, since it relies on those six, diverse dimensions, the index comprehensively captures the material aspect of countries' capabilities that the theory posits as being important to understand the effect of power on volatility. In particular, the focus on those six dimensions of power enables the index to capture not just actualized power, as focusing exclusively on the size of the armed forces, for example, would do, but also that power that can be mobilized for conflict, or the *in potentia* capabilities of each country.[21] Capturing these multiple dimensions of power, in turn, is crucial to comprehensively capture the degree to which relative power with respect to a counterpart can really expand the range of behaviors available to one single country toward a specific counterpart.

Moreover, because the index relies not just on one but on multiple dimensions, it eschews reductive understandings of the multifaceted nature of power, seeking instead to capture "the breadth and depth of the resources that a nation could bring to bear."[22]

Finally, using CINC scores allows me to calculate the ratio between each country's CINC score and that of its counterpart in a meaningful way, by comparing these two countries on the same set of characteristics. This ratio, in turn, enables me to compare countries on a diverse and consistent set of power characteristics. Such comparison between counties constitutes a fundamental step toward capturing relative power difference.

Like all measures of concepts as important and complex as power, the CINC ratio also has drawbacks. It is therefore important to understand how those drawbacks can affect inference in this case. The first drawback comes from the fact that in the classic CINC score, the size of the denominator changes depending on how many countries enter or exit the international system. This feature, in turn, makes it hard to make cross-temporal comparisons or understand when and why power shifts in major power transition moments. The same percentage of power in the international system possessed by one country can become more impressive as the number of countries in the system increases.[23] This is an important drawback of the measure, but it is less damning in the context of the study. By taking the ratio of a country's CINC score over that of its counterpart, the comparison with the system de facto disappears, and the measure captures how each country fares with respect to the other.

Another drawback of the measure, however, is that the CINC score does not establish a priori a weight for each of those categories. For this reason, countries with a similar CINC score can have different power configurations, some with more actual power, as opposed to power in potentia, and others with less. This drawback is more problematic if we want to use the CINC score to compare specific aspects of power, such as their military readiness, or if we use the score to rank countries in the international system based on their CINC score.[24] This drawback is less pronounced, however, when scholars simply use the CINC score to measure changes in power as a whole, as opposed to focusing on changes in specific power characteristics.

Measuring Heterogeneous Domestic Interests

My other variable of interest is the presence, in the domestic arena, of a heterogeneous set of interests that can influence states' behaviors toward other states. To measure the presence of this domestic interests configuration, I build a domestic interest index, H.

The index is built with three questions in mind. First, can different domestic groups access power? Or, put differently, can we expect different groups to alternate? I expect countries where this is the case to be, on average, prone to greater volatility than countries where it is not possible for different groups to alternate in power. Specifically, the index acquires the value 1 if there are institutionalized procedures in place for transferring power between different groups.[25] Argentina, South Korea, and Japan, at different points in time, all acquire the value 1 in the index. Second, if groups can alternate, do they represent a heterogeneous set of domestic preferences? Thus, I add one to the index if cleavages in society (on issues of race, religion, ethnicity, language, income, and geography) are reinforcing. Cleavages are reinforcing if knowing where one individual stands in terms of any of the indicators above (e.g., race) can tell us something about where that same individual stands in terms of other indicators above (e.g., ethnicity). Data on national cleavages come from the Cross-National Indices of Multi-Dimensional Measures of Social Structure (CIMMSS).[26] For example, Israel and Pakistan both acquire the value 2 at different points in time. This operation of distinguishing between different domestic group configurations is fundamental to capture the theory's claim that the presence of nonoverlapping interests can push groups to compete for the definition of foreign policy.[27] Finally, I add one more if the electoral system is proportional, as proportional electoral systems are more likely than other systems to represent diverging domestic interests.[28] For example, India and the Philippines both acquire the value 3 at different points of time in the dataset.

This index therefore has an additive nature: the various components combine together, and when they do their effect on volatility is amplified. This additive feature of the index is important to test my argument, which posits an additive relation between the various components of the domestic side of my argument. Given this feature, the index allows me to see whether, as I posit, volatility increases as a function of the degree to which the domestic environment represents heterogeneous domestic interests. In the argument I present, it is not the case that the effect of interests on volatility changes depending on institutions (or vice versa), as would be the case in an interactive model. Rather, interests have influence only if those institutions that allow for interest representation are in place. Representation is a necessary condition for interests to affect volatility. For this reason, here I do not use an interaction between these different indicators.[29] Moreover, the index allows me to avoid using a dummy variable to code regimes as either democratic or autocratic, with the risk of oversimplifying differences between such complex regimes. Instead, the measure proposed here emphasizes the specific features that enhance interest representation.[30]

Finally, a couple of this index's features warrant further discussion. To properly capture the presence of a heterogeneous set of interests, I avoid assuming a specific dimension or identity of the domestic constituencies as more salient than others. While this is common practice in studies of trade, it can be misleading when assessing the impact of multiple and heterogeneous interests in the conduct of foreign policy as a whole. Privileging one cleavage (like the religious or the ethnic one) over others when assessing the impact of the presence of a heterogeneous set of interests on foreign policy volatility would amount to arbitrarily assuming that one of these dimensions is systematically more salient than others. Instead, each foreign policy decision can have redistributive consequences on multiple dimensions—such as the economic, or ethnic, or religious dimension, and so on—and assuming one of these as the most salient one would amount to unduly assuming that that policy unequivocally mobilizes one identity over all the others. Second, to capture the degree to which the domestic interests are heterogeneous, I focus on the degree to which these cleavages are reinforcing rather than simply looking at the number of cleavages in society. I do so because if cleavages are reinforcing, rather than overlapping, then these multiple cleavages will identify different groups in society with very little interest overlap. It is precisely this feature that, according to the theoretical prepositions advanced, will increase volatility in states' behaviors.

Alternative Explanations

I also add controls to check for the alternative hypotheses that I describe in Chapter 2. Thus, to control for the impact of polarity (H3), I add a dummy that acquires the value 1 if events take place before 1989 and 0 otherwise. I control for leaders' characteristics by leveraging data from the Leader Experiences and Attributes Description (LEAD) dataset.[31] I add a dummy that is equal to 1 if a new leader assumes office in a given year (H4). I also add another dummy that acquires the value 1 if the leader had combat experience and 0 otherwise (H5a). Moreover, I include one dummy that acquires the value 1 if the leader is male and 0 otherwise (H5b). In addition, I control for characteristics of leaders that have often led observers to link their leadership style to be unusual or erratic and to not conform to international standards. In particular, I add a dummy to control for the leader's mental health.[32]

Next, I control for the presence of changes in the coalition of support, using the appropriate dummy from the Change in Source of Leader Support (CHISOLS) dataset (H6).[33] As for the presence of issues (H7), I include several controls. First, I control for both the number of contentious issues and their salience from the point of view of the main actor in the directed dyad. Then, I also control for both the number and the salience of contentious issues from the point of view of the dyad. In both cases, I leverage data from the Issue Correlates of War (ICOW) dataset.[34] I also control for the volatility of states' counterparts, lagging such indicator. It is possible that encountering volatility in the counterpart will increase a state's own volatility as reactive behavior, especially among rivals.[35]

Table 4.2 presents descriptive statistics for all of these variables. Descriptively, the data tell an intuitive story that is consistent with the main argument put forward by this book. Namely, none of the countries in each directed-dyad-year with volatility below 25th percentile has an interaction between power and interests that sit above 25th percentile. By contrast, all those directed-dyad-years where the interaction between interests and power is above the 75th percentile display levels of volatility above the 75th percentile. Similarly, in 30% of the years, India's volatility toward Pakistan resides on or above the 75th percentile of all the volatility observed in the dataset. But this is true only for 2% of the years when looking and India's volatility toward China. In the case of Cuba, in 99% of the years for which Cuba is in the sample, its volatility toward the US sits below the 75th percentile.

Results and Discussion

I structure my data in panel fashion, with M representing seventy-two observations (from thirty-six directed dyads, see Table 4.1) and T equaling the years during which each dyad constitutes both a strategic and an enduring rivalry. I start by estimating a simple model that just contains the main explanatory variables, power and interests, their interaction, and the opponent's volatility. Then, I estimate another model, this time adding all the alternative explanations. Finally, a third model instead adds additional

Table 4.2 Summary Statistics

Variable	Mean	Std. Dev.	Min.	Max.	N
Volatility	0.547	4.449	0	94.173	2,974
Relative Power × Het. Interests	10.577	41.838	0	479.861	2,344
Relative Power	11.866	39.97	0.002	479.861	2,936
Het. Interests	0.576	0.863	0	3	2,358
Opponent's Volatility	0.547	4.449	0	94.173	2,974
Issue Salience in Dyad	0.619	2.242	0	12	2,974
Issue Count in Dyad	0.152	0.578	0	3	2,974
Issue Salience	0.542	1.933	0	12	2,974
Issue Count	0.113	0.423	0	3	2,974
Leader's Mental Health	0.007	0.086	0	1	2,956
Leader's Gender	0.977	0.15	0	1	2,970
Leader's Combat Experience	0.373	0.484	0	1	2,950
Leader's Transition	0.165	0.371	0	1	2,970
Leader's Coalition Change	0.08	0.271	0	1	2,954
Cold War	0.071	0.256	0	1	2,974

controls that capture different nuances of the role that leaders and issues might play as well as the role of issues. Table 4.3 presents results from random effects models.[36]

The coefficients in Table 4.3 provide empirical support for the argument proposed in this book. The coefficients suggest that the effect of power on volatility depends on interests and that the effect of interests on volatility depends on power. In particular, the coefficients suggest that the presence of heterogeneous domestic interests with a say in external behavior is not a significant predictor of volatility when the ratio of power relative to a state's counterpart is zero. The presence of these interests is, however, a positive and significant predictor of increases in volatility when the ratio is bigger than zero. Thus, the shape that the impact of interests on volatility takes depends on relative power. Similarly, the coefficients for *Relative Power* and that for *Relative Power* × *H* differ, suggesting the influence of domestic interests on the impact of power on volatility. This feature, in turn, is one crucial component of the interactive nature of the relation between the presence of multiple and heterogeneous domestic interests and relative power superiority. In the presence of multiple and heterogeneous domestic interests having access to foreign policy, the models suggest, volatility in states' behaviors increases by 14.2% when going from a scenario of median (50th percentile) power superiority to one of greater

Table 4.3 Cross-Sectional, Time Series Models of Volatility in States' Behaviors

	Model 1	Model 2	Model 3
Relative Power ×	0.001***	0.002***	0.001***
Het. Interests	(0.000)	(0.001)	(0.000)
Relative Power	−0.002***	−0.002***	−0.002***
	(0.000)	(0.001)	(0.000)
Het. Interests	0.017	0.003	0.005
	(0.033)	(0.028)	(0.018)
Opponent's Volatility	0.429***	0.421***	0.420***
	(0.023)	(0.027)	(0.023)
Issue Salience (Dyad)		−0.042***	0.007
		(0.010)	(0.034)
Issue Count (Dyad)		0.134***	−0.063
		(0.038)	(0.132)
Leader's Gender		−0.212	−0.214
		(0.17)	(0.267)
Leader's Combat Experience		0.055	0.056
		(0.045)	(0.047)
Leader's Transition		0.032	0.037
		(0.07)	(0.078)
Leader's Coalition Change		−0.051	−0.052
		(0.086)	(0.096)
Cold War		−0.119***	−0.124***
		(0.03)	(0.03)
Issue Salience			−0.038*
			(0.022)
Issue Count			0.202*
			(0.121)
Leader's Mental Health			−0.072
			(0.059)
Constant	0.110***	0.188**	0.771**
	(0.018)	(0.085)	(0.354)
N	25,784	25,740	25,740

NOTE: Standard errors presented in parentheses beneath coefficient estimates. * significant at the .10 level, ** .05 level, *** .01 level.

(75th percentile) power superiority. Similarly, when power superiority is high (75th percentile), volatility increases by 85% going from a scenario where there are no heterogeneous interests controlling foreign policy to one in which there are. Moreover, overall volatility increases as the two indicators increase.

Given the nature of statistical interactions, however, it is impossible to gauge how interests and power affect each other's impact on volatility by only relying on coefficients.[37] Therefore, I plot both the marginal effect of relative power superiority on volatility for different values of domestic interests and the marginal effect of domestic interests on volatility for different values of relative power superiority. I discuss those graphs in turn.

Figure 4.1 shows the models' predictions for how relative power affects volatility given different domestic interest configurations. The figure presents the marginal effect of relative power on volatility for different levels of H. The plot highlights how the effect of power on volatility does indeed depend on the domestic interest configuration within each country. In countries where there are no multiple and heterogeneous interests contending for the definition of foreign policy ($H = 0$), increasing levels of power superiority does not affect volatility (left graph). By contrast, in a scenario where there are domestic interests with competing preferences that have access to foreign

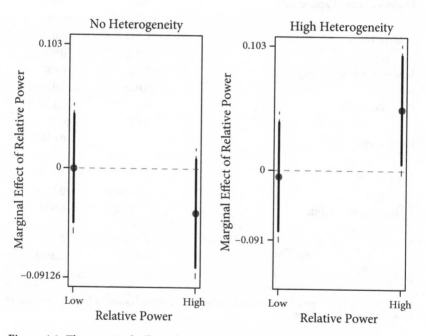

Figure 4.1 The marginal effect of relative power on volatility for different levels of multiple and heterogeneous domestic interests (H), with 90% and 95% confidence intervals. Relative power held at 25th and 75th percentiles, respectively.

policy definition ($H = 3$), greater relative power superiority systematically translates into greater volatility.

Thus, the scenario that emerges from the analysis is consistent with an explanation that emphasizes how competition between domestic interests can spark volatile behavior. Relative power superiority, per se, does not necessarily translate into greater volatility in the absence of such divided interests. This result is consistent with the idea that, while power gives countries access to multiple possible behaviors, power alone does not motivate countries to increasingly conduct themselves in a volatile manner. These findings also fail to support explanations, such as theories of foreign policy hedging, that might only rely on power to explain countries' erratic behavior. Since these results show that the effect of power on volatility is shaped by domestic interests, these empirical patterns suggest that theories only relying on power to explain volatility will be incomplete. For example, those approaches might have a hard time explaining when and how states decide to shift course and implement certain foreign policies and not others.

Figure 4.2 shows instead the models' prediction for how the impact of different domestic interest configurations on volatility changes depending on the level of relative power. In technical terms, the figure reports the marginal effects of the domestic indicator H on volatility for different levels of relative power. The figure shows the crucial interactive nature of the relation between relative power and the presence of a heterogeneous set of domestic interests. When there is low relative power (i.e., when *Relative Power* is held constant to the 25th percentile value, left graph), the presence of multiple and heterogeneous interests has no significant impact on volatility in foreign policy. Conversely, as the level of power superiority increases, the presence of multiple and heterogeneous interests significantly increases volatility.

This finding presents an important nuance in the way we understand the importance of the availability of options that relative power superiority grants states: although constituting an important component of the final outcome, domestic interests cannot predict whether one state will swing inconsistently between cooperation and conflict in its relations with one counterpart when relative power is equal to zero. While a diverse set of interests might increase states' propensity to engage in extreme behavior,[38] both cooperative and conflictual,[39] it is the actual availability of options in the international arena that determines whether this propensity will increase volatility. In this sense, analyzing states' relative capabilities can help explain the options available to them.[40] These results also lend credence to the point that relative power

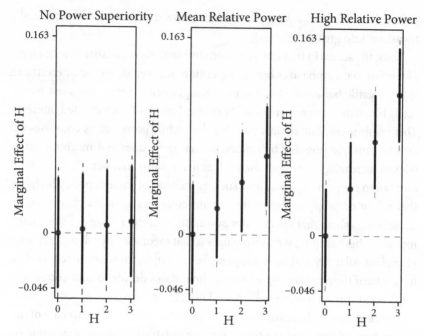

Figure 4.2 The marginal effect of the domestic indicator for heterogeneous interests (H) on volatility for different levels of relative power, with 90% and 95% confidence intervals. Relative power held at 25th, 50th, and 75th percentiles, respectively.

superiority acts as a permissive condition for volatility, by showing that in the absence of relative power superiority, divided domestic interests are not conducive to volatility.[41]

In sum, the models' results, as analyzed via Figures 4.1 and 4.2, do provide evidence in support of the posited interactive nature of the relation between power and interests that the theory posits. Namely, such evidence suggests two different and interrelated features emerging. First, the presence of multiple and heterogeneous domestic interests translates into greater volatility if one state has greater relative power with respect to its counterpart. Second, the presence of greater relative power translates into greater volatility if multiple and heterogeneous domestic interests are present and contend for the definition of a country's policy in the international arena. As the theory posits, the effect of interests on volatility depends on power and the effect of power on volatility depends on interests.

Moreover, both graphs suggest that volatility is higher when *Relative Power* is higher and *H* is higher as well, indicating that each factor produces greater volatility when interacting with the other.

Finally, these results also show that the effect of power and interests on volatility is robust to including possible alternative explanations, further lending support to my argument. Personal characteristics of the leader such as their gender and their combat experience, for example, when controlling for other factors relating to both the country and the dyad, do not predict volatile behavior. This is true also when looking at other characteristics of the leader. Leaders' mental health, for example, fails to explain what can be characterized as "unusual" or unexpected behavior. These results echo descriptive evidence from Chapter 3 on India's behavior toward Pakistan and China. There too, comparing to time periods where the same leader was in charge, India displayed different levels of volatility. In particular, volatility was higher in India's behavior toward Pakistan than in its behavior toward China, an observation that is consistent with the role that relative power plays in my argument. A similar result also emerges from the analysis of France's volatility toward the US in the next chapter. Changes in the coalition that supports the leader and transitions to a new leader also fail to predict volatility. These results, of course, do not rule out that a change in leaders or a change in their characteristics or in the coalition of support might catalyze change in a state's behavior toward their counterpart. Instead, they do show that, controlling for other factors, such change is not likely to take a volatile form.

Results show here that the presence of issues within the dyad has a mixed effect. When a country has issues with another country that are salient, it will behave in a more volatile fashion toward it, whereas the greater the number of issues the country has with another country, the less volatility its behavior will betray. However, when adding controls for the presence of issues that one country has toward the other member of the dyad, these dyadic effects disappear. These mixed effects of issues on volatility paint an interesting picture. Issue salience within a dyad might decrease volatility by giving states incentives to act in a more consistent manner, be it more cooperative or more conflictual. Instead, as the number of issues in the dyad increases, states might interact more often, and some of those interactions might be more likely to be volatile. However, these results should be taken with caution. Not only are these results mixed, but also rivals are perhaps the most obvious candidate for contentious issues to shape behaviors.[42]

The models do also suggest the relevance of reciprocity in explaining volatility, as the indicators for the counterpart's volatility are significant and positive across model specification. Volatility, in other words, attracts more volatility. These results are hardly surprising. First, these results echo previous findings that reciprocity effects are often present in International Relations, suggesting that countries often behave toward other countries according to a "tit for tat" strategy, mimicking the behavior that they perceive is directed toward them.[43] Reciprocity is also particularly strong among rivals, so if there is any group of countries in which we would find a significant effect of the counterpart's behavior, this group of countries would likely be it.[44]

Second, and perhaps more importantly, these results also emphasize how reciprocity is only part of the story, as even controlling for reciprocity power and interests are significant predictors of volatility. Indeed, that the interaction between relative power superiority and heterogeneous domestic interests is significant and robust even when one focuses on dyads whose relation is so pronouncedly dyadic emphasizes the strength of its effect on volatility. Finally, reciprocity might also not necessarily be the most satisfying part of the story. This is the case because reciprocity can only offer a circular explanation for volatility. It emphasizes how foreign policy behavior on the part of one country responds to previous behavior, without ever clarifying what the engine of that volatility is to begin with.[45]

Conclusions

This chapter has presented an empirical exploration of this book's argument on the origins of volatility. Leveraging the new measurement of volatility in international politics presented in the previous chapter, this chapter sought to establish whether the interaction of power and interests has consistently correlated with the occurrence of volatile behavior in international rivalries.

Three main findings have emerged from the analysis presented in this chapter. First, volatility emerges from the interaction between relative power in the international arena and the presence of a heterogeneous set of interests in the domestic sphere with access to the definition of foreign policy. Second, as this book's argument posits, both are important factors in explaining volatility and complement each other in important ways. Finally, the effect of power and interests on volatility is robust to controlling for alternative explanations, both those explanations that rely mostly on domestic factors and those that rely mostly on international factors. The differing levels of volatility in the behavior of one rival toward its counterpart shows how complex these relationships might be, and how much it is possible to miss if we only focus on conflict.

Results in this chapter open up new and important venues for research in international politics. First, these results echo recent findings on the limits of the assumption that states function as unitary actors in international politics, an assumption embraced in studies of foreign policy hedging, among others. Without considering the layout of domestic interests, this analysis has shown, it is not possible to predict volatile behavior. This, in turn, raises the question: Under what circumstances is assuming that states are unitary actors an acceptable simplification of the international arena? In other words, when does it pay to use this assumption? Second, these results also show the importance of further exploring the role of leaders in international politics. As the analysis in this chapter and evidence from other parts of this book suggest, volatility cannot be explained by idiosyncratic leaders, or even by leaders' transitions. Perhaps too often pundits attribute changes in states' behaviors to changes in leadership or on the peculiarly mercurial nature of states' leaders. Therefore, it becomes important to ask: Do leaders systematically affect *other* ways in which states' behaviors change? If so, how? Finally, this chapter shows mixed results on the presence of contentious issues and volatility, even in the case of rivalries, perhaps the ideal candidate to find this effect. So why is this the case? More research on how issues are made and come to be to begin with is needed.

The next chapter complements the empirical evidence provided in this chapter in important ways. First, it expands the range of relations over which the theory is tested by delving into the volatile relations between two historic allies, France and the US, between the 1950s and the 1960s. Studying volatility in alliance relations is particularly interesting, not only because alliances are often at the center of many studies of international politics, but also because when we think of volatility we are less prone to associate it to relations, such as those among allies, that are mostly cooperative. But even the relationships we traditionally think of as cooperative might vary greatly with

respect to the degree to which they include inconsistent shifts between cooperation and conflict. Second, the analysis in the next chapter leverages fine-
grained, declassified, and contemporaneous data on interactions between
those two countries and their decision makers to see how relative power superiority and divided domestic interests unfold in states' everyday behavior
to give rise to volatility in international politics.

5

Volatility and Allies

On October 1, 1966, a classified document landed on the desk of US President Lyndon B. Johnson. Officials in the State Department, the document stated, had concluded that the US had finally reached

> the nadir of post-war US-French relations: at present we can hope to do little more than (a) maintain appearances; (b) try to ensure that we understand each other; (c) consult on problems on those parts of the world, Middle East and Africa, where we still work together; and (d) look forward to better days.[1]

What makes these comments even more striking is the fact that they are describing US relations with France, its oldest ally. Just twenty years earlier, US troops had landed in Normandy to lead Allied forces in their successful attempt to liberate France from the Nazi occupation. The US and France had emerged from the rubble of that war as strong and committed allies. In the years following the end of the Second World War, France had become the second major beneficiary of the Marshall Plan, getting access to US $2.7 billion in aid to rebuild the country.[2] In the context of the technical assistance component of the plan, many French factory and farmer workers traveled to make six-month visits to US industries and farms and learn new agricultural and industrial techniques. The plan also included cultural and informational exchanges. In addition, the Marshall Plan provided assistance to France for building railroads and water systems in French North Africa.[3] During those same years, the US had also forgiven France's World War I debt. In 1949, moreover, France became one of the first countries to join the North Atlantic Treaty Organization (NATO). Through Article 5 of the North Atlantic Treaty, both the US and France had committed to consider an armed attack against the other as an attack against themselves and therefore to assist the country attacked, even with the use of force.[4] So what had happened in the intervening years? How did the relations between these two countries unfold in such a way to reach, according to US policymakers, their "nadir" in 1966?

Volatile States in International Politics. Eleonora Mattiacci, Oxford University Press. © Oxford University Press 2023.
DOI: 10.1093/oso/9780197638675.003.0005

This chapter will explore the years preceding the French withdrawal of all its armed forces from NATO's integrated military command in 1966. The analysis picks up in 1954, a watershed year for France, as I explain in greater detail below. France's behavior toward the US during this specific period of time constitutes an interesting case for studies of volatility. On the one hand, this is an alliance like other alliances. For example, almost 50% of all alliance members between 1815 and 2016 had a defense obligation to other members of the alliance, similar to the obligation present within NATO.[5] On the other hand, this is a unique case compared to others, because France actually decides to withdraw from the integrated NATO command, thus changing a key component of the agreement and of France's membership in it.[6] And because the years preceding this unusual decision on the part of France to abandon the alliance are also characterized by increasing volatility, this case can illustrate what the potential implications of volatility for states' relations can be.

Moreover, since the episodes this chapter retraces happened in the past, it is possible to reconstruct volatility with multiple sources, both primary and secondary. The diverse nature of the sources utilized, in turn, provides a deeper and richer account of the events as they unfolded. These sources provide more details on what variation in volatile behavior would look like in practice to those who witness such behavior as it unfolds. In addition, these resources also uniquely reveal how perceptions of volatility impacted decision makers' thinking and behavior, both publicly and covertly. In this sense, this multipronged approach provides a different way to corroborate the evidence on the role of factors such as power, interests, leaders, issues, and so on that emerges via statistical correlations.

Three main findings emerge from this chapter. First, an increase in French relative power interacted with the presence of a heterogeneous set of interests having access to the definition of foreign policy to produce increased volatility during the period 1954–1962. Second, while relative power did not recede to pre-1954 levels, a decrease in the access on the part of a heterogeneous set of interests to the definition of foreign policy after 1961 translated into a decrease in France's volatility toward the US. Third, alternative explanations such as those focusing on issues of leadership fail to explain when and why volatility changed during these years.

This chapter therefore extends the empirical investigation in this book in at least three ways. First, this chapter investigates volatility in the alliance context. Alliances are complex interactions, perhaps more so than rivalries, because, due to the overlapping commitments among them, it is quite common for allied countries to interact together across multiple theaters at once. This complexity makes alliances an inherently interesting case for studies of volatility. Moreover, since volatility is often associated with mistrust and conflict, alliances make for an important, if counterintuitive, context in which to investigate volatility. Second, the chapter also complements the previous chapter by taking a different empirical approach. It zooms in on one country's behavior toward another and it does so for a much shorter period of time: the twelve years between 1954 and 1966. This narrower focus makes it possible to engage in a more detailed analysis of how volatile behavior unfolds and what consequences it has on states' interactions. It also makes it possible to analyze how decision makers perceive and react to volatility. Third, in addition to event data, the chapter includes archival materials from multiple presidential libraries, newspaper articles published during those periods, debates in the National Assembly, public statements made by different actors, and declassified diplomatic documents published by the US State Department and the French Ministère des Affaires étrangères.

This chapter proceeds as follows. The next section details the salient areas for French foreign policy during the period under analysis, showing how French interests spanned the whole globe. Then, the chapter explains the configuration of power and interests in France during the period under analysis. After deriving expectations from my argument, the chapter presents evidence of varying degrees of volatility in French behavior toward the US. The next section illustrates how this book's argument can explain variation in France's volatility toward the US while alternative explanations cannot do so as well. The conclusions to the chapter discuss its value added to our understanding of volatility in international politics.

France in 1954

To provide a more detailed yet tractable in-depth account of volatility, the analysis focuses on the years immediately preceding France's decision to leave NATO.

In particular, the chapter starts during a crucial year of international transformation for France, 1954. During that year, a momentous defeat in Indochina at Dien Bien Phu had "shattering" psychological effects that outweighed its material implications and de facto put the final straw on the

French political willingness to remain in Indochina, where it had been since the end of the previous century.[7] Similarly, a recrudescence of terrorism in Morocco and Tunisia accelerated the rapid decline of the French colonial empire, an empire that had long constituted a crucial facet of France's image and role in the world. Elsewhere, rebels organized into the National Liberation Front (NLF), inaugurating one of the bloodiest conflicts of independence that would usher in an independent Algeria. Moreover, it was also in 1954 that France established a nuclear weapons program, en route to soon become the fourth nuclear weapons country.[8] In addition to these pivotal events, numerous leadership changes took place starting in 1954 (see Table 5.1). Given the numerous leaders in power and the presence of several salient issues in France's foreign policy, this is a particularly interesting period to show how explanations based on issues and leaders cannot quite capture variation in volatility to the degree that the interaction between power and interests can.

In the remaining paragraphs of this section, I retrace the main areas where France was active in the international arena, to better understand the context in which volatile behavior took place.

At the dawn of 1954, France's role in the international arena spanned several continents. Close to home, France was negotiating a new international economic community after concluding the treaty of Paris with Italy, West Germany, Belgium, Luxembourg, and the Netherlands to formally establish the European Coal and Steel Community (ECSC). During those same years, France and other European leaders, with the strong support of the US, made a significant push to establish the European Defense Community (EDC). The EDC, whose idea was first floated in 1951, would have amounted to the creation of a European army, eventually including also German units. This European army would have been placed under a European authority, equipped with both military and political functions. In this sense, the EDC sought to find a palatable solution to the thorny issue of Germany rearmament. As one of the occupying forces in those areas per the 1945 Potsdam Conference, France had also been involved in negotiations over the political future of Berlin and Germany.

Beyond the European continent, in Africa, the 1946 French Constitution had established the French Union, a political entity aimed at replacing the colonial system by creating a metropolitan France and overseas territories, with a president, a high council, and an assembly. Conflicts unfolding all over French colonies, however, would soon lead to independence for many of these countries and to the creation of the French Community, which replaced the French Union.

In Asia, France's military struggle in Indochina came to an end in 1954, after the devastating defeat at Dien Bien Phu in May of the same year. A referendum in France some time afterward recorded little interest on the part of the population in remaining in Indochina.[9] This major defeat came after years of struggles and propelled the French to move out of Indochina, though it hardly exhausted their political, cultural, and economic involvement in the area. The recognition of mainland China in 1964 marked the climax of the activities of France in the region during those years, opening rifts in the area not only with Taiwan but also with the US.

The late 1950s also witnessed an increase in French activities in the Western Hemisphere. Inspired by a desire to augment its political, economic, and diplomatic contacts with this area of the world, such an increase included a tour of multiple countries on the part of De Gaulle in Latin America, a famous visit in Quebec, and infamous trade negotiations with Castro's Cuba.

Finally, on a global scale, the newly minted United Nations (UN) also started to gain centrality in France's foreign policy, for two reasons. First, France was one of the five permanent members of the UN Security Council (UNSC) with veto power (one of the so-called Permanent Five). In the years to come, the UNSC turned into an important political arena for France, given the presence in the council of both its most powerful ally (the US) and its most powerful rival (the USSR). Second, the UN General Assembly (UNGA) became increasingly a venue where nonaligned countries or Third World countries took France to task on issues of decolonization. The UN also became one of the main theaters for the French involvement in global disarmament, at a time when France was starting a nuclear program of its own.

In sum, by 1954, France was active in the international arena on multiple fronts. These included the nascent European Community, the possibility of a European army, and the fate of the German territories, but also a transition to a postcolonial world, the renegotiation of its interactions with communist countries in multiple continents, and an evolving role within the UN. Such French activities in the international arena inevitably involved the UN, at least to some degree. Not only were France and the UN allies, but also US interests started extending across the globe during this time period. For example, the US was keeping a close eye on developments in Europe, deeply favoring a consolidation of the collaboration between the European

Economic Community (EEC) countries. France's politics toward its colonies abroad also was of interest to the US, as America was trying to prevent the spread of communism in Africa and in Asia by (also) presenting itself as an alternative to former colonial powers.[10]

France's Relative Power

France faced several challenges as it emerged from the Second World War: major disruptions to its transportation routes; several inefficient industry and commerce sectors; and high inflation due to the cost of war, the national debt, and an unbalanced national budget.[11] During the period under analysis, however, France's power relative to the US started increasing.[12] Figure 5.1 depicts France's relative power with respect to the US during

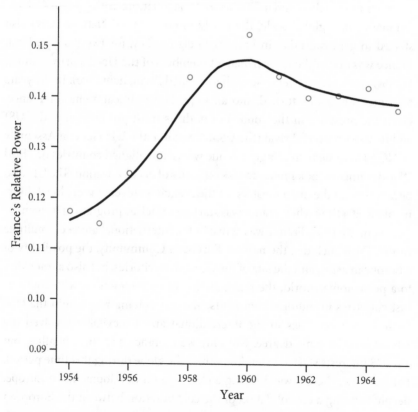

Figure 5.1 France's relative power with respect to the US, 1954–1966.

the period 1954–1966 as represented by the Correlates of War's Composite Index of National Capabilities (CINC) score.[13] As described in Chapter 4, the CINC score takes into account multiple indicators of material capabilities— total population, urban population, iron and steel production, primary energy consumption, military expenditures, and military personnel ratio.

During the first years of the time period under analysis, Figure 5.1 suggests, France's power relative to the US begins to rather rapidly increase. France's relative power slightly declines post-1960.[14] Such decline was mostly driven by the sharp reduction in military personnel that followed the conclusion of the Algerian War. Even so, France's power relative to the US in 1962 was much higher than in 1954 and never reverted to pre-1954 levels during this period. Indeed, throughout those years, France's military expenditures as a percentage of gross domestic product (GDP) went up.[15] Thus, even though France's power was, and remained throughout the years, a fraction of the US power, such relative power mostly increased during the years under analysis.[16]

France was often aware of the power differential between the two countries, archival documents show. The US, for France, was "the greatest power in the West."[17] Similarly, during his first meeting with US Secretary of State John Foster Dulles after becoming president, in July 1958, French President De Gaulle is reported to have compared France's "weakness" to US power, observing:

> The reasons for French weaknesses were well known: it had been subject to any number of foreign invasions and to 13 changes in regime in modern history. The United States was very rich and therefore powerful. If the United States had been invaded many times, had endured changes in regime and lacked modern natural resources, such as coal and petroleum, the United States might well be in the same position as France.[18]

At the same time, France was also very aware that its relative power was increasing. Such increase in its power relative to the US was perceived as a great opportunity for France to re-establish a stronger presence in the international arena. In the same conversation with Foster Dulles, for example, De Gaulle remarked: "The proof [of France's importance] is that you, Mr. Secretary, are here today and that I am also here."[19] American aid had made it possible to rebuild France and its colonies in the 1940s, and a great proportion of the investments from the growing economy during those years was being dedicated to military research.[20]

France's relative power vis-à-vis the US often emerged in conversations, such as the one above, where the two allies were bargaining over which course of action to choose. In particular, rising relative power tended to be perceived as shaping which options were available to France. For example, French decision makers interpreted a national nuclear arsenal as fundamental for France to explore a wide set of options "and enable France to regain flexibility in dealing with her allies as well as her opponents."[21]

France's Domestic Interests

During the period under analysis, France's domestic interests were characterized by non-cross-cutting cleavages across religion, ethnicity, race, income, and geography.[22]

Religion and income, for example, were mostly reinforcing, each identifying distinct groups with little or no preference overlap. Religiosity, for instance, was prevalent among wealthier individuals but not among the working class.[23] Geography and income cleavages were also reinforcing, creating distinct groups of individuals.[24] Those that lived in cities boasted better standards of living, as higher-paying industry work was concentrated in cities as opposed to the countryside.[25] Even when there were industries in mostly rural areas, they were systematically different from the ones present in the cities, as they were more consumption oriented and so had different import–export needs.[26]

Cities became more densely populated after the end of the Second World War as people searched for work in factories. This internal migration made the divide between the country and the city even sharper, as during those years the industrial sector grew way more than the agricultural one, translating into different priorities for the two sectors.[27]

In general, the North saw more economic development and greater access to natural resources than the South and the population in the South felt deprived, perceiving the North as being given privileged access to resources.[28] The ethnic composition of the North and of the South was also different, with more immigrants populating the South, as opposed to a more homogeneous, in terms of ethnicity and race, North.[29] Analysts remarked on the disparities among regions in terms of richer, more industrial areas being concentrated around Paris and in the Northeast during those years.[30]

Domestic interests had an important bearing on numerous policies that France pursued in the international arena. For instance, export-oriented technology firms, eager to find new markets, were a powerful force behind France's decision to recognize China.[31] As France's strengthening economic and production performance unfolded, some domestic commercial interests also played a considerable role "to inject momentum to the Sino-French rapprochement," as France's imports and exports became more appealing to China.[32] Indeed, trading and banking interests played a significant role in pushing for furthering contacts with several countries in the Soviet bloc.[33] The export-oriented agricultural sector in France sought to influence French colonial politics, pushing to abandon an empire that was seen as serving a very limited set of interests ("high finance, the Church, and the military caste") and to not do much good for other people.[34] French farming interests expected large gains from the European Common Market, but some sectors of the French industry were worried about it, and clashes between these forces influenced French policy over this very topic.[35] As exports from the agricultural sector started to increase and the transition from the French franc area (comprising present and former colonies) to the European Market took place, the impatience with the empire on the part of certain groups grew.[36]

Domestic interests were also vociferous in the context of nuclear developments, seeing such investments as a way "to cope with increasing domestic pressures to decrease domestic investments in conventional armaments."[37] Ideological clashes impacted the French decision to open to the Soviet Union,[38] whereas cultural attachments on the part of some groups to Algeria played a crucial role in the French decision to transfer troops that were deployed under NATO orders in Eastern France and Western Germany to Algeria, a mere three years after Dulles had asked for increased participation of European countries in the European defense within NATO.[39]

Domestic interests' access to foreign policy, however, changed over the course of the period under analysis. During the Fourth Republic, interests tended to be well represented, so much so that "even a small constituency in a few parts of the country was assured representation in the National Assembly, and thus each party could act as a spokesman for highly specific socioeconomic and political preferences."[40] Due to the creation of the Fifth Republic in 1958, each individual intending to become the president or a member of the National Assembly would need a broader electoral basis compared to the one needed in the Fourth Republic. This institutional change set the key condition for a decrease in domestic interests' access to the definition of foreign policy.[41] In particular, it made it possible for De Gaulle to increasingly take over control of French behavior in the international arena after the failed military coup in Algeria in April 1961.[42] But the loss of access brought about by this institutional change manifested itself in a gradual way.[43] De Gaulle's control further solidified after three referenda in 1961 institutionalized the image of the president as speaking directly to and on behalf of the whole population, as opposed to being only in conversation with specific interest groups.[44] As a result of these series of institutional changes, by 1962 De Gaulle went from being seen as the "arbiter" among different interests to the "guide of the nation."[45] Indeed, scholars have argued, these changes made De Gaulle increasingly able to insulate foreign policy from domestic interests.[46]

Theoretical Predictions

Given the power and interests configuration during this period as it emerges from the previous sections, volatility should be higher during the period 1954–1962 and then decreasing over the subsequent time period.

These expectations follow directly from the argument put forward in this book. During the period under analysis, the previous section has shown, France's relative power vis-à-vis the US increased compared to its 1954 relative power (see Figure 5.1 and subsequent discussion). An increase in relative power similar to that experienced during the period under analysis, the argument suggests, would create a permissive condition for increasing volatility. It would do so by expanding the range of options available to France in its behavior toward the US.

Precisely given this theorized function of power, however, power alone will not systematically translate into greater volatility. So it would be possible for power to be increasing but for volatility to not increase. This is the case because the catalyzing factor for volatility—that is, the factor that translates greater options into actual volatile behavior—is the presence of a heterogeneous set of interests that competes for the definition of foreign policy. Indeed, as the previous section shows, interests emerging from non-cross-cutting cleavages played an important role in the way France behaved toward the US during the period under analysis. Their access to the definition of France's conduct in foreign affairs, however, decreased, especially after 1962.

Therefore, by 1962, even though France boasted greater access to options than in 1954 given its relative power, we should expect volatility to have declined, as the impetus for such volatility declined.

The next section will show patterns of volatile French behavior in the period under analysis, explain how these patterns speak to this argument's expectations, and illustrate why alternative hypotheses cannot fully explain the observed patterns.

Retracing Volatile French Behavior

Figure 5.2 plots the levels of volatility registered in France's policy toward the US during the years under analysis.[47] Evidence comes from event data

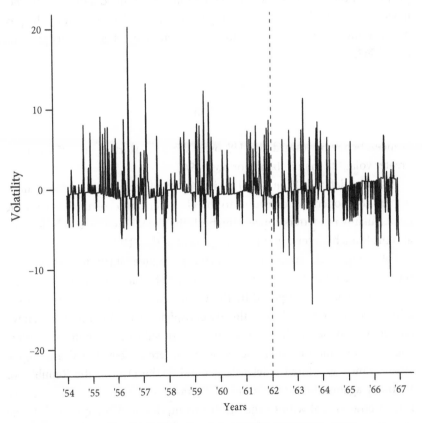

Figure 5.2 Volatility in France's behavior toward the US, 1954–1966.

capturing France's behaviors toward the US.[48] The figure suggests that, on average, volatility was higher pre-1962 than post-1962, consistent with the expectation that volatility would increase pre-1962 and decrease afterward. To boot, a nonparametric Wilcoxon signed-rank test rejects the null hypothesis of no difference between the means of the residuals before and after 1962 ($p \leq 0.001$).

But what, exactly, did these differences in volatility between the two time periods look like? The remaining part of this section illustrates these differences by leveraging contemporaneous and archival resources. It also complements the time series, event data approach used so far in the book by focusing on specific areas in which France interacted with the US. In particular, the next subsection focuses specifically on Vietnam, while the subsequent one deals more broadly with developments in the context of NATO (including dealings with communist countries and nuclear affairs). The purpose of these sections is to provide more fine-grained details on the behavior represented in Figure 5.2, unpacking such behavior with the help of primary and secondary sources, to show different levels of volatility pre- and post-1962.

Vietnam

France's behavior toward the US over Vietnam starting in 1954 betrays greater volatility than its behavior post-1962.

After the defeat at Dien Bien Phu in May 1954, for example, France made numerous cooperative overtures to the US, offering to collaborate with the powerful ally in matters concerning both the French presence in Indochina and the French leadership role in the project of the EDC.[49]

Following such cooperative overtures, France abruptly switched to refusing to cooperate with the US on issues of Indochina, now characterizing the conditions imposed by the US for cooperation as too onerous.[50] Differences with the US were already conspicuous by the time the Geneva conference opened in June 1954 and did not subside through the conference.[51] A few months after the Geneva conference concluded, in August 1954, France appointed a delegate general to the Democratic Republic of Vietnam, against the wishes of the US.[52] France also refused to take an active role in how to deal with China on this front, despite US requests.[53] At the same time, France suddenly dropped its support for the EDC. It soon refused to join it, even though the US had warned France of how disruptive it would be for the US if plans for the EDC were to fail and had complained that there had been broken promises before.[54]

However, just a few months later, in September 1954, France quickly switched again. French delegates traveled to Washington to ask the US for support to the continued French presence in Indochina, while agreeing to support Ngo Dinh Diem (as per the US request).[55] During the same month, France also opened to cooperation with the US on armaments.[56]

In December, France delayed US plans in Vietnam by suddenly objecting to its plans on how to divide the training responsibility between France and the US in the country (the Collins-Ely pact), even though France had signaled agreement on this issue before.[57] France, moreover, further opened to the Viet Min against US wishes.[58] In February of the next year, France switched on the Collins-Ely pact, finally agreeing to the US proposal. At the same time, France also relented on the issue of the Bangkok conference and Manila Pact after advancing severe critiques to the Southeast Asia Treaty Organization (SEATO) proposed by the US.[59]

At the Tripartite Talks in Paris from May 8 to 11, 1955, France expressed its strong opposition for the US decision to support Diem, even though, just a few months earlier, it had agreed to support him notwithstanding reservations on his fitness for leadership. However, French Prime Minister Edgar Faure switched back to cooperation, promising that although France was against Diem, it would accept the US proposal to continue to support Diem.[60] After forcefully denying accusations by US Secretary of State John Foster Dulles regarding French intentions to cooperate with North Vietnam back in March, by October 1955 France switched and concluded a commercial agreement with North Vietnam.[61]

Progressively, starting in 1962, volatility in the French behavior toward the US on Vietnam started to decrease, making room for more consistently conflictual behavior.

On August 29, 1963, France openly challenged US policy and preferences by publicly calling for the neutralization of Vietnam.[62] In August, France publicly declared it would support Vietnamese efforts to "throw off foreign influence and achieve unification."[63]

In November 1963, France did not join the US in recognizing South Vietnam as a country.[64] Contemporaneously, France agreed to provide aid to Cambodia when the country turned down US aid.[65] In January 1964, when recognizing China, France called again for the "neutralization of the former

French possessions in the Indochinese Peninsula [Cambodia, Laos, and North and South Vietnam] in cooperation with Communist China."[66]

In February 1964, further tensions emerged because the US perceived France as to some degree supporting the Chinese agenda in Vietnam and in the broader region, though the French denied it, and the US lodged public complaints directed at France for French declarations on Vietnam and neutralism.[67] Disagreements on US Vietnam policy continued in December 1964, with France questioning objectives, means, and the likelihood of success.[68] France publicly challenged the prevalent narratives of the origins of the Vietnam conflict, blaming the Americans for it while proposing disengagement and negotiation.[69] In March 1965, in response to new US bombings of North Vietnam, France openly asked for international negotiations to solve the crisis.[70] By February 1965, the American allies had grown increasingly frustrated with the French position on Vietnam.[71]

France officials also made public calls for closer cooperation on Vietnam between France and the Soviet Union.[72] In April 1965, France spoke in favor of a declaration of the nonaligned countries asking for peace in Vietnam, saying it had been France's position for a long time.[73] During a televised speech in April 1965, De Gaulle emphasized the importance of France's independence and condemned US behavior in Vietnam.[74] In February 1966, France voted against the US request that the UNSC add Vietnam to the topics for discussion. France's position was reaffirmed in another official statement disapproving of North Vietnam bombings.[75]

In sum, the historical record suggests that, while volatility was high before 1962, it declined afterward. Such pattern, the next section will show, also manifested itself within the broader area of NATO interactions.

France's Behavior within NATO

This section analyzes France's behavior toward the US in the broader context of the NATO alliance, for the period 1954–1966.

The Suez crisis arguably represents one of the most interesting examples of France's volatile behavior in the context of NATO. On July 29, 1956, in London, France agreed to meet with the US and the UK to talk about the crisis spurred by Nasser's decision in July 1956 to nationalize the Suez Canal Company.[76] During that meeting, French representatives explicitly connected the Suez crisis with Algeria, claiming events in both countries were intertwined in a North African crisis.[77] France seemed to be more severely hit by the crisis than the US, as 48% of its oil imports went through the strait, as opposed to 3% of American oil imports.[78]

France first threatened its American ally, in August 1956, to act militarily alone.[79] However, France subsequently switched positions, arguing for trying other methods first, such as negotiating with Nasser. Thus, France agreed to a meeting in London with Dulles and the UK counterpart to organize an international conference to deal with the events in Egypt.

In September 1956, France switched again, going behind the back of its US ally by holding secret consultations with Israel and the UK and making secret plans to invade Egypt and overthrow Nasser. Later, however, France decided to open to the US by agreeing on the US-proposed plan, which culminated in a new London conference whose final text was approved on September 21, with directives to create the Suez Canal Users Association.[80]

Days later, France publicly protested the ways the Americans portrayed their role in the Middle East.[81] During a meeting the next month, even though it had obtained cooperation from the US on a common line of action at the UNSC,[82] France decided not to disclose to the US its secret plans with Israel.

On October 29, 1956, Israeli forces attacked Egypt, advancing up to a few miles from the Canal. On October 30, France and the UK sent separate ultimatums to the Egyptian embassies in their respective countries, without first notifying the US.[83] France told the US it would not back down even though the US asked it to, refusing to halt its intervention in Egypt. Then, switching policies, France decided to be more cooperative with the US on this issue, sharing with the US the details of its role in inspiring Israel to attack Egypt and in colluding with Israel and the UK.[84] France also asked for reassurances regarding the alliance between the two countries.[85] On November 7, France made a further opening to the US, when French decision makers argued that France would welcome UN-sponsored troops.[86]

In December 1956 and throughout the first months of 1957, France opened up to cooperation with the US on matters of Algeria.[87] However, in March 1957, France switched, criticizing the US for meddling in Algeria when US Vice President Nixon visited Algeria and met with members of the NLF on March 20.[88]

Another interesting example of volatility emerges a few years later. Right after taking office in June 1958, De Gaulle reaffirmed French support for the current alliance with the US.[89] But just a month later, in July, De Gaulle criticized the alliance, characterizing it as obsolete and too limited in scope to prove useful anymore.[90]

In November 1958, in defiance of its US ally, France raised the tone of its critiques when De Gaulle publicly shared with NATO members the letter he had sent to President Eisenhower regarding NATO back in September 1958, in which he expressed his concerns about the obsolete nature of the institution.[91] In December, however, France joined the US ally in issuing a joint communiqué on Berlin, to respond to a Soviet one, even though it had just criticized the US posture toward the Soviet Union a few months earlier, in June 1958.[92]

By February 1959, however, France departed again from its position vis-à-vis the communist threat and decided not to join the US in sending an ambassador to Taiwan, even though previously, in November, it had expressed support of the US position during the crisis over the Quemoy and Matsu islands.[93]

After expressing pleasure with US openings on a possible reform of their partnership through NATO just one month earlier, in February 1959,[94] on March 7 the French government notified NATO of its intention to transfer its naval forces in the Mediterranean from the control of NATO to its own control, invoking its responsibilities in Algeria and complaining that the French fleet "did not enjoy the same freedom as the others," namely the US and the UK.[95] During the same month, France also opposed the installation in its territory of launching ramps, arguing it disliked not having control over them.[96] American officials perceived these French behaviors as particularly deleterious, potentially signaling disunity within the alliance at a moment when, due to the Berlin crisis, projecting unity was even more crucial than usual.[97]

From April 16 to 21, 1959, however, France agreed to meet the US and the UK for talks to take place in Washington, focusing on Africa. France had indeed asked in June 1958 for greater direct cooperation with the US and the UK on Africa. The French, however, quickly discarded the meeting agenda, even though they had previously agreed to it.[98] Moreover, in June 1959, Americans signaled their willingness to continue collaboration on Africa thinking that France would have been quite interested in the offer, but the French did not accept this offer.[99]

During discussions preceding a ministerial meeting of NATO from April 2 to 4, 1959, France switched to different contingency plans regarding Berlin than the ones it had proposed earlier on.[100] Even though, back in June 1958, France had seemed open to maintain a low profile and to be open to live with a divided country, while agreeing with the US on the importance of keeping Germany in the Western bloc,[101] now France advocated for greater firmness in showing the Western power's willingness to not tolerate a Soviet blockade. Such tougher stand constituted a switch from the behavior during previous months, when in the context of tripartite and quadripartite discussions, a compromise seemed to have been reached on a common plan.[102] Instead, by April, the French switched, arguing that those plans could lead to "a general European settlement adversely altering the relative power status of France vis-à-vis Germany or weakening the security of Western Europe."[103]

Shortly after inconsistently switching its position on Africa and Berlin, France agreed to meet with the US again on the sidelines of the Geneva conference, which took place in Paris toward the end of April 1959.[104] During this meeting at the sidelines, the French advanced cooperative openings for a common economic policy for underdeveloped nations between Western powers and the Soviet Union. To American decision makers, the plan seemed inconsistent with previous French behaviors. Indeed, in the preceding months, France had sharply criticized the Soviets when communicating with the Americans, accusing them of trying to divide Western allies and to leverage communism as a cover for their real agenda.[105]

Meanwhile, in May 1959, notwithstanding previous disagreements, France agreed to present a joint plan with the US to the Geneva conference on Berlin.[106]

In September 1959, Eisenhower visited Paris. On Berlin, the two presidents agreed on the minimal objective of not letting it fall into the hands of the Soviets.[107] Similarly, in October 1959, France agreed to a tripartite conference in Washington on issues of economic aid to Tunisia and Morocco. Shortly after, France also agreed to a tripartite meeting on Laos.

Soon, however, France switched again, inviting Khrushchev to visit France without consulting the US first, while also publicly challenging the US narrative of the Cold War.[108] At the UNGA, the French representative, in a clear critique of the US position on this topic, emphasized how pointless it was to ban testing if nothing was done on disarmament. During a press conference on November 10, De Gaulle even strongly cast doubts on the US allegiance to France.[109] De Gaulle's insinuations were bitter:

Who can say that [. . .] the two powers having the nuclear monopoly will not agree to divide the world? Who can say that if the occasion arises the two, while each deciding not to launch its missiles at the main enemy so that it should itself be spared, will not crush the others? [...] And who can even say that the two rivals, after I know not what political and social upheaval, will not unite?[110]

During the same press conference, De Gaulle accused the US of never going through with their original plan to put their nuclear weapons under the control of the UN.[111] Starting in January 1960, France switched, showing greater cooperative openness toward the US, on multiple camps. From January all the way into March, the French and US foreign ministers discussed the French request to establish tripartite talks to coordinate on issues of global politics. The Americans responded by proposing consultative arrangements in Washington.[112] After previous protestations against meetings including only Russia and the US, Paris agreed to host a summit exclusively between Eisenhower and Khrushchev on May 14, 1960, and the preparations for the summit started promptly.[113]

On February 18, 1960, France backtracked on its requests for tripartite talks with the US and the UK, which it had agreed to set up back in December 1959. American decision makers thought this choice was inconsistent with previous positions. Tellingly, President Eisenhower commented: "when our conversation took place, I thought that General De Gaulle was in complete accord and seemed to agree that the scheme could be set afoot without fanfare and without trouble. Just where it jumped the track I do not know."[114]

Starting in 1962, volatility in French behavior toward the US waned, and France started to more consistently oppose the US agenda within NATO and in the broader security context.

For example, in January 1962, it rejected US complaints about the impact of the formation of a force de frappe on Germany's nuclear ambitions while turning down US requests for more active participation of France on Berlin.[115] Meanwhile, in February 1962, disagreements between France and the US on the functioning of NATO and on the issue of nuclear weapons, which France insisted on framing as connected, continued. The French criticized the US proposal of a multilateral nuclear force as both unfeasible and unhelpful.[116] France did not participate in the disarmament conference, against the wishes of the US.[117] In May 1962, France also condemned the US decision to negotiate directly with the Soviet Union on Germany.[118] In October 1962, France still refused to contribute more troops to protecting Berlin and NATO.[119] In November 1962, during the Cuban missile crisis, after praising the US restraint, France warned the US about not partaking in political consultations with France and the UK (as the US had done during the Cuban missile crisis). France argued that the lack of such consultations in the event of a new Berlin crisis would have been very consequential.[120]

In July 1963, France congratulated Kennedy on the conclusion of the nuclear Partial Test Ban Treaty (PTBT) but downplayed the consequences of the treaty.[121] French policymakers defined the treaty as unhelpful and France reiterated its necessity to insulate itself from nuclear threats.[122] After the conclusion of the PTBT on July 25, 1963, the US publicly invited France to join in, arguing that France was indeed the fourth nuclear power.[123] Yet France turned down the invitation, arguing that it would only give up nuclear weapons if the US and the USSR were to do the same.[124] Instead, France publicly offered a counterproposal, a four-nuclear-power conference to discuss disarmament.[125]

France turned down the US offer to join the US and Great Britain in the Nassau agreement on the Polaris, on January 14, 1963.[126] In March 1963, to mark the disagreement with the US, the French foreign minister chose not to join the meeting at the Atlantic Council where members discussed the creation of a multilateral force.[127] In September 1963, France refused to sign the PTBT in Moscow, while still opposing, within NATO, a US-supported study of the long-term needs of the alliance. In October 1963, France also continued to voice its opposition to the multilateral force that the US supports.[128]

In April 1963, France opposed the US proposal for interallied forces, as well as multinational forces, both sponsored by the US during the ministerial council of the Atlantic Organization that same month.[129] Just a few days later, De Gaulle gave a speech on the creation of a national nuclear force.[130] In May 1963, at the meeting of the Atlantic Organization in Ottawa, after the declaration of no cooperation by France in January on the Nassau agreement, it became harder to coordinate increased cooperation on nuclear material. During the same month, the French foreign minister accepted an invitation to Washington, but no rapprochement took place between the policies of the two countries.[131]

In April 1964, De Gaulle announced his decision to retire French officials from the upper echelons of the naval interallied command.[132] In May 1964, France acted in opposition to the US in the UNSC by supporting Cambodia's request for a UNSC special session on US aggressions within Cambodian borders. France proposed an international conference on the issue of Laos and the Soviet Union agreed, but the US did not. In May 1964, France refused to try to "sell" the Multilateral Force (MLF) to the Soviets, as requested by the

Americans, arguing that France had the same reservations about the force as the Soviets did.[133] In September 1964, France did not participate in the naval military exercises of the multilateral Atlantic force.[134] Instead, De Gaulle visited South America, as it became clear that France wanted a presence in that region.[135]

During the same month, France also declined to participate in the military exercise Fallex in the context of the Atlantic Organization.[136] In August 1965, the disarmament conference in Geneva started again, but France decided not to participate.[137] In July 1965, France refused to join a new nuclear committee that the Americans proposed to create within the Atlantic Organization to study nuclear issues. In July 1965, France sent a verbal protestation to the US embassy, presenting pictures that showed a plane flying above the no-fly zone of Pierrelatte.[138]

During the same years, France's hostile behavior also concerned how to deal with communist countries.[139] In February 1962, without first coordinating with the US, France responded to a message by Khrushchev and asked for a meeting between the US, USSR, Great Britain, and France to talk about nuclear weapons.[140] In September 1962, the French resumed trade talks with the Soviet Union.[141]

On January 27, 1964, after numerous past reassurances to the US that France was not going to do so,[142] France recognized China. The US complained that the Soviet Union was given a "greater warning" about the incoming recognition of China than the US.[143] US decision makers further argued that France's decision to recognize communist China also had negative economic consequences for the US.[144]

In February 1964, France forced Taiwan to break diplomatic relations when it announced that it intended to exchange diplomatic missions with Beijing.[145] During the same month, the question of France trade credits toward another communist country, Cuba, gained salience in the relations between France and the US. France was supporting with credit guarantees those domestic interests exporting to Cuba, as part of a plan to improve relations with the Soviet Union and China. The US during this month considered halting US aid to France over this very issue.[146]

In March 1964, France joined the Soviet Union in abstaining on a UN resolution on the establishment of a military force in Cyprus. France also supported China being admitted to the World Health Organization. In January 1965, as the UN faced a financial and political crisis, France proposed going back to a great directorate, including the original Permanent

Five members of the UNSC—that is, including mainland China—even though the US did not recognize China as a UN member.[147] France also claimed that the UN had betrayed its original mission, due in no small part to US pressures to do just that, and that for that reason France refused to finance the mission in Congo, against US wishes.

France further challenged US preferences in the area when De Gaulle, during a press conference on January 31, 1965,[148] both praised the Chinese accomplishments and proposed, in spite of France's Southeast Asia Treaty Organization (SEATO) commitments, the "neutralization of the former French possessions in the Indochinese Peninsula [Cambodia, Laos, and North and South Vietnam] in cooperation with Communist China."[149] Giscard d'Estaing, French minister of economy and finance, announced a visit to Moscow to promote French products there.[150]

In March 1965, France continued concluding economic agreements, such as one on color TV, with the Soviet Union.[151] In April 1965, France also exchanged diplomatic pleasantries with the Soviet Union during a visit by Soviet Foreign Minister Gromyko to Paris.[152]

In November 1965, during a major UNGA debate on the admission of mainland China, France spoke in favor of admission.[153]

Interests and Power Produce Volatility

In sum, the previous section suggests that volatility in France's behavior toward the US decreased after 1962. The data suggest that this is so both when we look at event data in the aggregate and when we leverage archival sources to look instead at specific episodes occurring during the time period under analysis. In this section, I explain how these results are consistent with the argument of the book that an interaction between power and interests can increase volatility.

According to American analysts, the increase in France's relative power, including its nuclear weapons acquisition and its rising economic prominence in the EEC, had progressively changed the way France behaved toward the US.[154]

In particular, France's increasing relative power expanded the set of options available to the country to deal with the US. After shifting resources to military investments and instituting an autonomous nuclear weapons program, France brought to bear its progress on nuclear weapons when negotiating with the US on a range of issues, such as the withdrawal from NATO, the Limited Test Ban Treaty, and even disarmament.[155] In 1962, for example, a healthier economy with a higher GDP helped free resources to give France the option of paying back loans that the US had offered at different points in time, a gesture that the US greatly appreciated.[156]

In 1963, France had also become better able to offer military aid to Cambodia when Cambodia decided to reject US aid. This offer added some heft to France's numerous condemnations of US behavior in Vietnam and to its agenda to restore its prominence in that part of Asia.[157] After its GDP recovered, France could offer credits to Cuba and become in general more assertive when it came to their agenda to offer aid to developing countries. France had considered this initiative before but had not been able to engage in it, due to a lack of material resources. A more vigorous economy had also expanded the options that France had at its disposal to deal with China, because trade prospects were one of the aspects that attracted the Chinese to establishing contacts with France.[158]

Some of this increase in relative power also brought about an increase in soft power. For example, attracting China economically allowed France to gain a renewed prestige in developing countries—a prestige much needed at a time when French colonial history had become particularly cumbersome.[159] Similarly, acquiring nuclear weapons gave France access to the much-coveted "nuclear club" and contributed to France's public recognition as one of the great powers of the 1960s: the US, the USSR, and Great Britain.[160]

Relative power, as it increased, expanded the options available to France. This, in turn, made it possible for France to behave in a volatile manner. Power alone, however, cannot quite explain the pattern of volatility that unfolded in France's behavior during those years. Simply put, changes in volatility did not exactly match up to changes in power during those years. Volatility started decreasing around 1962, when France started behaving toward the US in a more consistently conflictual manner. Yet power followed a different pattern. While, as Figure 5.1 makes clear, relative power started leveling off after 1960, it did not decrease to its 1954 levels. But in 1962, France started behaving in a more consistent manner even though relative power did not decrease to its early 1950s levels.

This pattern therefore casts doubt on explanations that rely just on power as the cause for change in countries' behaviors, such as those on foreign policy hedging, as useful to explaining volatility. Instead, the case of France suggests another important component of the explanation of volatility: domestic interests.

Power and interests combined to produce volatility. For example, large swaths of the population, especially those living in rural, less industrialized areas, saw the French presence in Indochina as wasteful.[161] Yet a subset of commercial interests, mostly focused in cities, saw the importance of keeping a French presence in the area. In particular, certain industrial sectors were especially dependent on the colonial empire for markets, including the textile and machine tool industry, and thus had an interest in resisting decolonization.[162] Because of this interesting configuration, then, it stands to reason that France leveraged its growing power relative to the US to shift seemingly inconsistently between asking for help to disentangle itself from the former colony and making attempts to keep commercial contacts with both South and North Vietnam. Similarly, the presence of clashing domestic interests regarding the rearmament of Germany increased volatility in French behavior regarding the EDC.[163]

A similar pull and push emerged between agricultural and industrial interests in the EEC. France farming interests expected large gains from the Common Market, but some sectors of the French industry were worried about what the new regulations would entail for their market shares.[164] In fact, France leveraged its increasing power to shift seemingly inconsistently between favoring the promotion of integration among countries within the EEC, an outcome that the Americans favored, and pulling back on its commitments.

Some domestic groups such as the ones represented by the Communist Party supported a reconciliation with the Soviet Union.[165] However, others opposed opening up to the USSR for a common German plan, which made cooperation quite complex.[166]

During the Suez Canal crisis, shareholders played an important role in pushing France to take a position.[167] Instead, other domestic interests such as rural groups saw little to be gained in the involvement in the crisis. As access to power by these interests decreased, especially after 1961, the dynamic condition for volatility declined, likely bringing a decline in volatility as well.

Alternative Explanations

As Chapter 2 makes clear, it is possible to think of several alternative explanations of volatility in states' behaviors. This section explores why such alternative explanations are not able to capture variation in volatility as well as my argument does.

For example, it could be that the presence of specific issues between France and the US explains the increase in French volatility toward the US. More issues could have developed or issues could have become more salient post-1962 . The presence of issues might increase the opportunities to interact and thus increase the probability of volatile behavior. Similarly, salient issues might attract greater attention and thus spur both more cooperation and conflict.

Statistically, a series of tests of proportion comparing the issues present pre- and post-1962 shows that there is no significant difference between the two periods in terms of the number of issues that were present. Moreover, similar tests show that the incidence of traditionally salient issues such as military and economic issues does not seem to differ much between the two time periods.[168] Similarly, a close examination of the historical record does not provide sufficient evidence for this issue-based explanation. As the discussion above illustrates, declassified and contemporaneous sources suggest that issues that were present and salient in 1954, such as what to do with communist countries, Europe's integration, the German question, nuclear weapons, NATO, and the transition of French colonialism, do not disappear in the years after 1962, when volatility decreases.

Not only do these similar issues appear to be recurrent throughout the time period 1954–1962, but also the previous discussion suggests that France and the US often created issues dynamically, coupling and decoupling bigger issues to serve their political purposes.

In particular, France did see relations between France and the US as comprising very many topics or issues: "Berlin, NATO, the UN, Franco-American nuclear relations, the Far East, Africa, the Middle East, Latin America, economic relations between the US and Europe and the dollar."[169] Yet what constituted an "issue" often morphed as a function of political calculus. Examples abound. French decision makers, at different points in time and to serve their domestic agenda, alternated between connecting France's policies in Africa with the larger struggle against communism taking place both in Africa and in Europe (e.g., in the case of Suez) and arguing that those policies in Africa were the domain of domestic politics and had little to do with foreign policy.[170] At different times, French officials presented the issue of what to do with the Soviet Union and what to do about the German question as linked or as disjoint.[171]

The political determination of what constituted an "issue" for consideration was politically motivated and dependent on the (previous) decision to cooperate or not. Refusing to cooperate or proliferate and thus rejecting invitations to participate in the Limited Test Ban Treaty, France argued that disarmament and proliferation were linked and should have been treated as two faces of the same coin, though Americans disagreed with the linking of these two concepts.[172] During conversations between foreign ministers, in 1959, Americans linked the fate of the US fighter squadrons—part of NATO forces in France—to developments in Berlin so as to achieve cooperation with France on this matter.[173] Unwilling to provide such cooperation, the French linked instead the question of US fighter squadrons to the French request for permanent tripartite talks, to the lack of US support for France in Algeria (and to the domestic turmoil of 1958 that resulted from that), and to the need for atomic cooperation between the two countries.[174] The American secretary of state retorted that

> he was sorry the French had linked the atomic stockpile question with the three other questions listed above, as he thought the need for the atomic stockpile was in connection with the common defense, whereas the other three points were ones which should be discussed but disassociated from the atomic stockpile.[175]

By contrast, leader-based explanations can take multiple forms. First, some leaders' attributes (e.g., their combat experience) might make them more prone to behave in a volatile manner. Yet, the seven leaders in power during the time period with greater volatility differ when it comes to their military background. Three of the seven had a military education, but only five of them had combat experience.[176] This suggests, in turn, that there is no direct correspondence between combat experience and volatility. As for gender, the case does not present variation, thus becoming less helpful to rule out or provide support for a correlation between these leaders' characteristics and volatility.

Second, changes in leadership do not seem to provide a satisfactory explanation of volatility. During the period 1958–1960, no leadership transition took place, yet volatility was still high (see Table 5.1). Similarly, a decrease in volatility does not simply correspond to a change in leadership. To begin, De Gaulle took office in 1958, but volatility does not appear to decrease until after 1961. Indeed, contemporary observers and scholars noted great continuity between the policies of De Gaulle and those of his predecessors before 1962.[177] Rather than a sudden switch in French politics following De Gaulle's ascent to power, observers perceived a slow transformation that took years. By August 1961, in a letter to US Ambassador Gavin, Nicholas Wahl compared 1961 De Gaulle to 1958 De Gaulle, noticing the effects that time in power had had on his approach to power and on his vision for France: "Three years in power have considerably affected his general view of France's future and his estimation of his own role in influencing the course of her history."[178] This observation emphasizes the role of institutions in shaping leaders' perceptions and behaviors.

Another possible leader-based explanation can argue that it is not so much the change in leadership that brought volatility but rather the change in the coalition that supported the leader. Table 5.1 presents a list of all French leaders, by year. In the third column, the table codes as 1 those instances when a new leader transition is accompanied by a change in the coalition supporting the leader (as measured by changes in party membership of the leader). The fourth column reports instead the coalition of parties that supports the leader for that year.[179] As it emerges from Table 5.1, a change in coalition takes place only in 50% of the years when we note higher volatility (in four out of the eight years in which volatility tends to be higher). Moreover, in some of the instances in which the leadership change is accompanied by a change of supporting coalition (e.g., in 1954, in the transition between Laniel and Mendès-France), the only thing that changes is the affiliation of the leader in terms of the party, not the whole coalition of parties that supports the leader. A period of lower volatility does coincide with no coalition change in the period between 1962 and 1966, Table 5.1 shows. However, in reality, there was continuity in the coalition supporting the leader even before that date (since 1958), but volatility did not start declining until 1962. As I explain below, such decrease is due to the change in domestic interests' access to the definition of foreign policy that happens at the end of 1961.

Another possible explanation has to do with changes in the polarity of the system during that period. Figure 5.3 therefore leverages the CINC score to shed light on whether there are significant changes in bipolarism during that period compared to the duration of the Cold war, 1948–1991. The plot on the left-hand side, in particular, depicts the ratio of the US and Soviet CINC score for the duration of the Cold War, comparing material capabilities between the two superpowers. The plot on the right-hand side, in contrast, depicts the US and Soviet material capabilities as a percentage of

Table 5.1 List of French Leaders, by Year, with Party Affiliation and a Dummy for the Presence of a Change in the Source of Leader Support

Leaders	Year	Change	Coalition
Laniel, Mendès-France	1954	1	IND/MRP/RSP/GAUL, RSP/MRP/IND/GAUL
Mendès-France, Faure	1955	0	RSP/MRP/IND/GAUL, RSP/MRP/IND/GAUL
Faure, Mollet	1956	1	RSP/MRP/IND/GAUL, PSF/RSP/GAUL
Mollet, Bourges-Maunory, Gaillard	1957	1	PSF/RSP/GAUL, RSP/PSF/GAUL, RSP/PSF/GAUL/MRP/IND
Gaillard, Pflimin, De Gaulle	1958	1	RSP/PSF/GAUL/MRP/IND, MRP/RSP/IND/GAUL, GAUL/MRP/PSF/RSP/IND (De Gaulle), UNR (De Gaulle)
De Gaulle	1959	0	UNR
De Gaulle	1960	0	UNR
De Gaulle	1961	0	UNR
De Gaulle	1962	0	UNR
De Gaulle	1963	0	UNR
De Gaulle	1964	0	UNR
De Gaulle	1965	0	UNR
De Gaulle	1966	0	UNR

Note: GAUL=Gaullist party; *IND=Independent*; MRP=*Mouvement Républicain Populaire*; PSF=*Parti Social Français*; RSP=*Parti Socialiste Révolutionnaire*; UNR=Union for the New Republic

the total world capabilities for each year of the Cold War, to see if there are changes in the degree to which power is concentrated in the hands of these two superpowers. In both plots, a nonparametric loess curve suggests that those quantities follow a similar, declining trend throughout the years and do not exhibit any sharp change in trend during the years under investigation. Primary documents also confirm that throughout the period under analysis French decision makers perceived the US and the USSR as being the two most powerful countries in the world.[180] No sharp variation in bipolarism seems to coincide with the start or end of volatility.

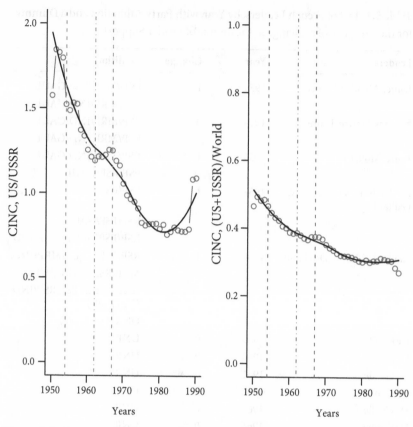

Figure 5.3 Composite Index of Military Capabilities (CINC) score for the US and the Soviet Union during the Cold War. *NOTE: Loess curves in black. Vertical lines, in gray, denote, respectively, 1954, 1962, and 1966.*

France Exits NATO: 1966

In March 1966, France notified the US ambassador that France was withdrawing from NATO's military structure and ordered the headquarters of NATO's Allied Command Operations (SHAPE) out of France. France wanted, De Gaulle argued, to recover on its territory the full exercise of its sovereignty.[181]

This French decision would present notable costs for Americans, US officials predicted in now-declassified documents. It would make it harder to convince other allies to increase their contribution to NATO. It would also raise the specter of a renewed German domination of the continent. Moreover, it was expected to have broader ramifications, potentially killing off the Kennedy Round's prospects within the GATT while complicating Western countries' policies vis-à-vis the USSR and Eastern Europe.[182]

Declassified documents also suggest that before France left NATO, the increasingly volatile French behavior augmented US uncertainty. For example, by 1960, regarding matters of the alliance, Eisenhower expressed that he could not "quite understand the basic philosophy of France today" as France seemed to advance proposals that "appear [...] incompatible."[183]

American decision makers expressed their increasing inability to leverage France's past behavior to correctly predict major French decisions, such as the one to recognize China and the one to leave NATO.[184] Indeed, when trying to discern France's agenda, those decision makers admitted at times to having "absolutely no clue."[185]

Such uncertainty, in turn, increased US distrust of France, likely contributing to spoiling the relationship between the two countries. After years of volatility, in May 1962, relations between the US and France were "in parlous conditions."[186] By 1963, US decision makers perceived France and the US as "political competitors pursuing divergent goals."[187] American officials perceived French political objectives "in [a] number of important respects" as "different from and [...] in fact in conflict with our own."[188] The prevalent feeling among decision makers was that, especially on Vietnam issues, France had "disregard for American interests."[189] By 1965, US decision makers felt it safer to embrace a defensive posture toward France, fearing that France, if the occasion arose, would try to publicly embarrass the US.[190] The American public too grew distrustful and in July 1966 American citizens by and large no longer judged France as a "dependable ally of the US."[191]

Strikingly, volatility had strained relations so much that French leadership suggested taking a quite radical approach to rebuilding trust: starting over from scratch, taking small steps, and cooperating on small projects.[192] This suggestion to taking cooperation step by step so as to build more trust seems to reveal the depths of the rift that had emerged between the two countries.

Commenting on the state of the relations between the two countries, the US ambassador in France, Bohlen, argued in March 1965: "French Government has not behaved in fashion befitting an old ally in recent weeks."[193]

Conclusions

In 1966, relations between the US and France, the quote at the beginning of this chapter suggested, might have reached their nadir. After several months of conflicts and disagreements, in March 1966, the US ambassador to France concluded: "to pretend that our relations were normal [. . .] is illusory."[194] Some scholars have gone as far as saying that France was "the greatest threat to Western unity in the Cold War," and even a greater threat than Communism.[195] It was only in 2009 that France joined NATO again as a full-fledged member.[196]

Leveraging primary sources as well as event data to retrace France's interactions with the US over the time period 1954–1966, the chapter has provided more in-depth evidence of the unfolding of volatility in the behavior of one country toward another. Growing relative power became a permissive condition for volatility, while access to the definition of foreign policy by a diverse set of interests catalyzed it. Alternative explanations, focusing, for instance, on issues or on leaders, fail to account for the variation in volatility registered during those years.

In addition to tracing what volatility might look and feel like for actors facing a volatile counterpart as events unfold, this chapter has also expanded the empirical reach of the book by showing that volatile behavior, although often associated with mistrust and conflict, is not just the realm of rivalries. Complex relations such as those between allies might indeed provide an especially fertile ground for observing volatility.

In showing how an increase in the volatility of an ally's behavior has repercussions for the other ally, the chapter has expanded on our understanding of alliances. Present studies have investigated several aspects of alliances. As a consequence, we have learned a lot about when countries decide to form alliances, how countries choose which type of commitment the alliance should entail, and whether countries come through in their commitments, among other topics.[197] But we know less about how relations unfold through time and, in particular, when they are more likely to become volatile. Yet understanding how relations unfold can become crucial to explaining alliance features, such as which alliance commitments last and for how long. While the decision to pull back from alliance commitments is complex and multiple factors contribute to it, findings in this chapter suggest that it will be fruitful to investigate how volatility can often matter a great deal in these matters.[198]

This chapter also challenges current understandings of volatility in states' behaviors in important ways. Perhaps most importantly, this chapter shows how the theory applies to cases and times of so-called "politics as usual": not just during or before major crises, but rather in the very conduct of foreign policy. By tracing the relation as a whole, as opposed to just looking at certain sectors of foreign policy, such as the economic sector, the chapter shows how intertwined various aspects of a relation are, how much political activity goes into defining crucial areas of cooperation or conflict, and how many connections are lost when we focus exclusively on conflictual or cooperative behaviors.

In sum, the empirical section of this book has presented evidence from multiple scenarios and with multiple methodological techniques to support my argument on where volatility in states' behaviors comes from. But what, if any, is the value added of learning more about volatility in states' behaviors toward other states? The next chapter takes on precisely this question, presenting the conclusions to the book.

6

Conclusions

Volatility presents traditional approaches to the study of international politics with a catch-22.

On the one hand, in order to gain a firmer grasp on key processes in international politics, scholars need to be able to explain volatility. Volatility is at the root of many of the phenomena we study, as it potentially transforms international politics in visible and unwelcome ways. In particular, since volatile behavior lacks clear patterns, it erodes trust (the bedrock of sustained cooperation) while intensifying conflict.

On the other hand, in order to explain volatility, it is crucial to better understand key processes in international politics. In particular, it becomes necessary to find new, different ways to conceptualize interactions in the international arena. To date, however, scholars have mostly restricted their analysis to looking at central tendencies in countries' behaviors. Even when studying change, most scholars have largely focused on change that is consistent over time. This focus has limited International Relations (IR) scholars' ability to study volatility, with the result that the field is lagging behind other areas of study in the field of Political Science and beyond. Instead of explaining volatility, IR scholars have simply coped with it by dismissing it either as inexistent or as constant background noise. Neither of these approaches, however, is well equipped to explain why volatility increases in some cases but not others.

As the first systematic exploration of volatility in states' behaviors, this book has sought to address this catch-22 by adopting a new perspective on states' behaviors in the international system—a perspective that focuses on how diverse states' behaviors can become over time. This book therefore also provided a new conceptualization of volatility in states' behaviors, a tool to measure it, and an explanation for where it comes from. It has advanced the argument that volatility in international politics emerges from the interaction of two distinct processes taking place at different levels. At the international level, growing relative power equips countries with more options when interacting with other countries. Greater relative power in the form

Volatile States in International Politics. Eleonora Mattiacci, Oxford University Press. © Oxford University Press 2023.
DOI: 10.1093/oso/9780197638675.003.0006

of nuclear weapons acquisition, for example, can increase the availability of conflictual options for a state. It can also open up more cooperative options, for example, by providing the state with valuable "bargaining chips." Power alone, however, does not explain volatility. This is the case because power provides countries with options, but it does nothing to determine which options will be used and whether countries will shift inconsistently between the available options. Relative power, in other words, operates as a permissive condition—it makes volatility possible. The second crucial process to explain volatility resides instead within countries themselves. Domestic groups often compete to impose their preferred foreign policy actions. When the interest configuration within a country is such that preferences diverge—that is, when cleavages are reinforcing—competing interests will push and pull countries' activities in different directions in the international arena.

In sum, power and interests interact, producing unruly behavior in the global arena. In particular, the further apart the preferences of those domestic groups with a say in defining foreign policy, the more diverse their preferred courses of action will be in foreign policy, on average. The greater a country's relative power, the more likely that those opposing domestic preferences will be put into practice. The outcome of the interaction between interests and power, therefore, is increased volatility in states' behaviors toward other states.

Unlike accounts that rely exclusively on power to explain countries' behaviors in international politics, this argument specifies what actually catalyzes volatility. Hedging accounts, for instance, argue that the greater the relative power that a country can rely on, the more likely the country is to explore different, even opposing policies in the international arena. While this perspective can explain what countries can do by focusing on the options that power gets them, they are less well suited for exploring what volatility actually looks like, and why countries might act in a volatile manner in some cases but not others. Similarly, accounts that emphasize the presence of issues—that is, areas over which political actors can negotiate—cannot explain volatility because they do not explain where these issues come from to begin with. Finally, accounts that build on leaders' traits and experiences, while often important to explain change, are insufficient to capture volatility because they cannot explain both what makes volatility possible and what spurs it.

This book has then provided empirical evidence for its argument that volatility emerges from the interaction between power and interests.

Chapter 3 has presented a new measurement and, using examples of major states' behaviors, leveraged it to illustrate how volatility can change over time and across cases. Chapter 4 has applied a large-N analysis design to the study of international rivalries. Finally, Chapter 5 has extended this exploration by leveraging declassified and contemporary primary sources to shed light on one specific manifestation of volatility: France's behavior toward the US in the years preceding France's decision to leave the North Atlantic Treaty Organization (NATO).

Properly understanding volatility has crucial reverberations. At the most fundamental level, it enriches our theoretical understanding of the international system by adding an important missing piece to our representation of global affairs. Volatility is different from other forms of change that are well studied, such as cycles or trends. In particular, what sets volatility apart is the inconsistency of changes in states' behaviors. Inconsistency makes change hard to predict for the counterparts to the volatile state, therefore hampering their attempts to use the past as a guide for the future.

Another reverberation is that, as I argue in this chapter, volatility's by-products, including distrust and conflict escalation, can be dispelled to some degree by a more accurate understanding of where volatility originates. Volatility does not need to become a black hole at the center of the global arena, preventing policymakers from seeing through.

A New Perspective

What are the payoffs, in practice, of explaining volatility in states' behaviors? The remaining pages of this book are dedicated to answering this question. In particular, the rest of the chapter is divided into three parts.

The first section resumes the discussion from the introduction of volatility's damaging repercussions in international politics: its effects on crucial phenomena such as trust and escalation. It then shows how understanding the root causes of volatility can change states' incentives and potentially stave off its most pernicious consequences.

Then, I explain how this book's findings on the connection between power and interests on the one hand and volatility on the other can illuminate different paths of research for addressing some of the mixed findings in the field of IR. I focus in particular on those studies that analyze consistent state behaviors and their implications for international politics—studies of compliance, reputation, credible commitments, and audience costs.

The final section traces instead future directions for research on volatility. It outlines several ways in which the theory and findings in this book can help extend the study of volatility in IR beyond volatility in states' behaviors. In particular, it points toward the study of nonstate actors and of the international system.

What Can Volatility Tell Us?

One of the valuable aspects of understanding where volatility originates is that such understanding can help reduce the incidence of most of volatility's unintended consequences— those unintended consequences with systemic repercussions that political scientist Robert Jervis calls "systems effects."

But how can knowing the origins of volatility reduce these unintended consequences? As Jervis makes clear, decision makers are reflexive actors. As such, they react not just to their counterparts' actions but also to their own interpretations of such actions. Therefore, when dealing with a volatile counterpart, actors will likely react not just to the actual behavior they encounter but also to the uncertainty that volatility generates.[1]

By the same token, however, precisely because decision makers are reflexive, becoming aware of such system effects changes their impact. This awareness, in other words, "enables people to compensate for the results that would otherwise occur."[2] Consider, for example, domino theory. Its central tenet is that an actor with a reputation for backing down will attract more aggressive behavior from its counterpart. But when decision makers are made aware of and understand this central tenet, then they will take actions to prevent the projected outcome.[3] Such actions, in turn, will potentially reduce the negative consequences of domino theory, possibly contributing to preserving a country's reputation for resolve. When decision makers are aware of domino theory's implications, in other words, we see those implications develop less frequently.

Just as making decision makers aware of domino theory's predictions might attenuate the negative externalities the theory identifies, so too might informing decision makers about the origins of volatility alleviate (at least in part) the uncertainty that volatility can generate.

In the next sections, therefore, I will illustrate how understanding volatile behavior as emerging from power and interests can potentially stave off its worse consequences.

Volatility and Strategy

As discussed in the introduction, volatility, presenting decision makers with inconsistent change in their counterpart's behavior, complicates efforts to plan for the future by looking at the past—a task that is essential for strategizing.[4] Since volatile behavior is behavior that is subject to random fluctuations, decision makers struggle to parse out the "signal" from the "noise." In other words, they scramble to decipher the information that is actually helpful for them in terms of making decisions and elaborating strategies.[5] Thus, volatility has the potential to dissuade decision makers from elaborating strategies to begin with, by making the uncertainty that they must face feel overwhelming.[6]

Knowing where volatility comes from, however, can uniquely mitigate these challenges in multiple ways. First, contextualizing volatile behavior as emerging from an interaction between interests and power helps dispel suspicions that volatile behavior reflects a concerted effort to deceive. Such suspicions, scholars suggest, complicate efforts to elaborate a strategy.[7]

Second, information such as that provided on the origins of a counterpart's specific behavior, some analysts have argued, can even be crucial for moving from the realm of uncertainty to the realm of risk. Drawing on the Knightian distinction between the two, this shift from the realm of uncertainty to the realm of risk allows decision makers to more accurately estimate how plausible some future scenarios will be.[8] In turn, refining predictions when dealing with great uncertainty is key to elaborating realistic and successful strategies.[9]

Indeed, being able to better forecast increases in volatility, even without completely eradicating doubts as to what specific behavior to expect next, could provide a powerful antidote to what some scholars have referred to as the major challenge to the elaboration of sound strategies: the power of habitual thinking. Habitual thinking discourages strategy updating in response to current events.[10] When decision makers elaborate strategies according to the logic of habit, "collective ideas come to be seen as obvious, axiomatic choices made from unexamined assumptions."[11]

Being able to foresee a surge in inconsistent behavior without knowing what it will look like can counteract the logic of habit in strategy creation, keeping decision makers on their toes.[12] Given the importance of keeping decision makers' focused on constantly elaborating and tweaking strategies in order to minimize their biases,[13] the exercise of predicting volatility can help produce sounder, more robust strategies.

Volatility and Trust

By making it harder to leverage the past to predict the future, volatility also challenges states' willingness to trust their volatile counterparts. Yet since trust, at a fundamental level, "involves particular beliefs about the motivations of others,"[14] knowing where volatility comes from can uniquely affect its impact on trust by shaping such beliefs. This is true whether we embrace a situational or a dispositional understanding of trust.

According to situational accounts of trust, actors will observe behaviors and impute intentions when deciding whom to trust. Trust, in these accounts, is understood as "strategic" because it is based on the situation in which the actors are involved.[15] For example, in a classic depiction of strategic trust, trust will develop if the actor to be trusted can send costly signals, defined as signals that are "so costly that one would hesitate to send them if one were untrustworthy."[16] When an actor acts in a volatile manner, thus shifting inconsistently toward more cooperation or more conflict, it might be hard amidst the inconsistent fluctuations to get a clear idea of whether any of those actions constitute a costly signal. Knowing that the origins of the behavior lie at the interaction of interests and power, however, potentially changes the calculation. It makes it easier to assess whether volatile behavior is costly because it gives background information as to where such behavior originates. This new way to look at states' behaviors then raises an important question that studies of strategic trust have yet to address: when will actors' ability to contextualize the behavior they observe be enough to overcome the obstacles to trust?

According to instead to dispositional accounts of trust, the decision to trust someone's counterpart depends on specific, innate traits. This type of trust is moralistic: it constitutes a judgment about someone else's character—indeed, "a belief that others have consistent personalities and traits that do not vary by situations."[17] It differs, therefore, from strategic trust, which entails a judgment based on evidence of behavior. So what determines what evidence will be used to evaluate an actor's character? Will it be evidence of the inconsistencies in its behavior, or evidence of the consistency of the origins of such behavior? Results in this book suggest that understanding where volatility comes from can generate a paradoxical answer to this question. Namely, volatile states could become some of the most trustworthy actors in the international arena. This is the case not so much because their past behavior can be leveraged by observers to predict their future but, rather, because their counterparts will likely become able to correctly interpret their present and future behavior as closely reflecting the interaction between interests and power considerations animating them. In other words, volatile states might become trustworthy if observers understand where their volatile tendencies come from, because these states are likely to be interpreted as accurately displaying their motives when acting in a volatile manner.

Trust is a fundamental building block for lasting cooperation. In this capacity, it has an impact on key international phenomena we care about, including reconciliation between rivals, the endurance of alliances, counterproliferation, detente between opposing superpowers, and the spread of multilateralism.[18] If, as I have argued here, knowing where volatility comes from can significantly tame its negative implications regarding trust, then understanding volatility as emerging from the interaction of power and interests will also have important implications for these crucial international phenomena that trust affects. In the realm of counterproliferation, for example, understanding the origins of volatility can help countries cooperate with nuclear-ambitious states in a way that better considers the conflicting domestic forces that influence those countries' behaviors.[19]

Volatility and Escalation

Volatility, as Chapter 1 discusses, complicates efforts to use the past as a predictor of future behavior. For this reason, volatility sows fear, potentially fueling escalation. For example, it was likely the increase of volatility in Iranian behavior toward the US in the 2010s that led the violence between the two countries to escalate to the point where the US sponsored the assassination of Major General Qassim Suleimani in 2020.[20]

Knowing where volatility comes from, however, can tame its effects on escalation. This is the case because escalation is based on how a state interprets its opponent's behavior.

Escalation is, at least in part, socially constructed: in order for a state's behavior to count as escalatory, others have to interpret it as such.[21] Information on where the opponent's volatile behavior originates can change such an interpretation. Understanding that volatility originates from the interaction between power and interests can contribute precious knowledge to this interpretation process. Seeing the world through the eyes of the enemy can increase the probability of stopping or even reverting escalation.[22]

Since escalation can produce unwanted consequences, including violence, knowing where volatility originates can also have broader reverberations. Studies of escalation have traditionally been preoccupied with predicting the impact of escalation on the fate of alliances, on power distribution, and, of course, on the occurrence of conflict. To date, such studies have focused on material causes for escalation, including capabilities, alliances, territorial proximity, contested territory, and so on.[23] We know far less about how information about the likely cause of inconsistent behavior can successfully stave off the process of escalation altogether. Results in this book suggest that the effect might be very significative indeed and that this might be a very productive line for further research.

Broader Implications for Research

In addition to potentially taming volatility's negative consequences, illuminating the origins of volatility can also shed light on other, important aspects of the international arena. In practice, what can learning more about the sources of inconsistent behavior tell us about current debates in international politics regarding the importance of consistent behavior? What are we missing about inconsistent behavior that may change how we see the role of consistent behavior in the international arena? This section explores these questions.

Volatility and Compliance with International Organizations

At times, states decide to consistently comply with international treaties and regulations even when doing so entails renouncing, at least in part, their sovereignty. At other times, however, they do not, thus behaving in an inconsistent manner. What explains this variation?

Scholars do not agree on how to answer this question.[24] According to some, a great deal of the observed compliance can be explained by the fact that countries select themselves into agreements to begin with, choosing only to commit to those agreements whose provisions they can respect without changing many of their current behaviors.[25] Such a choice often reflects the power or status of a country. Thus, treaties do not really constrain states; they simply screen them.[26] Others have argued that treaties actually change states' calculus for compliance,[27] either by activating the power of international norms and reputation or through the role of domestic institutions and interests.[28]

Findings in this book, however, suggest that these disagreements might subside if we adopt a richer understanding of noncompliant behavior.

First, for example, scholars tend to see power and interests as alternative explanations for noncompliant behavior. But inconsistency in behavior is a function, this book argues, of both. So, compliance is likely to be dependent on both. Countries with the "right" combination of power and interests will be more prone, at times, to not comply with existing obligations. We should thus explore how the influences of interests and of power on compliance interact, as opposed to studying these influences as separate phenomena (as studies of screening vs. constraining effects tend to do). Moreover, while at present most studies focus only on studying compliance with a single treaty at the time, findings in this book point to the value of leveraging variation in states' volatility and looking at patterns of compliance across cases. If it is the interaction between interests and power that explains compliance, then it is likely that this interaction will have similar effects on countries across treaties. In other words, the same (volatile) countries will be more likely, on average, to become noncompliant across treaties.

Second, precisely because interests and power interact, alternative processes might explain noncompliance at different points in time. For example, when competing interests gain access to foreign policy and when relative power increases as well, we could see countries stop complying with existing treaties and regulations and act in inconsistent ways, even in the presence of pro-compliance norms. But when the configuration of power and interests changes, pro-compliance norms might once again exert a stronger pull on states and lead them to comply.[29]

In this sense, understanding the root causes of inconsistent behavior can provide us with a more sophisticated understanding of states' noncompliance with international treaties and obligations—one that goes beyond existing scholarly disagreements and explains a greater number of empirical cases.

Volatility and Reputation

Findings in this book on what increases volatility can have important implications for the ways we understand and study reputation, potentially opening new questions for research. Reputation is a belief that observers hold regarding what guides their counterpart's behavior. When an actor has a reputation for being resolute, for example, it means its counterpart sees it as being willing to go through with its threats and promises, even to the point of risking war.[30] Similarly, if an actor has a reputation for its commitment to human rights, for example, its counterparts might see it as willing to systematically stand up for the protection of human rights.

Reputation plays a big role in studies of international politics, because decision makers, scholars perceive, spend a notable amount of resources to prop up their reputation.[31] Reputations for being resolute or for being honest, for example, often play an important role in investigations of deterrence theory.[32]

Notwithstanding the big role reputation plays in accounts of international politics, scholars disagree on the extent to which reputation shapes states' interactions, presenting mixed findings.[33] Some scholars find that leaders and states can develop reputations and that those reputations do matter in international politics.[34] Others find instead that reputation has not mattered historically, that its effects fade over time, or that it cannot even be developed.[35]

The reason for these mixed findings might stem from the fact that inconsistent behaviors, this book shows, are rooted in both power and interests, the former providing the willingness and the latter providing the opportunity for volatile behavior. Therefore, actors engaging in behaviors that are inconsistent with their reputation might justify such inconsistency in different ways. They can argue to observers and counterparts that their behavior is indeed quite consistent with their interests and/or with their power configurations. Conversely, actors might prefer to embrace their volatile, inconsistent behaviors and present themselves as "mad men."[36] In addition, some counterparts might be more likely than others to believe actors' attempts to create such narratives regarding their reputations. Power and interests affect perceptions of reputation, but not for everyone.[37] For example, if actors make the argument that their inconsistent behavior consistently follows domestic interests, when is this justification effective in building reputation? In other words, who is more or less likely to believe these framing attempts? If reputation is often in the eye of the beholder,[38] countries facing similar constraints and opportunities could be more likely to give each other the benefit of the doubt.

In a way, findings in this book urge us to recast our debates on reputation. The most effective question to ask is not as much whether reputation matters, but how it enters actors' calculations—when, in other words, actors frame their behavior as consistent with their interests, if not their past, and when their counterparts buy these frames. This recasting exercise can enrich our understanding of how actors in international politics use reputation in their everyday activities.

Volatility and Credible Commitments

Commitment problems emerge when states have an incentive to cheat in the future on commitments they take in the present.[39] Because of this incentive that actors face, their counterparts have to take a gamble, deciding whether to cooperate in the present while knowing that cooperation might not last into the future. States that engage in more volatile behaviors can be at a greater risk of showing commitment problems, and thus this book's results have implications for research in this area.

Scholars have focused in particular on the role of domestic institutions as tools to decrease commitment problems. Findings have been mixed. Some suggest that democratic institutions make countries better at committing credibly because they increase the costs of reneging on previous commitments.[40] Others emphasize, however, that since democratic institutions can better represent domestic interests than autocratic institutions, they potentially make democracies less able to make credible commitments regarding the future.[41]

This book's findings on the origins of volatility point to important new directions to solve this impasse regarding the role of institutions. They suggest that institutions on their own likely do not affect the ability to project credible commitments. Their impact instead depends both on the domestic configuration of states' interests and on states' relative power.

First, greater relative power suggests that countries will have more options at their disposal. Having more options might make them better able to give up on their existing commitments if their agenda requires it.

Second, domestic institutions differ not just in their features but also in the type of domestic interests they represent. In some cases, they might represent a set of heterogeneous domestic interests that, in turn, can catalyze more volatility and thus make countries less able to take on credible commitments. But in other cases, domestic institutions might give voice to fairly homogeneous interests instead. In other words, institutions might affect the ability of a country to commit credibly to future behavior differently depending on the interests they represent.[42]

States' ability to systematically stick to their commitments is likely to depend not just on institutions but also on interests and power, given what we know about volatile behavior. Taking these complex effects into account might help shed light on states' credibility in international politics.

Volatility and Audience Costs

The study of volatility can also offer important insights into another area of study in International Relations that focuses on the presence of patterns: the study of audience costs. Leaders, audience cost theories posit, pay a price with their domestic audiences if they back down and do not do what they said they would do on the international stage.[43]

Audience costs play a crucial role in the study of IR. By highlighting how policymakers' behaviors in the international arena impact their domestic arena, audience costs connect the domestic and the international realms.[44] And yet, scholars disagree on whether audience costs matter or not.[45]

Results in this book renew this debate, by presenting two challenges to the way in which we currently understand audience costs. First, they remind us that we should not assume that domestic audiences are monolithic. Since, as this book demonstrates, inconsistencies in states' behaviors develop when decision makers appease conflicting interests, then such inconsistencies will be welcomed by those sectors of the population (or audience) that benefit from them. In other words, variation in the degree to which audiences punish leaders for their inconsistencies could depend on the fact that those inconsistencies might serve different proportions of the population differently. By underplaying the domestic dividends of conflict, we might have been ignoring a fundamental source of information on how different domestic audiences react to inconsistencies.[46]

Second, these findings challenge us to rethink the ways in which institutions can shape audience costs. To date, the literature on audience costs has explored how institutions can publicize leaders' inconsistencies, which is key to catalyzing audience costs. Within democracies, institutions, in particular the existence of an opposition and of a free press, can make inconsistencies more visible, thus increasing audience costs.[47] Notably, autocratic institutions are just as able as democratic institutions to generate audience costs.[48]

Yet, this book shows, institutions play another, fundamental function in relation to audience costs. In addition to publicizing inconsistencies, they allow different interests access to the definition of foreign policy. When the interests represented do not overlap, the book shows, inconsistent behavior is more likely to develop. Therefore, institutions are not simply important for publicizing leaders' behaviors. They are also an important source of that behavior because they channel domestic interests. This feature, in turn, suggests that, when institutions reflect a heterogeneous set of domestic interests, they might provide leaders with an incentive, paradoxically, to act inconsistently in order to consistently cater to differing interests. How do these two functions that institutions play (publicizing leaders' behaviors and channeling domestic interests) interact with one another? Exploring this facet of how institutions work can complexify our understanding of how they shape audience costs, making our grasp of audience costs firmer in the process.

Taking Volatility Seriously

This book has focused on a particular facet of volatility, exploring what makes states behave in an increasingly volatile manner toward their counterparts. But the study of volatility can (and should) be expanded to other areas in international politics. This section further extends the study of volatility. In particular, in the remaining pages, I explore how the new insights that emerge when studying volatility between states can enrich two major areas of inquiry within international politics: systemic politics and nonstate actors.

Systemic Politics

Volatility in states' behaviors has the potential to shape the international system as a whole. When countries act in an increasingly volatile manner, their increased volatility is likely to reverberate throughout the system, moving beyond interactions between a volatile state and its counterparts. Thus, there are at least three very interesting areas in which to further explore volatility at the international level.[49]

First, volatility could contribute to emerging system properties. One such property is the level of segregation within a system.[50] Since volatility generates uncertainty, countries might seek to reduce interactions with volatile states. Indeed, declassified documents in the previous chapter suggest that US decision makers considered reducing interactions with a volatile France to curtail the damage that France's behaviors were inflicting on US policies abroad. This finding, then, raises an important question: How much volatility is too much volatility? In other words, when does volatility make observers tip and choose to reduce interactions with volatile states? And do different actors have different tipping points? Moreover, the decision on the part of volatile states' counterparts to limit interactions with the volatile states might feed back into the ability of volatile states to be volatile. For example, it may reduce volatile states' opportunities to find cooperation partners, leaving them with mostly conflictual options. If this is the case, volatility's externalities would give rise to a thermostat-like system: volatile behavior in the system would balance out over time, with each increase in volatility bringing about isolation for volatile actors (segregation) that would, in turn, decrease the occurrence of volatile behaviors.

Second, and relatedly, an increase in the incidence of states' volatile behaviors can also change the fundamental culture of the system, another emerging property of the system. If and when multiple countries become increasingly volatile, such volatility has the potential to shape social practices and interactions in the international arena. It could be the case, for example, that members of the international system, rather than isolating volatile states, become more used to their behavior, and that therefore volatile behavior becomes quite normalized when multiple states engage in it. Perhaps if the number of volatile states in the system reaches a critical mass, it will become expected for states to act with some degree of volatility. Such different expectations regarding volatility, in turn, could potentially lead volatile states' counterparts to embrace a different understanding of their international landscape, one characterized by a greater sense of unpredictability. Thus, changes in the culture of the international system such as the one described here could affect major patterns of cooperation and conflict in the system.[51]

The third area in which investigating states' volatile behaviors can be helpful is the study of system polarity. Scholars have long debated whether a unipolar international system is more or less prone to conflict.[52] Some have argued, for example, that conflict is more likely during periods of unipolarity, both because the unipole might disengage from certain geographic regions (so that local conflicts in the region are no longer constrained) and because multiple revisionist states—now with no clear patron—might opt for fighting the unipole directly.[53] But what happens if we increase the prevalence of volatile states in the international system? In particular, if it makes conflict more likely, does volatility mean a shorter duration for the unipolar moment? The unipole, for instance, might wind up squandering its resources if forced to intervene in multiple conflicts abroad.

For all these reasons, exploring in greater depth what periods of increased incidence of volatility mean in terms of transformation of the international system promises to shed light on important system dynamics that have so far been left unexplored.

Nonstate Actors

Another promising area of research on volatility in international politics looks beyond states to focus on volatility in nonstate actors' behaviors.

In particular, the study of violent nonstate actors, commonly referred to as rebel groups, represents a particularly rich area for expanding the study of volatility, due to the role that power and interests play in influencing these actors' political agenda. Scholars have found that rebels' relative capabilities vis-à-vis the state they are fighting determine the range of behaviors at their disposal.[54] These findings suggest that these same relative capabilities might also impact how volatile their behavior will be. Moreover, rebel groups are to be understood as complex organizations, whose preferences and actions reflect internal competition between different interests seeking to achieve their preferred outcome.[55] This feature of rebel groups suggests that competing interests might work as engines of volatility. Indeed, research has shown that competition between different interests within rebel organizations affects various outcomes, such as their control over territory, members, and resources; their choice of violent or nonviolent tactics; and their choice of allies.[56]

Given the role that power and interests play in shaping rebels' behaviors, what would be the value added of extending the study of volatility to nonstate actors such as rebels, then? Three areas of research seem to be particularly promising.

First, studying volatility in rebels' behaviors can help make sense of the mixed findings emerging from studies on the role of rebels' capabilities. Greater relative capabilities make rebels better able to mobilize resources to achieve their objectives,[57] extract concessions,[58] and spread their insurgency.[59] They also decrease the probability of overthrowing the government,[60] increase the length of the conflict,[61] and make rebels more willing to settle for a mediated settlement to end the war.[62] What explains these diverging conclusions on the role of capabilities?

Findings in this book suggest that these mixed conclusions stem from the fact that capabilities are only part of the story and therefore their effect on most of these outcomes will only be indirect. When rebels have increasing relative power vis-à-vis the government, they have the potential to behave in a more volatile manner. But only a fraction of rebels with increasing capabilities will start acting in a more volatile manner toward the government—those rebels with competing interests. So, relative power will translate into volatile behavior for some rebel groups but not others. And because volatility might increase mistrust and escalation, rebels' volatile behaviors can have serious effects on the duration of the conflict, how it ends, and whether it will reoccur. Therefore, capabilities might only have an indirect effect (via volatility) on numerous facets of civil wars, including duration and outcomes. Similar levels of observed rebels' capabilities might yield quite different effects.

Studying volatility can also uniquely shed light on another important facet of civil wars: the way in which rebels relate to civilians during conflict. So far, studies have shown that rebels' behaviors toward civilians can range widely, including actions as disparate as intentionally targeting civilians and providing key welfare services for them.

Scholars have tried to explain why rebels choose these tactics. For example, some scholars have shown that rebels with greater relative capabilities might have greater access to civilian targeting. Thus, they might be more likely to engage in this activity as a conflict strategy even though it violates international norms.[63] Welfare-like services (or rebel governance), by contrast, have been found to be particularly appealing to rebels seeking to achieve independence and to establish their legitimacy in the eyes of the local population or of foreign actors.[64]

Results from this book, however, have shown that cooperative behaviors (such as providing welfare-like services) and conflictual ones (such as targeting civilians) should be understood as two sides of the same coin. Instead of studying these behaviors in isolation, we should investigate when and why rebels are more likely to stick to one tactic and when and why they are more likely to shift inconsistently between them. In other words, what makes rebels more volatile toward civilians, and thus more prone to shift inconsistently between cooperation and conflict? Insights in this book suggest that the answers to these questions may lie in an interaction between rebel groups' capabilities and their interests. And, in turn, how does such volatility affect the effectiveness of their strategies? For example, providing public goods while targeting civilians might reduce the legitimation benefits of engaging in governance.

Another promising area for research concerns the relationship between rebels and foreign actors. Foreign actors play a crucial role in civil wars because receiving support from them can significantly shape these wars' outcomes.[65]

Thus far, scholars have investigated in great detail why countries might opt for supporting insurgent groups in other states. Some have argued, for example, that it has to do with both rebels' relative capabilities and the presence of transnational constituencies.[66] Others have argued that rebels constitute a means for foreign countries to oppose the governments engulfed in civil wars while avoiding direct confrontation.[67] Still others have delved into the ways rebels reach out to foreign audiences and actors to establish connections with third-party states and ask for their support.[68]

While we know that third-party support is often likely to unfold over multiple time periods, we know far less regarding how the interaction between third parties and rebels unfolds. In other words, we do not know much about the ways in which rebels behave toward external parties. This topic is particularly interesting because present research suggests that there is some interest overlap between rebels and third parties, but also that such interest overlap is not perfect. For this reason, rebels have an incentive to stick to their own agenda as much as possible, to be at least a bit independent of the intervening third party.[69] So we can expect that rebels, while mostly cooperative toward external actors whose support they need, could at times also deviate from such cooperation.[70] When will rebels' behaviors exhibit greater volatility? In other words, when are rebels likely to shift more inconsistently between cooperation and conflict toward potential third-party interveners? Findings in this book suggest that the answer to this question will have to do with rebels' relative capabilities and the internal configuration of those interests that have access to the definition of their policy. Illuminating volatility toward external parties can also illuminate what cooperation between rebels and external actors might look like and the conditions under which it might end. To the extent that volatility erodes trust, it might also change the type of support that rebels receive, and thus how effective such support is.

In sum, investigating volatility in rebels' behaviors can shed light on important new areas of research that have been left underexplored thus far. It has the potential to delve deeper into mixed findings on issues as central to the study of these groups as their behaviors toward the government, local populations, and even third parties.

Moving Forward

This book has put forward the first systematic account of volatility in states' behaviors toward their counterparts. It has proposed an explanation for when countries behave in unruly, inconsistent ways, and it has tested this explanation empirically. A stronger grasp on volatility, this concluding chapter has argued, has several payoffs: it can contribute to ameliorating volatility's worst consequences; it can provide the missing piece to numerous IR puzzles; and it can illuminate fertile grounds for further investigations of volatility in other areas of international politics, including systemic politics and non-state actors' behaviors. By delving into an important facet of interactions between countries, this book contributes to our efforts to more precisely map the global arena.

Moreover, a better understanding of volatility in states' behaviors will hopefully inspire us to reconsider our own assumptions about international politics. IR studies have almost exclusively investigated consistent forms of change, studying, for example, how actors become consistently more conflictual toward others (escalation) or consistently less conflictual (reconciliation). The study of volatility thus pushes us to reconsider our deeply held assumptions on how change unfolds in the international arena. In addition, by looking at dynamics between events instead of simply focusing on events themselves, volatility pushes us to think of cooperation and conflict as being on a continuum—and to explore the various shapes that dynamics on that continuum can take.

The potential upsides of understanding volatility in international politics, however, go even further. Human beings have a natural distaste for the lack of clear patterns that characterizes volatility. The uncertainty that volatility stokes fuels fear, which, in turn, often encourages decision makers to engage in self-defeating behavior.

Such a strong and perhaps even innate aversion toward volatility's by-products, however, can lead scholars and practitioners down a dangerous path in IR, in at least two ways. First, it often prompts scholars and practitioners to ignore the inconsistent forms that change can take. The risk here is that they overemphasize the consistent nature of change. This excessive emphasis might mask the complexity that characterizes the international system, ultimately shaping scholars' recommendations and policymakers' behaviors in counterproductive ways. The use of analogies to understand conflict, for example, betrays a cyclical understanding of history that might leave us unable to notice what is really unique about the current situation and thus lead decision makers to fight the wrong war.[71] An appreciation of volatility in international politics is a welcome counter to these tendencies.

Second, if, as the normative implication of our distaste for volatility would imply, volatility is bad and to be avoided, then this might lead us to prefer predictability (or stability) to volatility every time. In IR, this perspective might translate into a greater appetite for the type of stability in foreign policy that is likely to come from very centralized regimes. Most recently, many have noted how the Chinese can more easily focus on providing a stable and predictable, if assertive, foreign policy.[72] Such a penchant for stability, however, comes at a cost. Tellingly, China uses the expression "stability maintenance" to refer to its policy of forcibly integrating minorities, a policy that has costed many human lives.[73] It might be instead advisable to resist the lure of "the false certainty of order and control."[74] And yet, such stability might become all the more appealing in times when citizens of democratic countries become increasingly wary of the uncertainties that the need to give representation to a large and often diverse population can cause, as polling data from the US in 2020 seemed to suggest.[75]

Properly understanding where volatility comes from in international politics and what it represents can stave off our often self-defeating and dangerous aversion to it. This book has taken the first step in that direction.

Appendix

Event data used in Chapter 4 come from the Conflict and Peace Data Bank (COPDAB) and World Events/Interactions Survey (WEIS) data sets (Azar, 1979; McClelland, 1978; Pevehouse and Goldstein, 2006).[1]

COPDAB data are present from 1948 to 1978.[2] WEIS data are present from 1966 to 1978.[3] Events are coded according to multiple categories and subcategories.

To prevent adding heterogeneity and/or discontinuities within a time series by using different sources, I follow Haber and Menaldo (2011, appendix). Specifically, I create two distinct weekly time series, both extending from 1966 to 1978—one from COPDAB and another from WEIS—and I analyze their time series features. Therefore, after checking for the presence of unit roots, stationarity, or fractional integration, I apply a Box-Jenkins procedure to make sure that the series coming from different sources are able to pick similar interactional dynamics (i.e., a similar auto regressive integrated moving average, or ARIMA[p,d,q], process). Then I use splicing to ensure that the final time series is homogeneous (see Reuveny and Kang, 1996, 290 and Colaresi, 2004 for further technical details on this procedure).

A Note on Scaling

Event data aim at including multiple states' behaviors. Thus, such data categorize each behavior as an instance of broader categories of events, such as, for example, expressing the intent of cooperating militarily, attacking with the military, and so on. This creates nominal-level data. Scaling these data consists of going one step forward and actually creating a continuum of cooperation and conflict, and assesses how cooperative or conflictual each event is. In this book, I scale the event data from the different sources with the Goldstein (1992) scale. This is the most widely used scale for event data (Schrodt, 2007, 4) and ranks all the categories on a continuum from most conflictual (−10) to most cooperative (10). For instance, the category "to apologize" is weighted as 2.0, because it is considered to be twice as cooperative as "to ask for clarification," which instead is weighted as 1.0 on the scale. To create the Goldstein (1992) scale, Goldstein gathered a panel of experts and calculated the mean values of the value proposed for each behavior by those experts. Scaling makes it possible to take into consideration the substantial differences in the degrees of cooperation and conflict that each foreign policy event presents. It also makes it possible to use interval-level methods on nominal-level data (Schrodt, 2007, 4).

An alternative to weighted event data is event data counts. Both scale event data and event data counts build on the same *ontologies*—that is, the category typology that assigns a number to each type of event. However, event data group all events simply into four categories: verbal and material cooperation and verbal and material conflict.

Scaled data are to be preferred to the alternative, event counts, for three reasons. First, the task of scaling events is not that far removed from the task of categorizing an event. In other words, deciding that an event constitutes an instance of expressing one's intent of cooperating militarily entails an exercise of abstraction that requires no smaller of a judgment call than declaring that expressing the intent of cooperating is half as cooperative a gesture as retreating militarily. In other words, creating a four-category event count is no less arbitrary than creating a scale. In practice, it amounts to scaling a set of categories as being equally cooperative: to use the example provided above, the category "to apologize" would be considered equivalent to the category "to offer material support." So, using event counts does not spare the researcher from scaling data; it simply forces them to scale all the events in the verbal cooperation categories as the same. Second, using four categories, like event counts do, requires reducing dramatically the degree to which our data reflect the actual empirical variation in the real world. This is the case because there the procedure of cramming together all instances of verbal cooperation, for instance, amounts to putting in the same category the expression of an intent to cooperate militarily and making an optimistic comment about the interaction between states, although these two expressions have potentially very different implications for countries. Finally, weighted event data have been found to correlate strongly with counts of material conflict.[4]

The advantage of using weighted event data is that it is possible to build a continuum with foreign policy actions while keeping different events distinct, therefore, for example, drawing a distinction between the imposition of economic sanctions and a military attack (which, with event counts, would be crammed within the same category of material conflict and weighed the same way). Event data counts, instead, weigh both events similarly, thus failing to distinguish between the two. For these reasons I opt for weighted data over event count data.

Measuring the Dependent Variable Using the Box-Jenkins Procedure

I operationalize volatility as the standard deviation of the squared residuals from a Box-Jenkins procedure applied to the time series of the foreign policy of country A toward country B. Below, I describe the procedure I follow.

First, I gather event data on each of those rivalries. I merge data from different sources and I scale the data using the Goldstein (1992) scale, as I described above. For each dyad (i, j), I build a time series of the foreign policy actions carried on by i and directed toward j, as well as a time series of the foreign policy actions carried on by j and directed toward i for each year in the time interval.

I then determine the time dynamic in the data employing the Box-Jenkins procedure *Step One*. The first stage entails finding out what dynamics are present in the time series. To this end, I leverage correlograms to visually inspect auto- and partial autocorrelation functions (respectively, ACF and PACF) applied to the time series. Such graphs speak to the degree to which events depend on past events that took place earlier and, as such, can inform the model specification later on. For example, if the ACF and PACF correlograms suggest the presence of a seasonal effect, then it makes sense to explore seasonal, autoregressive moving average (SARMA) models. If instead the tests suggest the presence of fractional integration, then autoregressive fractional integrated moving average (ARFIMA) models also will be explored.

Before estimating and comparing several models, however, I check for the presence of stationarity in the data. In particular, I triangulate between several tests. Each test explores the presence of stationarity in the data through different perspectives, by testing different null hypotheses. Specifically, I employ the following tests: the Dickey-Fuller test and the augmented Dickey-Fuller test, each testing the null of unit roots; the Kwiatkowski-Phillips-Schmidt-Shin (KPSS) test for the null of absence of a unit root test; and the nonparametric Phillips-Perron test. If all tests reject the hypothesis of stationary data, I differentiate the time series.[5] Since each test presents a different null hypothesis, if the tests yield different results, I instead also check for fractional integration.

These procedures taking place before estimating the models inform the subsequent decision of what model to estimate, the third stage of the Box-Jenkins procedure. For example, if the ACF and PACF correlograms suggest the presence of an autoregressive dynamic whereupon past interactions affect the present one in a decaying fashion, then it is important to estimate models with a different number of lags, so as to identify how far into the future the impact of past events extends for—one, two, three, or six time periods, for instance. Then, to choose the best-fitting model specification, it is also important to triangulate again between multiple tests, including tests of residuals such as the Q test, comparison of the Akaike and Bayesian information criteria (AIC and BIC), and the significance of the coefficients associated with the different lags. The aim of such triangulation is to find the model that best specifies the time dependencies in the data while avoiding overfitting.

The Box-Jenkins procedure that I just described, therefore, identifies different types of change in the data, parsing out the degree to which shifts in a state's behavior toward another are explainable by, for example, inertia (by measuring the presence of an autoregressive process), escalation or de-escalation (by measuring the presence of a moving average process), cycles (by measuring seasonality), and so on.[6] In technical terms, from the Box-Jenkins procedure, there emerges an ARMA(p,q) for a time series y_t with p autoregressive (lagged dependent variables) and q lagged moving-average terms:

$$y_t = \mu + \gamma_1 y_{t-1} + \gamma_2 y_{t-2} + \ldots + \gamma_t y_{t-p} - \theta_1 \varepsilon_{t-1} - \ldots - \theta_q \varepsilon_{t-q} \tag{1}$$

where μ is the intercept and e_t, the disturbances, are called innovations.[7] In sum, *Step One* allows me to deductively identify the specific dynamics characterizing the behavior of each country toward one of its counterparts—in other words, this step answers the question of whether the change that we observe is consistent and is explained by the presence of trends, cycles, and so on.

This step is essential because it enables the analysis to acknowledge that not all change in international politics is a symptom of volatility, and that instead such change can come from sources other than volatility (such as escalation, inertia, etc.).[8] For example, shifts between cooperation and conflict could depend on specific events that are set to take place during specific times. Every January since 1992, for instance, India and Pakistan have exchanged the list of nuclear installations and facilities, per the Agreement on the Prohibition of Attack against Nuclear installations signed in 1988. This might constitute a shift toward cooperation, but one that happens just at specific points in time, due to recurring deadlines that make it predictable. Therefore, the Box-Jenkins procedure would identify the cyclical component of such changes in states' behaviors and avoid conflating it with volatility.

Moreover, the Box-Jenkins procedure makes it possible to isolate the presence of volatility without confusing it with other determinants of change in countries' behaviors.

It is in fact quite reasonable to think that change in states' behaviors comes from multiple processes and only some of those processes are related to volatility. For example, Figure A.1 presents a simulated time series where change is driven by the presence of a trend and of a cyclical (or seasonal) component (top graph). The Box-Jenkins procedure would then make it possible to parse out the trend component of the change (second graph from the top) and the seasonal one (third graph from the top). The residuals from a correctly specified Box-Jenkins procedure, therefore, would identify the shifts between cooperation and conflict that are instead inconsistent (bottom graph).

As Figure A.1 makes clear, therefore, using a "one-solution-fits-all" approach such as taking directly the standard deviation of the time series of states' actions toward their counterparts or taking the difference between two contiguous time periods would not produce a valid measure. Not only would this be incorrect, because we would be labeling

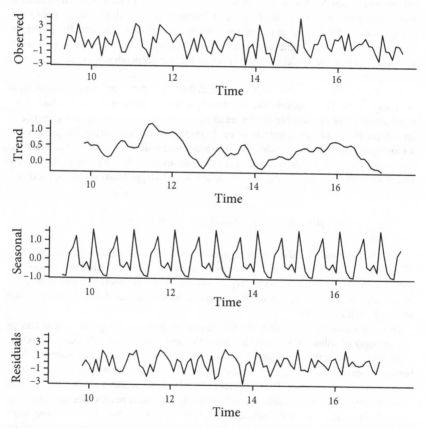

Figure A.1 Simulated ARIMA (1,0,1) model with seasonal component (2,0,1). *Note: The top graph shows the series as it appears. The graphs below decompose such series, focusing, respectively, on the trend, the seasonal component, and the residuals that emerge from the series once the trend and the empirical component are taken into account.*

change as volatile even though it is not volatile, but also it would amount to inflating the presence of volatility in the series. A systematic comparison of 1,000 simulated time series with a trend and a seasonal component and their residuals, for example, shows that taking the standard deviation of the whole series without first taking into account these other sources of change systematically leads to overestimating volatility in 99.6% of the cases.[9]

Once the Box-Jenkins procedure identifies the best model for the time series, I estimate the residuals from the procedure. Those residuals emerge by subtracting the original time series from the one estimated taking into account the different dynamics present in the data as emerging from the Box-Jenkins procedure. The difference between observed changes and estimated ones identifies all the change in the data that is not consistent with the presence of trends, inertia, cycles, and so on. This change represents, therefore, inconsistent shifts between cooperation and conflict—that is, volatile behavior. Thus:

$$\varepsilon_t = \hat{y}_t - y_t \tag{2}$$

Therefore, the outcome of the procedure described here is a new time series that traces those shifts toward more cooperation or conflict that cannot be explained by consistent forms of change such as trends or cycles. While, as with all residuals emerging from a correctly specified Box-Jenkins procedure, the mean of each series of residuals is equal to zero, values of the standard deviation of series vary. In particular, values that display volatility are much bigger compared to values of the standard deviation for less volatile series. This feature suggests that volatile series tend to experience events that are further apart from the mean than less volatile series do.

What do such series of volatile behavior look like exactly? Plotting them is useful to see that volatility unfolds through time. Figure A.2 plots a comparison of 100 simulated time series of residuals displaying different levels of volatility (left panel). Darker colors indicate greater volatility. Figure A.2 (right panel) zooms in on just ten randomly selected simulations, differentiating between those with less (light colors) and those with more (darker colors) volatility.[10] Figure A.3 (left panel) plots the mean plus and minus the standard deviation for each of the simulated series in Figure A.2. Figure A.3 (right panel) instead plots the mean plus and minus the standard deviation of a series of the difference between the absolute values of the observations at time t and time $t-1$ in each of the simulated series in Figure A.2, squared. Once again, darker colors represent higher volatility.

The figures usefully represent two important features of volatility. First, series displaying greater volatility (i.e., those with greater variance, see Figure A.3, left panel) present greater shifts toward cooperation or conflict than series displaying less volatility. In Figure A.2, darker, more volatile time series tend to reach further toward the higher and lower points on the vertical axis, which correspond, respectively, to more cooperative and more conflictual behaviors.

Second, focusing on what happens between contiguous time periods, on average, shifts between more cooperation and more conflict from $t-1$ to t tend to be both bigger and harder to predict in more volatile series than in less volatile series. As a reminder, Figure A.3 (right panel) plots the mean plus or minus the standard deviation of the difference between the absolute value of observations at time t and time $t-1$ in each of the simulated series in Figure A.2. As the plot reveals, the average of differences between contiguous time periods tends to be higher in series with more volatility (darker colors) than in

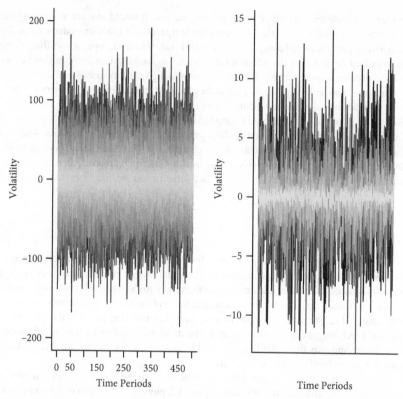

Figure A.2 Comparison of 100 simulated time series of residuals displaying different levels of volatility (left panel) and of 10 simulated time series randomly sampled from those 100 (right panel). Darker colors indicate greater volatility.

those with less volatility (lighter colors). Moreover, those differences also tend to be more spread out with respect to the mean in series with more volatility than in series with less volatility.

Together, therefore, Figure A.2 and Figure A.3 (right panel) suggest that more volatile series tend to experience bigger and less predictable shifts than less volatile series.

Summarizing Volatility

Measuring volatility as the residuals of a Box-Jenkins procedure applied to time series is useful to capture the exact timing at which inconsistent shifts take place. However, in order to get a sense of just how volatile a series is, it is also possible to get a sense of how big, in the aggregate, these shifts were during a certain period of time. Most of the phenomena we study in international politics, such as political regimes, economic growth, military capabilities, and so on, vary meaningfully on a yearly basis rather than a weekly or monthly basis, so it is important to have a sense for how volatile a year will be. In addition, it is hard to understand which series display more volatility or less volatility just

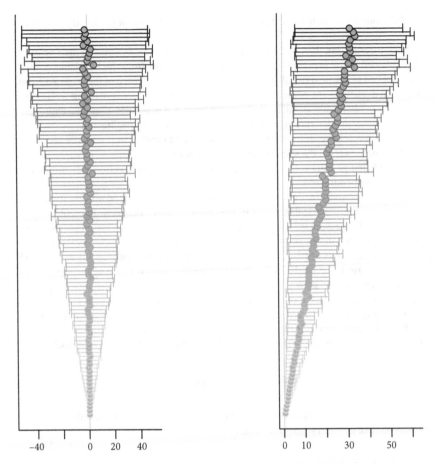

Figure A.3 Comparison of 100 simulated time series of residuals displaying different levels of volatility. Darker colors indicate greater volatility. *NOTE: The plot to the left represents the mean plus and minus the standard deviation for each of the simulated series in Figure A.2. The plot to the right represents the mean plus and minus the standard deviation of a series of the difference between the absolute values of the observations at time* t *and time* t − 1 *in each of the simulated series in Figure A.2, squared.*

looking at the time series of the residuals. Therefore, I also estimate the standard deviation of these residuals, squared.

The standard deviation of the residuals offers a compact measure of how far each observed behavior is with respect to the average observation. The greater the standard deviation of these residuals, the greater the level of volatility experienced by each country in each year, as Figure A.2 and Figure A.3 (left panel) also show. I square the residuals because what I am interested in is summarizing how big the inconsistent shifts toward more cooperation and more conflict are, not so much whether the shift was toward cooperation or conflict. The outcome of these steps is an estimate of how much unexplained change in the behavior of one state toward another deviated from the mean unexplained change in a given year.

Such measure can then be used to compare different series in terms of their volatility. As explained in the previous section, residuals that emerge from the Box-Jenkins procedure applied to a time series all have a mean value of zero, but each of them has a different standard deviation. The higher the standard deviation, the more spread out with respect to the mean observations will be. Indeed, as Figure A.3 makes clear, more volatile series tend to display greater variance. In particular, as the simulations illustrate, for each time series, the greater the shifts between cooperation and conflict in a year, the greater the volatility of the series, the standard deviation of that series. Therefore, by capturing how spread out change will be, the standard deviation of the residuals effectively summarizes the volatility encountered.

There is also another, important benefit to employing the standard deviation of the residuals. In the empirical analysis in this book, I move between different temporal aggregations to measure volatility, leveraging both weekly and monthly measures. At present, there is no consensus on what the optimal unit of analysis is for interactions between states. In other words, do relations between states vary meaningfully at the weekly, monthly, quarterly, or yearly levels? However, there is evidence that aggregating data to the yearly level might skew the inference drawn from the data.[11] Therefore, keeping the time series analysis at a temporal level that is less aggregated than the yearly level makes it possible to avoid misrepresenting dynamics in the data by avoiding temporal aggregation while at the same time getting a sense, through summary statistics, for how much volatility was registered in the relevant period under analysis when using covariates.[12]

Monthly Data

Finally, Table A.1 replicates the analysis in Chapter 5 using a country-month unit of analysis in place of a country-year unit of analysis.

Table A.1 Cross-Sectional, Time Series Models of Volatility in States' Behaviors (Monthly)

	Model 1	Model 2	Model 3
Relative Power ×	0.001**	0.001**	0.002*
Het. Interests	(0.000)	(0.000)	(0.001)
Relative Power	−0.001***	−0.001***	−0.001
	(0.000)	(0.000)	(0.001)
Het. Interests	0.02	0.015	−0.038
	(0.025)	(0.019)	(0.037)
Opponent's Volatility	0.297***	0.297***	0.628
	(0.018)	(0.017)	(0.405)
Issue Salience (Dyad)		−0.019***	−0.073
		(0.006)	(0.081)

Table A.1 Continued

	Model 1	Model 2	Model 3
Issue Count (Dyad)		0.061***	0.193
		(0.021)	(0.256)
Leader's Gender		−0.075	−0.546
		(0.087)	(0.37)
Leader's Combat		0.027	−0.197
		(0.026)	(0.121)
Leader's Transition		0.028	−0.073
		(0.035)	(0.112)
Leader's Coalition Change		−0.059	−0.032
		(0.041)	(0.059)
Cold War		−0.101***	−0.074
		(0.018)	(0.05)
Issue Salience			−0.049
			(0.055)
Issue Count			0.420*
			(0.218)
Leader's Mental Health			−0.03
			(0.059)
Constant	0.110***	0.188**	0.771**
	(0.018)	(0.085)	(0.354)
N	25,784	25,740	25,740

NOTE: Standard errors presented in parentheses beneath coefficient estimates. * significant at the .10 level, ** .05 level, *** .01 level.

Notes

Chapter 1

1. These included the lifting of US travel restrictions to Cuba in March 2015 and the removal of Cuba from the US list of state sponsors of terrorism in May 2015. In July 2015, the US embassy in Havana and the Cuban embassy in Washington reopened for the first time since 1961.

2. It was seen, for example, as "the most vivid manifestation yet of [. . .] a world in which the United States sets aside historic feuds to broker a more stable global order." "The Cuba Obama Will See is Changing, but Much Remains the Same," *Washington Post*, March 17, 2016. Commentators saw the rapprochement as potentially consequential for the whole Latin American region and argued it could possibly have ripple effects even beyond that region. See, for example, "Obama Hopes Cuba Gamble Has Regional Payoff," CNN, March 24, 2016; "US Normalization with Cuba: Is North Korea Next?," Brookings Institution, December 18, 2014.

3. "Statement by the President on Cuba Policy Changes," White House Press Release, December 17, 2014.

4. "PM Modi Lands in Lahore on a Surprise Visit, Meets Pakistan PM Nawaz Sharif," *Indian Express*, December 25, 2015.

5. "Narendra Modi of India Meets Pakistani Premier in Surprise Visit," *New York Times*, December 12, 2015. This "richly symbolic gesture," some commentators added, was likely to "add momentum to a tentative reconciliation process between the nuclear-armed neighbors." "India's Narendra Modi Makes First Visit to Pakistan for Chat with Nawaz Sharif," *Wall Street Journal*, December 25, 2015.

6. For a scholarly investigation of why face-to-face meetings are so momentous in international politics, see Holmes (2013).

7. The literature on the study of international rivals is very rich; se, for example, Bennett and Nordstrom (2000); Diehl and Goertz (2001); Maoz and Mor (2002); Colaresi and Thompson (2002a, 2002b); Colaresi (2004, 2005); Colaresi, Rasler, and Thompson (2007).

8. "Twenty-Fifth Person at US Embassy in Cuba Is Mysteriously Sickened," *New York Times*, June 21, 2018. While President Trump reinstated travel and business restrictions, in part as a reaction to the attack, diplomatic connections as well as the newly reinstated direct flights and cruise ship routes from the US were left in place.

9. "Indian Prime Minister Narendra Modi Begins Key China Visit," BBC News, May 14, 2015. See also Rana (2015, 328).

10. These conflicts were over border disagreements, Tibet, and Chinese support for Pakistan, among other issues. "Indian Prime Minister Visits China," Brookings Institution, May 14, 2015.

11. In the following years, Modi held other high-profile meetings with Xi, often aimed at avoiding tension escalation at the border or overcoming other sources of conflict. "Xi Jinping and Narendra Modi Met Again This Month. Here Are 4 Things to Know about Sino-Indian Relations," *Washington Post*, October 22, 2019. To be sure, contentious issues have not disappeared in the years since Modi's visit (especially at the border), and they have continued to color the (complex and multifaceted) relations between these two countries. Perhaps most famously, border clashes took place again on the Line of Contact between 2020 and 2021, claiming the lives of twenty-one Indian soldiers. But already by April 2021, tensions had de-escalated as per the mechanisms previously put in place to defuse such conflict, as Indian leaders lauded such developments. "Pangong Lake: India and China Complete Pull-Back of Forces," BBC World News, February 21, 2021. However, India's behavior before and since has not seemed to shift inconsistently toward more cooperation or more conflict with China to the same degree as it has with Pakistan. "Indian Prime Minister Visits China," Brookings Institution, May 14, 2015. Observers, however, warn that it is possible that these rather steady behaviors might change in the near future as India's relative power vis-à-vis China increases. Indeed, relative power is a critical predictor of volatility in states' behaviors, as this book argues. "Arriving at a New Normal in India-China Relations," *Hindustan Times*, July 3, 2020.

12. International Crisis Behavior database (Brecher et al., 2016) and Correlates of War, Militarized Interstate Disputes (MIDs) database (Jones, Bremer, and Singer, 1996).

13. In particular, India had exchanged numerous leadership visits with China, put in place mechanisms to deal with the existing border dispute, increased the number of people traveling between the two countries, and promoted economic ties.

14. Rasler, Thompson, and Ganguly (2013).

15. I (mostly) use "behaviors" in the book to indicate what I am studying, as opposed to "foreign policy." In common parlance, the two expressions could be used interchangeably. In current studies of IR, states' foreign policy and behaviors are germane, but not quite the same. First, foreign policy indicates a collection of behaviors of one state toward another. I intend to focus on single episodes of states' actions toward their counterparts to retrace the time series of such behaviors and investigate the dynamics in such time series. Second, through the field of "foreign policy analysis," the study of foreign policy has progressively focused more and more on the process that generates states' behaviors, often (though not always) in place of focusing on the content or outcome of those processes. In this book, however, it is the outcomes, the actual behaviors, that I focus on (for a review of the field of foreign policy analysis, see Garrison, 2003). In this sense, this study is also different from studies that focus instead on grand strategies. Every grand strategy helps make sense of the complexity of international politics by establishing an overarching goal and ranking possible behaviors according to which ones will be most helpful for achieving such goal. But such abstract plans often do not survive first contact with the complex web of

domestic and international interests with a stake in countries' foreign policies, to paraphrase Prussian army commander Helmuth von Moltke. In the 1990s, for example, the US considered different general principles to guide its behavior toward China, pondering both a "containment" and an "engagement" grand strategy (Shambaugh, 1996). Containing China meant aiming to decrease Chinese influence in the international arena. A containment grand strategy therefore prescribed actions such as engaging in proxy wars against Chinese allies. To engage China meant instead to integrate the country into the existing structure of multilateral organizations, for example, by aiding the Chinese accession to the World Trade Organization (WTO). US behavior toward China during the years when containment and engagement grand strategies were discussed was characterized by a diverse set of behaviors: trade agreements, human rights violations complaints, the so-called "third Taiwan crisis," and so on. It is precisely these kinds of manifested behaviors that countries engage in, rather than the abstract principles that may guide them, that I study in this book.

16. Khong (1992).

17. Hobson (2000) provides a review of the study of states in IR, highlighting the presence of a "first state debate" and a "second state debate." While the first state debate mostly unfolded in the 1970s and focused on "the degree of autonomy that states have from non-state actors and social processes," the second state debate revolved around state/society relations. Many theories have placed states at their core (Lake, 2008).

18. This definition of cooperative and conflictual action follows the one proposed by Goldstein (1992).

19. The literature on rivalries is vast. For some examples, see Goertz and Diehl (1995); Thompson (1999); Maoz and Mor (2002); Diehl and Goertz (2001); Colaresi (2004); Colaresi (2005); Colaresi, Rasler, and Thompson (2007); McLaughlin Mitchell and Thies (2011); and so on.

20. In particular, lower values represent material conflict (respectively, military, economic, and then diplomatic). Examples include a military attack, economic sanctions, or a reduction of diplomatic contacts. Moving upward on the lower half of the axis, we would find, respectively, military, economic, and then diplomatic actions (in this order) that are all verbal and conflictual (e.g., military, economic, and diplomatic threats). Then, above those, we would find, respectively, diplomatic, economic, and military actions (again, in this order) that are verbal and cooperative (such as proposals to cooperate in these various fields), and finally diplomatic, economic, and military actions that are material and cooperative (such as joint military exercises, diplomatic exchanges, trade agreements, etc.).

21. "Joint Statement between the United States and the Republic of Korea," White House, June 30, 2017. "US and South Korea to Stage Huge Military Exercise despite North Korea Crisis," *The Guardian*, August 11, 2017.

22. Ward (1981, 233); see also Stoll (1984).

23. Nincic (1990). Policymakers themselves are well aware of cyclical change patterns in countries' behaviors in response to regularly reoccurring events such as elections. Perhaps most famously, a hot mic captured US President Barack Obama de facto acknowledging such patterns when, eight months before the presidential elections of

2012, he reassured Russian President Dmitry Medvedev about the increasingly firm US stand on missile defense in Europe by arguing: "after [my] election I have more flexibility." "Microphone Catches a Candid Obama," *New York Times*, March 26, 2012.

24. See, among others, Colaresi, Rasler, and Thompson (2007).

25. Kirby, Li, and Ross (2006); DiCicco (2011).

26. Across the many contexts in which it is employed in studies of IR, the concept of instability always refers to the recurrence of crises or violent disputes. This is the case whether the concept of instability is investigated in the context of regional interactions (Kapur, 2008; Narang, 2010), in the domestic realm (Nincic, 2010), or even in instances of nuclear weapons acquisition (Hart, 1960; Snyder, 1965; Jervis, 1993).

27. For a definition of stability as lack of severe conflict between states, see Gaddis (1986). The concept of stability is mostly, but not exclusively (see Diehl and Goertz, 2001, 3), used to describe a property of relations between states at the systemic level, rather than the dyadic level: the concept of stability incapsulates the lack of changes in the distribution of power and resources (Niou, Ordeshook, and Rose, 2007, 64–68).

28. Davenport, Melander, and Regan (2018, 16).

29. The display of force was indeed involved during a dispute over the Tokdo Islands in 2005. See MID dataset, version 5.0.

30. Adler (1997, 258).

31. Goertz, Diehl, and Balas (2016).

32. Mastanduno (1997).

33. Ross and Jiang (2001).

34. Ganguly (1995).

35. Many meanings of uncertainty exist both in our theories of international politics and in the international arena (Rathbun, 2007). The uncertainty that volatility generates is closer to the idea of ambiguity or analytic uncertainty as defined by Rathbun (2007). This is the case because the meaning of volatile behavior is hard to interpret for actors observing such behavior. Observers also have a hard time using the past to predict future behavior. Irreducible uncertainty has been defined as uncertainty that cannot be eliminated, either because it arises from uncontrollable factors such as the weather or an act or god (Bas and Schub, 2017) or because it is an emerging property of the interaction (Friedman, 2019). But whether uncertainty over volatile behavior can be resolved or not is an empirical question, as I discuss more in the conclusions to this book.

36. Knight (1921).

37. Nelson and Katzenstein (2014, 362). See also Kertzer (2017).

38. Holmes and Nolte (2019, 1). For a review of the heuristics and biases that individuals rely on in uncertain environments, see Stein (2010).

39. Lerner and Keltner (2001).

40. Ellsberg (1961).

41. In particular, for more examples of ambiguity aversion, see Kahn and Sarin (1988); Viscusi and Chesson (1999); Chow and Sarin (2001); Du and Budescu (2005); Pulford and Colman (2007); Hey, Lotito, and Maffioletti (2010).

42. See, for example, "Advisor Top-of-Mind Index Survey," EatonVance, Spring 2019 Report.

43. The index is calculated from the price inputs of the S&P 500 index by the Chicago Board Options Exchange, to estimate what the market predicts volatility will be in the next thirty days. See Whaley (2000).

44. Gray and Potter (2012).

45. Kriner and Schwartz (2009).

46. Tang (2008).

47. Jervis (1976, 58–110). According to Jervis, while the spiral model of conflict is rooted in fear, the deterrence one is rooted in greed.

48. A difference-in-means test comparing the difference in the hostility level reached in disputes initiated against a volatile and a nonvolatile counterpart finds that both the level of hostility reached in the dispute and the level of hostility reached by the targeted country are significantly higher if the target is volatile (respectively, at the $p = 0.003$ and $p = 0.02$ level). Data come from the COW's MID dataset.

49. Escalation too can give rise to unwanted, self-defeating, unanticipated behavior. But scholars suggest that escalation is rooted more in perceptions of risk rather than in perceptions of uncertainty, possibly because escalation is a type of change that follows a pattern. See, among others, Morgan et al. (2008, 7–45) and Dixon (1996). As such, fear developing from escalation has different implications.

50. Hoffman (2006).

51. Larson (1997).

52. Güvenç and Özel (2012, 543).

53. This is clearly the case for strategic trust. In strategic definitions of trust, the actual behavior of the counterpart within a specific situation plays a crucial role in determining whether such counterpart can be judged as being trustworthy (Uslaner, 2002). Yet the ability to predict whether cooperation will be reciprocated based on past behavior also plays a role in the context of generalized trust. While generalized trust is more "dispositional" than "situational"—that is, generalized trust resides mostly in the eye of the beholder—"generalized trust is not inconsistent with distrust of specific others who have proved themselves to be unreliable and dishonest patterns" (Rathbun, 2011, 24). This claim suggests that, since volatile actors often prove unreliable because their past behavior cannot be fruitfully used to predict the future, volatility can also erode generalized trust. I will return to this very claim in the concluding chapter of this book.

54. Betts (2000).

55. Fitzsimmons (2006, 131).

56. McMaster (2015, 197).

57. Jervis (1998, 10). In particular, there are two types of system effects: interdependencies between actions and emergent properties. Jones-Rooy and Page (2012) explain them, respectively, as "how one actor's choices affect another's choices" and "how micro-level actions produce (intentionally or otherwise) macro-level behaviors that in turn influence the system" (see also Jervis, 1997).

58. Jervis (1998).

59. Monteiro (2012b, 344).
60. Studies of electoral volatility look at shifts in the number of votes that parties obtain in consecutive elections (Lipset and Rokkan, 1967; Pedersen, 1979; Bartolini and Mair, 1990; Roberts and Wibbels, 1999; Heath, 2005; Madrid, 2005; Birnir, 2007; Mainwaring and Zoco, 2007) or even changes within the history of voters' identification with a specific party across elections (Keele and Wolak, 2006). Studies of party volatility look at the degree to which parties change within a political system (see, among others, Sikk, 2005). Trade volatility instead refers to shifts in the amount of trade registered between two countries across years (Rose, 2005; Mansfield and Reinhardt, 2008; Gray and Potter, 2012). Similarly, economic volatility describes the difference in the gross domestic product (or other measures of economic performance) of a country through time (Henisz, 2004; Leblang and Mukherjee, 2004, 2005; Fatas and Mihov, 2005; Down, 2007; Klomp and de Haan, 2009; Nooruddin, 2011; Campello and Zucco, 2020). Exchange rate volatility indicates sudden changes in the value of one currency with respect to another (Chowdhury, 1993; Hays, Freeman, and Nesseth, 2003; Moore and Mukherjee, 2006; Leblang and Bernhard, 2006). Climate volatility has been used to measure those deviations from mean rainfall and temperature values often associated with conflict (Jones, Mattiacci, and Braumoeller, 2017; Schmidt, Lee, and Mitchell, 2021). Finally, the concept of volatility has also been used in the context of transitional justice to capture the degree to which countries inconsistently commit to the principles of transitional justice, therefore measuring inconsistent shifts between progressive and regressive events (Bates, Cinar, and Nalepa, 2019).
61. Perhaps the closest to the idea of explaining volatility that scholars of IR have come is represented by the study of turbulence, a concept that in common parlance is used to refer to unsteady change, just like volatility is. Several studies seek to explain turbulence, though turbulence means something different from volatility. In particular, these studies define turbulence as the domestic turmoil that emerges as the effect of international processes such as globalization. See, in particular, Rosenau (1990) and Nieman (2011).
62. On bureaucratic politics, see the seminal contribution of Allison (1971, 162–181). See also Halperin and Clapp (2007) for a detailed retracing of the power struggle between those holding public office. For more recent investigations of the bureaucratic model, see Garrison (2007) and Jones (2017).
63. Henry Kissinger quoted in Ferguson (2015, XXIX).
64. For a review of the emergence of issue areas in the study of international politics, see Evangelista (1989). See also Brecher, Steinberg, and Stein (1969) and Potter (1980).
65. Diehl in Hensel et al. (2008, 118). Emphasis added.
66. Goddard (2009).
67. Hensel et al. (2008, 122–24); McLaughlin Mitchell and Thies (2011). At other times, conflict is achieved by accumulating what had previously been separate aspects of a relationship into one issue, for instance, by combining territorial claims and ethnic animosities (Dreyer, 2010).
68. On linking alliances and trade, see Long and Leeds (2006), Davis (2009), Poast (2013), and Poast (2012). On issue linkage and diplomacy, see Henke (2017). On dynamic

issue linkage across time, see Huelshoff (1994). On the advantages of issue linkage, see Tollison and Willett (1979). For a review of this literature, see Warner (2016). Scholars have long recognized that the practice of generating issues is quite common in IR. For example, issue linkage has been labeled "an ancient and accepted aspect of diplomacy," a "prominent and venerable practice," and even "central to international relations theory" (respectively, Wallace, Sebenius, and Tomz in Poast, 2012, 277). Conversely, when countries seek to reduce cooperation, they deconstruct areas of interactions into separate issues. For example, states can opt to frame defense spending and alliances as separate issues, one belonging to the domestic sphere and the other to the international one (Schelling, 1980, 32). Countries can also seek to manipulate opportunities for cooperation with their counterpart by engaging in "issue-redefinition," whereupon, for example, one domain traditionally associated with the economic interactions (such as trade agreements) can be redefined as being about a different area of interaction altogether, for instance, national security (Friman, 1993, 389).

69. McLaughlin Mitchell and Thies (2011).
70. On changes in Chinese behavior in the international arena after the acquisition of nuclear weapons, see, among others, Burr and Richelson (2001) and Jones (2001).
71. On the effects of nuclear weapons on conflict behavior, see Horowitz (2009) and Bell and Miller (2015). On the effects of nuclear weapons on status, see Gartzke and Jo (2009). On the effects of nuclear weapons on crisis behavior, see Beardsley and Asal (2009).
72. Bell (2015).
73. Schwartenbeck et al. (2015, 1). To minimize surprises, individuals "minimize the complexity of the models they use to generate [. . .] predictions" (FitzGerald, Dolan, and Friston, 2014, 1).
74. Hindsight bias is rooted in human beings' preference for recognizing and seeking out patterns (Mattson, 2014). Engaging in sense-making, individuals seek to "impose meaning on their own knowledge," even twisting their memory of past events to fit what they already know, as opposed to leveraging past events to learning more about unforeseen circumstances they may have encountered (Roese and Vohs, 2012, 411).
75. Braumoeller (2006).
76. Goertz, Diehl, and Balas (2016).
77. Jervis (1988, 68).
78. Galtung (1969).
79. Davenport, Melander, and Regan (2018, 14–16), for example, point out that often studies of international politics characterize peace as the absence of conflict, a choice that limits our ability to capture the changing "quality of peace."
80. On the way in which states have been progressively abandoning traditional forms of conflict, see Fazal (2018). On how "gray zones" and "liminal warfare" are becoming more common than traditional wars and challenging observers' and decision makers' ability to capture dynamics in the international system, see also Kilcullen (2020).
81. Shannon (1948).
82. The lack of consistent information as a condition for conflict is one of the most pervasive assumptions in the field. See Rathbun (2007) for a thorough discussion. The risk

in these cases is that the field gets trapped in cognitive entrenchment, defined as "a high level of stability in one's domain schema" (Dane, 2010, 579).

83. Jervis (1976); Blainey (1988); Keohane (1984); Wendt (1999).

84. Grynaviski (2014) argues instead that false interpersonal beliefs can, in some circumstances, lead to cooperation.

85. On the centrality of conceptualization for theorizing and for measuring, see Sartori (1970) and Goertz (2006).

Chapter 2

1. See Barnett and Duvall (2005) and Baldwin (2002) for a review. In the classic, foundational definition by Robert Dahl, power is fundamentally about how actors interact with one another, consisting of "A getting B to do something B would not otherwise do" (Dahl, 1957, 203). Baldwin (2016, 12), in his review of the concept of power as applied in IR studies, writes: "although alternative definitions abound, none has been so widely accepted as this one." According to Hans Morgenthau, power is at the very core of international affairs: "international politics, like all politics, is a struggle for power" (Morgenthau, 1950, 25).

2. Thus, to explain volatility, I use a rather narrow definition of what counts as power. In terms of the conceptualization of power offered by Barnett and Duvall (2005), I focus on compulsory power. Compulsory power denotes relationally specific influence—that is, power is exerted from one actor directly onto another, as opposed to institutional power, which instead works in a diffused manner—and operates through the interactions between these actors (as opposed to working through social relations of constitution, as in the case of structural power).

3. For a detailed timeline of the events leading to the nuclear deal with Iran, see https://www.armscontrol.org/factsheets/Timeline-of-Nuclear-Diplomacy-With-Iran.

4. Gallup, https://news.gallup.com/opinion/gallup/184169/deal-reached-iranian-rela%20a spx. Last accessed: July 14, 2022

5. Gallup, https://news.gallup.com/poll/181742/nuclear-talks-progress-iran-favorab%20a spx. Last accessed: July 14, 2022.

6. President Obama in "Iran and the Obama Doctrine," *New York Times*, April 6, 2015.

7. See, for instance, Horowitz (2010).

8. Jervis (1978); Hopf (1991); Glaser and Kaufmann (1998). For a review of the debate, see Levy (1984) and Lynn-Jones (1995).

9. A country considering launching a nuclear attack will usually have to acquire nuclear weapons, as well as certain ballistic missile capabilities (Mettler and Reiter, 2012).

10. On how countries' behavior depends on symmetry vs. asymmetry in nuclear power, see, for example, Beardsley and Asal (2009) and Bell and Miller (2015).

11. Gilpin (1981).

12. Gelpern, Horn, and Trebesch (2021).

13. Bell (2015).

14. Duque (2018). In other words, these material capabilities tend to be fungible, in that they can not only enhance hard power but also increase their soft power by enhancing their prestige. For a review of fungible power, see Baldwin (2002). For the fungible nature of material capabilities, see Art (2009).

15. COW's National Material Capability Dataset (Singer et al., 1972) and COW's Diplomatic Exchanges Dataset (Bayer, 2006).

16. Reynolds (1996).

17. Park (1997).

18. Palmer and Morgan (2011); Mattes, Leeds, and Carroll (2014).

19. See, for example, Goh (2006).

20. Waltz (1979). See also the rich literature on foreign policy substitution: Bennett and Nordstrom (2000) and Clark, Nordstrom, and Reed (2008).

21. On the relation between distributive and redistributive mechanisms, see Braumoeller (2006, 275).

22. See, for instance "Military Cuts Threaten Virginia's Pentagon-Dependent Economy," Bloomberg News, http://www.bloomberg.com/news/2011-11-17/military-cuts-threaten-defens html.

23. On the domestic roots of a country's nuclear weapons strategy, see Solingen (1994).

24. See Morrow and Carriere (1999), Mahapatra (1998), and Kapur (2000). On the different implications of the nuclear weapons acquisitions for different sectors of society, see Ganguly (1999).

25. On the role of domestic interests on positive liberal IR theory, see Moravcsik (1997).

26. Fordham and Kleinberg (2011).

27. Kleinberg and Fordham (2013).

28. Milner and Tingley (2011).

29. See, respectively, Colaresi (2005) and Mitchell and Prins (2004).

30. Trubowitz (1998).

31. Fordham (1998).

32. Solingen (2007).

33. Davis and Moore (1997).

34. Mattes, Leeds, and Carroll (2014).

35. Narizny (2003) argues that governments consider how internal vs. external balancing will affect their constituencies when deciding between increasing defense spending or joining an alliance, while Leeds, Mattes, and Vogel (2009, 464) suggest that domestic groups might prefer certain allies over others based on shared ethnic background. See also Narizny (2007).

36. Lektzian and Patterson (2015).

37. Lipset (1963); Rokkan (1967).

38. Lane, Ersson, and Ersson (1999, 41) in Selway (2011).

39. See Horowitz (1985) and Citrin (2001).

40. See Horowitz (1985) and Citrin (2001).

41. Cross-cuttingness is akin to the concept of statistical independence, as explained by Selway (2011).

42. It is important to notice that, contrary to common wisdom, the presence of diverging domestic preferences does not systematically lead to political paralysis. See, for example, Gordon and Landa (2017).

43. Compensation can take the form of side payments. Side payments are material or symbolic repayments (e.g., verbal condemnations of country B, threats, etc.) to dampen the adverse consequences that certain interest groups might perceive a specific foreign policy choice imposes on them. See Friman (1993, 388) for an excellent review on the literature on side payments. The two-level game approach also models the effects of domestic side payments on the elaboration of foreign policy, but it does so by concentrating on how the possibility of side payments makes reaching agreements more likely. For applications of this two-level game approach insight, see Chapman, Urpelainen, and Wolford (2012) and Weiss (2013), among others.

44. Mayer (1992, 806) writes that therefore, "more often, internal side-payments must be made in the coin of a nonmonetary issue linked to the negotiation."

45. Blake (2013).

46. FDIs have at times been opposed on grounds of being tools that facilitate former colonizers' access to local resources, potentially perpetuating colonialism in some form. See Makino and Tsang (2011) and Levis, Muradoğlu, and Vasileva (2016).

47. Mayer (1992, 795).

48. Smith (2015, 53).

49. Frieden (1988).

50. For an investigation of the relation between human rights and trade, see Hafner-Burton (2005), and for one specifically on China and the US, see Drury and Li (2006).

51. Snyder (1991).

52. For example, according to this account, overexpansion in Wilhelmine Germany emerged from "the marriage of iron and rye." As a consequence, "Junkers got grain tariffs that antagonized Russia; the navy and heavy industry got a fleet that antagonized Britain; and the army got an offensive war plan that ensured that virtually all of Europe would be ranged among Germany's enemy" (Snyder, 1991, 97–99).

53. In particular, for logrolling as theorized by Snyder to occur, two conditions have to be in place. First, logrolling tends to mostly take place when the interests involved are small. It is precisely their smallness that prevents them from achieving their favorite policy on their own, compelling them to seek alliances with other interests. Second, according to the logrolling principle, the policies favored by one group cannot be incompatible with those of other groups; otherwise, the alliance between the small interests cannot take place. In the specific example, grain tariffs and a brand new fleet were quite compatible policies, and therefore Junkers could tolerate the heavy industry's ambitions well and form an alliance with them that resulted in overexpansion. Other studies explore logrolling in foreign policy, though Gilli, Li, and Qian (2018, 4) argue that "the empirical literature on logrolling is not that rich, probably because the proof of the existence of logrolling depends on the record of the trading of favors, which may not exist (Evans 1994) or may be difficult to acquire (Buchanan and Tullock 1962)." Stratmann (1992) presents evidence of logrolling on some agricultural US congressional voting. Crombez (2000) shows the presence of logrolling in

member-states voting on EU policies. Copelovitch (2010) uncovers indirect evidence of logrolling among G5 countries on issues of International Monetary Fund lending.

54. Hyde and Saunders (2020).

55. See, among others, Narang and Talmadge (2018) and Gray (2013).

56. Morrow et al. (2008, 393). According to selectorate theory, when the coalition of people whose support the leader needs to stay in power (winning coalition, W) is small compared to the section of the population that has a say in the choice of the leader, as defined by the electoral rules (selectorate, S), the leader will try to stay in power by choosing policies that provide W with private goods. Conversely, when W is large with respect to S, then the leader will provide public goods, that is, goods that benefit all members of the society (Bueno De Mesquita et al., 1999; Bueno De Mesquita and Smith, 2005).

57. On the redistributive implications of investing in different sectors of the military, see Heginbotham (2002).

58. Specifically, Weeks (2012, 329) points to the uneven distributional consequences for domestic groups of goods largely theorized as public, such as winning wars. Kennedy (2009), on the other hand, demonstrates the weakness of the external validity of the concept of selectorate. See also Magaloni (2008) and Clarke and Stone (2008). For a critique of the concept of a public good as used in the selectorate theory, see Bell (2011).

59. Tsebelis (2011).

60. Ehrlich (2007) also points to the incapability of veto player theory to explain change, focusing in particular on explanations of magnitude and direction of change. Tsebelis (2011, 33) specifies this limitation clearly in his theory: "I will be able to identify the conditions where change of the status quo is difficult or impossible (policy stability is high), but I will not be able to predict actual change." Mansfield, Milner, and Pevehouse (2007) use veto player theory to explain stability, conceptualized as the probability of a preferential trade agreement (PTA) not being signed. By contrast, Henisz (2004) argues that volatility is brought about by the absence (or a reduced number) of veto players—that is, all those actors that have to agree in order for a new policy to be implemented. According to the literature on public choice, in contrast, policy change—or cycling—is propelled by the presence of heterogeneous preferences, of multiple alternatives that can be paired against each other, and of a simple majority rule. See Arrow (1951) and McKelvey (1976).

61. On this point, see Tsebelis (2011, 20–30).

62. On how factors interact in theoretical statements, see Braumoeller and Goertz (2000).

63. The permissive/precipitant cause approach is similar to the permissive/efficient cause framework specified by Waltz (1959), in that it emphasizes the relevance of parsing out the presence of enhancing and triggering causes. However, in this case I use the term "precipitant" (Ross, 2012, 66) rather than "efficient" cause because for Waltz (1959), the efficient conditions for the outcome of interest are the accidental, immediate, pretext conditions for the outcome of interest, whereas in my theory the presence of multiple and heterogeneous interests at the domestic level is to be understood as a systematic propellant for volatile action, rather than an accidental one. In this

sense, precipitant causes are closer to the idea of catalyzing (or contingent) causes put forward by Thompson (2003).

64. Cioffi-Revilla (1998).

65. Morgenthau (1950, 40).

66. Rose (1998).

67. See Schweller (2004, 1994). For neoclassical realism, domestic environments work as an "imperfect transmission belt" (Lobell, Ripsman, and Taliaferro, 2009, 4) for the stimuli that the international system produces.

68. Such as the ones put forward by Trubowitz (1992, 1998) and Moravcsik (1997).

69. Rose (1998, 146).

70. In addition, there is a tendency in the neoclassical realist approach to see the military realm as distinct from the economic one: Sterling-Folker (2009) claims that the security realm is plagued by tribalism between citizens holding different national identities, in a way that the economic realm is not. I drop this dichotomization between security policy and economic policy, put foreign policy on a conflict–cooperation continuum, and test empirically for what brings about inconsistent shifts between cooperation and conflict throughout the different realms.

71. Most and Starr (1984); Bennett and Nordstrom (2000); Clark, Nordstrom, and Reed (2008).

72. On the centrality of this assumption in studies of foreign policy substitutability and on why it is deleterious, see Milner and Tingley (2011, 40).

73. Studies in this tradition have instead investigated whether the presence of multiple and heterogeneous interest groups have made a country's policy choices in the international arena consistently more conflictual (Clare, 2010; Kaarbo and Beasley, 2008; Beasley and Kaarbo, 2014), more or less peaceful (Leblang and Chan, 2003; Palmer, London, and Regan, 2004; Kaarbo and Beasley, 2008; Kaarbo, 2012; Elman, 2000), or more or less capable to achieve the country's own objectives in the international realm (Clare, 2010).

74. Ganguly and Thompson (2011, 15) argue that when foreign policy is shaped by domestic interest groups that gain from the implementation of different foreign policies, the outcome is a "confusing" foreign policy, shifting between different policies to accommodate that diverse set of interests (Ganguly and Thompson, 2011, 15). Their conceptualization of factional politics investigates how domestic competition shapes foreign policy in the aggregate, across single policy choices. So unlike coalition politics scholars, the authors do not focus on whether factional politics makes states more or less likely to engage in specific behaviors, such as forming alliances or waging wars. Nevertheless, by ignoring the role of relative power, the factional foreign policy approach does not answer a crucial question to explain volatility: when domestic interests groups fight, what options are they really fighting over? This is an important question to answer because without an understanding of the set of options available to each group, it becomes hard to explain when and why a state's behavior in the international arena becomes more or less confusing.

75. Koga (2018, 2).

76. Kuik (2016, 505). There are multiple definitions of hedging strategies. Kuik (2016, 505) defines hedging as "a multiple-component approach situated between the two ends of the balancing–bandwagoning spectrum," entailing "the adoption of two sets of mutually counteracting policies, namely the 'returns-maximizing' and 'risk-contingency' options" (see also Koga, 2018). The definition by Goh (2005, 2) is more generic. Hedging is defined as "a set of strategies aimed at avoiding (or planning for contingencies in) a situation in which states cannot decide upon more straightforward alternatives such as balancing, bandwagoning, or neutrality."

77. Cheng-Chwee (2008, 163) defines hedging as "a behavior in which a country seeks to offset risks by pursuing multiple policy options that are intended to produce mutually counteracting effects under the situation of high-uncertainties and high-stakes."

78. The occurrence of mixed signaling, involving both positive and negative inducements, has also been investigated as a way to increase the probability of success for deterrence strategies. See, for example, Huth (1988, 1999).

79. Tunsjø (2013).

80. Medeiros (2005); Goh (2006); Foot (2006); Lim and Cooper (2015). But see Tessman (2012).

81. Koga (2018, 7–8).

82. Medeiros (2005).

83. On the domestic sources of the switch, and in particular on the role of nationalist and pro–free trade groups, see Saltzman (2015) and Easley (2017).

84. Smith (2015, 25).

85. Saunders (2011); Rathbun, Kertzer, and Paradis (2017); Yarhi-Milo, Kertzer, and Renshon (2018).

86. Lupton (2020) and Licht and Allen (2018).

87. Krcmaric, Nelson, and Roberts (2020).

88. Similarly, a business background, for instance, can decrease leaders' willingness to share expenses with allies (Fuhrmann, 2020), while leaders that participated in rebellions are more likely to pursue nuclear weapons (Fuhrmann and Horowitz, 2015).

89. Horowitz, Stam, and Ellis (2015).

90. Post and Sen (2020).

91. Koch and Fulton (2011).

92. On the importance of accounting for the likely endogeneity of leaders' characteristics, see Krcmaric, Nelson, and Roberts (2020).

93. On spurious correlations between states' performances and leaders' gender, and on the role of states' capabilities, see Piscopo (2020).

94. On the role of the coalition of interests that supports leadership on foreign policy behavior, see, for example, Potrafke (2009) and Dreher and Jensen (2013).

95. Mattes, Leeds, and Carroll (2015). On the relevance of leaders' coalitions of support more broadly, see Mattes, Leeds, and Matsumura (2016).

96. Diehl in Hensel et al. (2008, 118).

97. Hensel et al. (2008, 122–24); McLaughlin Mitchell and Thies (2011).

98. Goddard (2009).

99. The test is performed on data presented in Chapter 4.

100. Braumoeller (2006) shows how most studies embrace the distribution of a variable, and as such embrace a mean-centric approach.
101. See Braumoeller (2006) for a discussion of the value added of theories of variance.
102. Other exceptions to the episodic conception of international relations include studies theorizing the determinants of trends in foreign policy behavior (Hopf, 2002) or analyzing specific contexts of cooperation (Goldstein and Pevehouse, 1997; Goldstein et al., 2001).
103. See studies of foreign policy substitutions for an example.
104. Tilly (2001); Tilly and Goodin (2006). The concept of process as identified by Tilly (2001) is similar to the idea of mechanism concatenation discussed by Gambetta (1998), and even to the idea that Falleti and Lynch (2009) advance on the importance of thinking of mechanisms as interacting in a specific context. For a critique of Tilly (2001), see Bunge (2004) and Demetriou (2012).

Chapter 3

1. Schedler (2012, 22). Similarly, Carmines and Woods (2005, 10) describe measuring as "the process of linking abstract concepts to empirical indicants."
2. Morton and Williams (2010, 260). On the importance of there being consistency between concepts and measurements, see Goertz (2006, 95–128). On measuring, see also Jackman (2008).
3. Adcock (2001, 530). Gerring (2001, 155–62) discusses both validity and reliability of measurements at length.
4. In particular, I use the Conflict and Peace Data Bank (COPDAB), the World Events/ Interactions Survey (WEIS), and the Integrated Crisis Early Warning System (ICEW) data (Azar, 1979; McClelland, 1978; Pevehouse and Goldstein, 2006; Boschee et al., 2015).
5. "Trump to North Korean leader: My Nuclear Button 'Is Bigger & More Powerful,'" Reuters, January 2, 2018, https://www.reuters.com/article/us-northkorea-missiles-trump-button/trump-to-north-korean-leader-my-nuclear-button-is-bigger-more-powerful-idUSKBN1ES029. Last accessed: July 14, 2022.
6. The name of this ontology is CAMEO, which stands for Conflict and Mediation Event Observations, and it is available at http://eventdata.parusanalytics.com/cameo.dir/CAMEO.CDB.09b5.pdf. Last accessed: July 14, 2022.
7. Brecher and Wilkenfeld (1997) and Jones, Bremer, and Singer (1996), respectively.
8. ICB crisis number 435, Version 10, (Brecher, Wilkenfeld, et al., 1997).
9. Looking at countries' behaviors as a whole, I build on the approach adopted by other theories that seek to understand the broader dynamics characterizing foreign policy, such as studies of foreign policy portfolios (Palmer and Morgan, 2011) and substitutability (Bennett and Nordstrom, 2000; Clark, Nordstrom, and Reed, 2008).
10. Goldstein (1992). See appendix for examples and details. For recent uses, see Jones and Mattiacci (2019).

11. It is possible to think of the scale feature as performing a similar function as the "intensity" variable that is often present in other datasets, including the Correlates of War's MID and the ICB datasets.

12. Data comes from ICEWS (Boschee et al., 2015).

13. For a list of studies that use this procedure see, for example, Nooruddin (2011, 66).

14. Thyne (2009, 69).

15. Mansfield and Reinhardt (2008).

16. Mitchell and Moore (2002) identify strong autoregressive dynamics in rivalries.

17. Mastanduno (1997).

18. For a similar concern regarding the measurement of growth-rate volatility and a similar solution to the problem see, for example, Nooruddin (2011, 67).

19. Box and Jenkins (1970) first introduced the Box-Jenkins procedure. For a succinct discussion, including a reflection on the crucial role of parsimony in the procedure, see Enders (2008, 76–79). For a comprehensive step-by-step explanation of how the procedure works, see Box-Steffensmeier et al. (2014, 22–67).

20. See, in particular, Box-Steffensmeier et al. (2014, Chapters 2, 5, and 7).

21. The event data used in these graphs come from the ICEWS dataset (Boschee et al., 2015). I select in particular actions from government members of the source state to other governments' members of the target state. See the ICEWS codebook for details.

22. For details, see the ICEWS codebook.

23. Specifically, Figure 3.2(c) and Figure 3.2 (d). plot the five-week moving standard deviation of the residuals that emerge from a Box-Jenkins procedure applied to the time series in, respectively, Figure 3.2(a) and Figure 3.2 (b).

24. In both cases, the modal behavior toward the US corresponds to verbal conflict, such as public denouncing of US behavior.

25. See, for example, Kapur (2005) and Edelman, Krepinevich, and Montgomery (2011) among others.

26. On the difference between secret and public events, see also the literature on audience costs (Slantchev, 2006; Tomz, 2007; Weeks, 2008).

27. On performativity, see Austin (1975) and Goffman (1959).

28. On the differences between countries' overt and covert actions and on how overt actions more credibly signal intentions and goals, see in particular McManus and Yarhi-Milo (2017), Carson (2016), and Carson and Yarhi-Milo (2017).

29. See, for example, Putnam (1988). On how public behaviors become an asset for decision makers who want to push forward their own international agenda, see also Colaresi (2012).

30. Countries also vary dramatically in how they store declassified documents and how they make them accessible. Each country's "history, legal tradition, administrative culture, and social and political reality" determine whether countries address issues relating to records and archives in one single piece of legislation or in several laws, whether what counts as a "record" depends on the medium used, whether the scope of archived sources is limited to government bodies' records or also includes organizations performing public functions, whether those records are managed by a centralized organization such as National Archives, to whom such an organization

responds, and so on. All of these factors, in turn, affect the amount and quality of information that becomes available ("Principles for Archives and Records Legislation," International Council on Archives, 2004, 5).

31. Mark Trachtenberg, "Declassification Analysis: The Method and Some Examples," 2014. http://www.sscnet.ucla.edu/polisci/faculty/trachtenberg/documents/doclist. html (Last accessed: July 14, 2022). Moreover, historians have demonstrated that the information redacted changes with time, often profoundly altering the conclusions that analysts and scholars reach regarding those documents.

32. "Several major conditions impede the use of recorded emails: an absence of centralized oversight; a lack of understanding and knowledge of record-keeping requirements; a reluctance to use record email because of possible consequences; a lack of understanding of SMART features; and impediments in the software that prevent easy use." Adam Mazmanian, "SMART Tool Failed to Cure State Email Woes," Government Computer News, March 16, 2015. As new informational technologies increase the communication and exchange of information between actors, the communication that might have taken place over a single phone call might now take place through an email chain, and not all of those email chains will be made available. Therefore, we might be moving away even more from the ideal data collection procedure for secret events.

Chapter 4

1. If the same increase in volatility could be explained by relative power regardless of the domestic context, for example, then the analysis would lend credence to theories of hedging, which suggest that power alone can predict volatility. By the same token, if the impact of the configuration of domestic interests on volatility was the same whether the country displayed relative power superiority or not, then theories that only focus on the domestic configuration of interests would be better able to predict volatility than the theory put forward in this book.

2. "When India's Foreign Policy Is Domestic," Brookings Institution, April 3, 2013.

3. Jones, Smith, and Khoo (2013, 12–39).

4. For a detailed discussion, see Smith (2015, 22–50).

5. The study of war has been central to the study of International Relations (Jervis, 1988, 68).

6. Thompson (2001, 588). See appendix for further details.

7. Colaresi, Rasler, and Thompson (2007, 89).

8. See, for example, Diehl (1998) and Diehl and Goertz (2001).

9. Cranmer, Desmarais, and Menninga (2012).

10. On focused comparisons, see George and Bennett (2005, 67).

11. Achen (2005, 337).

12. Achen (2005, 338).

13. Thompson (2001, 560).

14. For a definition of enduring rivalries, see Diehl and Goertz (2001, 19–25). On the different definitions of rivalries and the differences and similarities between such definitions, see Colaresi, Rasler, and Thompson (2007). See also Colaresi, Rasler, and Thompson (2007, Table 2.2) for an exhaustive list of these dyads.

15. To only rely on perceptual approaches such as those encapsulated in the definition of strategic rivalries implies including rivalries such as the one between Argentina and Paraguay, together with rivalries such as the one between the US and the Soviet Union and Pakistan and India, even though the actual behaviors of these dyads in the international arena appear quite different.

16. In the appendix, I describe the procedure I use to merge together data from different sources. Event data on states' behaviors are available after 1992 through ICEWS (Integrated Crisis Early Warning System). Indeed, I use ICEWS data in Chapter 4. However, I decide not to leverage it here for several reasons. First, the ICEWS data do not start until 1995. Using it would then create a discontinuous time series that will likely affect the final results from the Box-Jenkins procedure (Box-Steffensmeier et al., 2014). Such procedure, in turn, is key to isolate volatility, as Chapter 3 illustrates. Second, most of the rivalries as coded by the sources I use end on or before 2001, suggesting that using ICEWS would only be possible for six years at most. Thus, in this case, adding more data does not necessarily improve the validity of the analysis. For these reasons, in order to keep the analysis rigorous, I choose to end the analysis in 1992.

17. Repeating all the analyses with a lag does not change the results.

18. Version 5, Singer, Bremer, and Stuckey (1972); Singer (1988). The Codebook is available at http://www.correlatesofwar.org/data-sets/national-material-capabilities.

19. See CINC Codebook, pp. 2–3. Available at http://www.correlatesofwar.org/data-sets/national-material-capabilities.

20. As the codebook to the data indicates, these indicators were selected "for being both meaningful at any given time and that had roughly the same meaning across this broad time range" (Codebook, p. 2). Available at http://www.correlatesofwar.org/data-sets/national-material-capabilities.

21. On the importance of capturing both actual and potential capabilities, see also Kugler and Domke (1986).

22. See COW CINC Codebook, p. 2. Available at http://www.correlatesofwar.org/data-sets/national-material-capabilities. Last accessed: July 14, 2022. Definitions of power that mostly rely on one component, by contrast, might not adequately capture the complexity of the process. Organski (1981), for example, proposes to rely on gross domestic product (GDP) per capita over a country's population to measure the power of a country. Such measure, however, cannot capture the actual military power of a country, as two countries with a similar GDP might make very different choices regarding how much to invest in the military. For a comprehensive review of the traditional literature on how to measure power in International Relations, see in particular Kugler and Domke (1986) and Tellis et al. (2000, 25–33).

23. Bear Braumoeller, "Has the American Military Fallen Behind?," Monkey Cage, *Washington Post*, May 4, 2016.

24. Bear Braumoeller, "Has the American Military Fallen Behind?," Monkey Cage, *Washington Post*, May 4, 2016.

25. This concept is operationalized via the variable *XRCOMP* in the Polity dataset (Marshall and Jaggers, 2002). This variable acquires five values, including the value 3 for competitive selection.

26. Selway (2011).

27. Selway (2011) codes whether a cleavage is reinforcing or not as the probability that knowing something about category A will tell us something about category B. The closer that probability is to 1, the more reinforcing the cleavages are. I adopt a conservative measure of the presence of reinforcing cleavages and code a country as having reinforcing cleavages if all cleavages are reinforcing and the probability of each is above 75%.

28. Data comes from the Democratic Electoral Systems (DES) dataset.

29. In addition to being theoretically less precise, interaction terms would also be less efficient. Since the index is composed of three elements and since those elements would then be interacted with the measure for relative power superiority, keeping those elements separate and then interacting them would amount to including thirteen variables in the regression. This is the case because interacting four variables, *A, B, C, D*, would amount to including all of the following terms of the interaction: *A, B, C, D, ABCD, ABC, AB, AC, AD, BCD, BC, BD, CD* (Braumoeller, 2004).

30. On the importance of a more complex understanding of regime type in international politics, see in particular Hyde and Saunders (2020).

31. Ellis, Horowitz, and Stam (2015).

32. This worry about mental health problems leading to erratic behavior was exemplified, for instance, in the discussions about US President Donald Trump and his conduct of foreign policy. Among others, see, for example, David Rothkopf, "The Greatest Threat Facing the United States Is Its Own President," *Washington Post*, July 4, 2017, and Richard Patterson, "Trump's Personal Pathology Is America's Foreign Policy," *The Bulwark*, December 6, 2019.

33. Mattes, Leeds, and Matsumura (2016).

34. Hensel and Mitchell (2007).

35. I check for H2 looking at the lower-order term coefficient for relative power.

36. For each model specification, I use a fixed effects model and a random effects model (Greene, 2003, 287–302). The Hausman test fails to reject the null hypothesis that the random effects model is consistent, suggesting that the random effects model should be preferred to the fixed effects model. Thus, I present results from random effects models. Moreover, standard errors are clustered by country.

37. On how to interpret interactions, see Braumoeller (2004); Brambor, Clark, and Golder (2006); Berry, Golder, and Milton (2012).

38. Snyder (1991).

39. Beasley and Kaarbo (2014).

40. On this point, see also Palmer and Morgan (2011).

41. The presence of permissive conditions makes the outcome possible, while their absence makes the outcome highly unlikely if not impossible.

42. On the relevance of contentious issues in rivalries, see in particular Colaresi, Rasler, and Thompson (2007).
43. See, among others, Colaresi, Rasler, and Thompson (2007).
44. Thompson (2001).
45. The result on polarity should also be taken with caution, as the dummy is coded as 1 only for the three years after 1989.

Chapter 5

1. Memorandum for the President from the Department of State, Subject: Call from French Foreign Minister, October 1, 1966. Papers of Lyndon B. Johnson President, National Security File (hereinafter, NSF), Country File: France, Box 173, Lyndon B. Johnson Presidential Library (hereinafter, LBJPL).
2. Summary Statistics and Map of Aid by Country, 1952, George C. Marshall Foundation, https://www.marshallfoundation.org/library/documents/ marshall-plan-payments-millions-european-economic-cooperation-countries/. Last accessed September 13, 2021.
3. Examples of Marshall Plan Aid, George C. Marshall Foundation, https://www.mar shallfoundation.org/marshall/the-marshall-plan/history-marshall-plan/ examples-marshall-plan-aid/. Last accessed September 13, 2021.
4. Article 5, The North Atlantic Treaty, Washington, DC, USA, April 4, 1949.
5. Alliance Treaty Obligations and Provision (ATOP) dataset (Leeds, Ritter, Mitchell, and Long 2002).
6. Only one-third of all alliance members during the period 1815–2016 experienced a change in the terms that bound them to the alliance (source: ATOP). The twenty-year rule contemplated in Article 13 of the NATO treaty stated that parties could cease to be members only twenty years after the treaty had been in force. Thus, France could not completely withdraw from the alliance. The decision to withdraw from the integrated command, however, was rather consequential. In his response to De Gaulle's letter informing him of the decision to withdraw, Johnson gives us a sense of the scope of the implications of the French decisions, arguing: "We continue to believe that if the Treaty is to have force and reality, members of the Alliance should prepare the command structures, the strategic and tactical plans, the forces in being, and their designation to NATO in advance of any crisis and for use in time of crisis" (Johnson Letter to DeGaulle, March 22, 1966). Available at https://www.nato.int/nato_static_fl2014/assets/pdf/pdf_history/20190401_e1-france-LBJ-response-to-deGaulle_032 266.pdf. Last accessed: July 14, 2022.
7. Mack (1975, 178).
8. Singh and Way (2004).
9. Larkin (1997, 240–41).
10. See, for example, McMahon (1981).
11. Hanrieder and Auton (1980, 116).

12. On France's power growth, see also Leon (1976, 1011).

13. Singer (1988). In particular, Table 5.1 plots the ratio of the French and American CINC scores.

14. The black line in the graph represents a nonparametric loess curve to highlight the trend developing over those years under analysis.

15. Morse (2015, 161–62).

16. In 1954, France started its nuclear program but did not perform its first nuclear test until 1960, and operational weapons did not become available until the end of 1964 (Frederic Joliot-Curie, Irene Joliot-Curie, Lew Kowarski, and Hans Halban, "French Nuclear Program," Atomic Heritage Foundation, February 14, 2017). The CINC score would not register nuclear weapons becoming operational, so arguably France's relative power was even greater than that depicted in Figure 5.1.

17. Memorandum of President's Conversation with Mr. Chaban-Dalmas, March 14, 1961, Papers of President Kennedy, NSF, Countries: France, Box 70A, John Fitzgerald Kennedy Presidential Library (hereinafter, JFKPL).

18. Memorandum of Conversation, Paris, July 5, 1958, Foreign Relations of the United States (hereinafter, FRUS), 1958–60, Volume VII, Part 2, Western Europe, ed. Glenn W. LaFantasie (Washington, DC: Government Printing Office, 2010), Document 34.

19. Memorandum of Conversation, Paris, July 5, 1958, FRUS, 1958–1960, Volume VII, Part 2, Western Europe, ed. Glenn W. LaFantasie (Washington, DC: Government Printing Office, 2010), Document 34. In the same document, De Gaulle also makes predictions as to the fate of US power: "General de Gaulle replied that he [. . .] hoped that the United States would maintain its strength and its liberal spirit. Each nation had its day. `Yours is now—you and the Russians.' He hoped that the United States would remain as it was today. He thought it would, at least for his lifetime."

20. Larkin (1997, 183–84).

21. Hanrieder and Auton (1980, 104).

22. These are the categories utilized in Selway (2011).

23. Larkin (1997, 211–12).

24. Larkin (1997, 201–2).

25. See in particular Williams (1958, 333).

26. Kemp (1980, 1219). The commerce-oriented tertiary sector workers focused in Paris (Kemp, 1980, 1219).

27. During those years, the fraction of the French population that lived in Paris increased from one in eleven to one in six, augmenting the divisions between those that lived in the cities and those that lived in the countryside (Larkin, 1997, 201–2). See also Kemp (1980, 997–98, 1012–13, 1232).

28. Larkin (1997, 201–2).

29. Larkin (1997, 201–2).

30. Kemp (1980, 1327–28).

31. CIA Special Report, "New Emphasis in French Foreign Policy," February 28, 1964, 19, Papers of Lyndon B. Johnson President, NSF, Country File: Finland, France, Box Number 169, LBJPL. Important political (leftist) and economic sectors pushed for recognizing China, France decision makers acknowledged. Memorandum of

Conversation, February 3, 1959, FRUS, 1958–1960, Volume VII, Part 2, Western Europe, ed. Glenn W. LaFantasie (Washington, DC: Government Printing Office, 2010). Document 93.

32. Martin (2008, 57).

33. Badel (2012, 75–77).

34. Larkin (1997, 223).

35. Hanrieder and Auton (1980, 123).

36. Larkin (1997, 184).

37. Hanrieder and Auton (1980, 103).

38. Telegram from the Embassy in France to the Department of State, April 24, 1965, FRUS, 1964–1968, Volume XII, Western Europe, ed. Glenn W. LaFantasie (Washington, DC: Government Printing Office, 2010), Document 46.

39. On the special role played by Algeria for some groups, see Hanrieder and Auton (1980, 143) and Zelikow and May (2018, 65). See also Institut de France (1956, 197–201).

40. Hanrieder and Auton (1980, 154–55).

41. Larkin (1997, 305).

42. Institut de France (1961, 634).

43. Institutional changes constitute a helpful and salient tool to capture changes in access to foreign policy across different cases, as the previous chapter shows. However, the ability that case studies afford to take a closer look at the specific case under analysis makes it possible to advance more nuanced statements aimed at better describing and pinpointing the actual time of the change within a specific case by leveraging both primary and secondary sources.

44. "The referendum ceremony not only has the function of periodically affirming the legitimacy of the head of state. It also enhances his freedom of action by putting other political forces out of the political game. It isolates a privileged actor: his freedom of action is thus much greater than it would otherwise be [. . .]. [They] [referenda] served to both mobilize the public and to give the leader autonomy to pursue his goals unencumbered by divisional party politics" (Morse, 2015, 187). Madelin (1997, 445–47) also makes the point that during the Fifth Republic De Gaulle became increasingly able to conduct foreign policy without being at the mercy of domestic interests.

45. "A change in rhetoric that defines the actual change in practices" (Morse, 2015, 109, footnote 5).

46. Menon (2000, 50).

47. In particular, Figure 5.2 plots the residuals from a Box-Jenkins procedure applied on the weekly time series of France's behavior toward the United States. These residuals therefore represent all change in France's behavior that cannot be explained by factors such as trends and cycles in the behavior (which have already been stripped by the Box-Jenkins procedure). See Chapter 3 for a description on how volatility is measured and for where those residuals come from.

48. Conflict and Peace Data Bank (COPDAB) data (Azar, 1979).

49. Institut de France (1954, 340). France also hosted a visit by US Secretary of State John Foster Dulles, who traveled there to meet with French Foreign Minister Georges Bidault and discuss details of such cooperation. Travels of the US Secretary of State,

John Foster Dulles, US Office of the Historian. See also Windrow (2013) and Irving (1975).

50. Institut de France (1954, 377–79).

51. The Pentagon Papers, Gravel Edition, Volume 1, Chapter 3, Sections 1–3.

52. B.C. (1956, 51).

53. Document 79: M. Hoppenot, Chef de la Mission Permanente de la France auprès de l'Organisation des Nations Unies, a Mendès France, Ministère des Affaires Étrangères, 19 aout 1954.

54. Institut de France (1954, 416). See also Document 78, M. Henri Bonnet, Ambassadeur de France a Washington, a M. Mendes France, Ministère des Affaires Étrangères 19aout 1954, Documents Diplomatiques Français, Ministère des Affaires Étrangères, 1958, Tome II, 21 Julliet–31 Decembre.

55. The Pentagon Papers, Gravel Edition, Volume 1, Chapter 4, Section 1, 179–214.

56. Institut de France (1954, 442).

57. The Pentagon Papers, Gravel Edition, Volume 1, Chapter 4, Section 1, 179–214.

58. Institut de France, 1954, 250–57.

59. Telegram from the Delegation at the SEATO Council Meeting to the Department of State, Bangkok, February 23, 1955, midnight, FRUS, 1955–1957, East Asian Security; Cambodia; Laos, Volume XXI, ed. Glenn W. LaFantasie (Washington, DC: Government Printing Office, 2010), Document 19. See also Institut de France (1955, 338).

60. The Pentagon Papers, Gravel Edition, Volume 1, Chapter 4, "US and France in Indochina, 1950–56" (Boston: Beacon Press, 1971), Section 1, 179–214.

61. Institut de France (1955, 218–19). In November, the final declaration of Geneva emerged, though France and the US have substantial disagreements on that. The Pentagon Papers, Gravel Edition, Volume 1, Chapter 3.

62. Institut de France (1963, 287).

63. Luthi (2014, 117).

64. Institut de France (1963, 309).

65. Martin (2008, 72–73).

66. "DeGaulle Proposes China Join a Plan to Neutralize Vietnam, Laos, Cambodia; Policy Defended; General Asserts Link with Peking Is Vital to Ease Tension," New York Times, February 1, 1964. See also Telegraph from Paris Embassy to Secretary of State, February 1, 1964, Papers of Lyndon B. Johnson President, NSF, Country File: France, Box Number 169, LBJPL.

67. Telegram from the Embassy in France to the Department of State, February 19, 1964, FRUS, 1964–1968, Volume XII, Western Europe, ed. Glenn W. LaFantasie (Washington, DC: Government Printing Office, 2010), Document 26. On the complaints, see Nodis for Ambassador from the President, February 25, 1964, Papers of Lyndon B. Johnson, President, NSF, Country File: France, Box Number 169, LBJPL.

68. Memorandum of Conversation, Paris, December 17, 1964, 1964–1968, FRUS, Volume XII, Western Europe, ed. Glenn W. LaFantasie (Washington, DC: Government Printing Office, 2010), Document 38.

69. Memorandum of Conversation, Paris, December 17, 1964, 1964–1968, FRUS, Volume XII, Western Europe, ed. Glenn W. LaFantasie (Washington, DC: Government Printing Office, 2010), Document 38.

70. Institut de France (1965, 229).

71. Memorandum of Conversation, February 19, 1965, FRUS, 1964–1968, Volume XII, Western Europe, ed. Glenn W. LaFantasie (Washington, DC: Government Printing Office, 2010), Document 43.

72. Telegram from the Embassy in France to the Department of State, March 11, 1965, FRUS, 1964–1968, Volume XII, Western Europe. Document 45.

73. Institut de France (1965, 237).

74. Institut de France (1965, 245).

75. Institut de France (1965, 220–21).

76. The Suez Canal Company was a private company with headquarters in France and whose main shareholder was the British government.

77. Zelikow and May (2018, 178, footnote 9).

78. Institut de France (1956, 334).

79. Zelikow and May (2018, 178–79).

80. Zelikow and May (2018, 185).

81. Institut de France (1956, 374).

82. Zelikow and May (2018, 189–90).

83. Zelikow and May (2018, 266).

84. Zelikow and May (2018, 282).

85. Pinault sent a cable to the US to ask "in an unequivocal manner that the clauses of the [North] Atlantic Treaty would come into play immediately in the case of a Soviet attack on the allies of the United States." Zelikow and May (2018, 270, footnote 35).

86. Institut de France (1956, 397). On November 30, Great Britain and France evacuated Suez, giving in in no small part to the oil pressures and blackmail that the US had imposed on them (Institut de France, 1956, 412).

87. Pinault agreed to meet with Dulles to talk about Algeria and their own alliance in December 1956 (Institut de France, 1956, 423).

88. Institut de France (1956, 219).

89. Institut de France (1958, 354).

90. Institut de France (1958, 370). See also Memorandum of Conversation, July 5, 1958, Department of State, Central Files, FRUS, 1958–1960, Western Europe, Volume VII, Part 2, ed.Glenn W. LaFantasie (Washington, DC: Government Printing Office, 2010), Document 34. French decision makers linked a possible reform of NATO to the broader discussion of French and US global interests. See Document 294, M. Couve De Murville, Ministère des Affaires Étrangères à M. Alphans, Ambassadeur de France à Washington, Paris, 28 octobre 1958, Documents Diplomatiques Français, Ministère des Affaires Étrangères 1958, Tome II, Julliet–Decembre.

91. "Letter from President de Gaulle to President Eisenhower," Paris, September 17, 1958, FRUS, Western Europe, Volume VII, Part 2, ed. Glenn W. LaFantasie (Washington, DC: Government Printing Office, 2010), Document 45.

92. Memorandum of Conversation, July 5, 1958. FRUS. Department of State, Secret. Department of State, Central Files, 611.51/7-558. Secret. FRUS, 1958–1960, Western Europe, Volume VII, Part 2, eds. Glenn W. LaFantasie (Washington, DC: Government Printing Office, 2010), Document 34. See also Four Power Communique on Berlin, December 14, 1958.

93. Memorandum of Conversation, February 3, 1959, FRUS, 1958–1960, Western Europe, Volume VII, Part 2, ed. Glenn W. LaFantasie (Washington, DC: Government Printing Office, 2010), Document 93.

94. Telegram from Secretary of State Dulles to the Department of State, Paris, February 6, 1959, FRUS, 1958–1960, Western Europe, Volume VII, Part 2, ed. Glenn W. LaFantasie (Washington, DC: Government Printing Office, 2010), Document 95.

95. Institut de France (1959, 344). See also Memorandum for the Record by the President's Assistant Staff Secretary (Eisenhower), March 3, 1959, FRUS, 1958–1960, Western European Integration and Security, Canada, Volume VII, Part 1, ed. Glenn W. LaFantasie (Washington, DC: Government Printing Office, 2010), Document 192.

96. Institut de France (1959, 345). These uncooperative moves on NATO were linked to French protestations of the US decision to abstain on a resolution on the right of the Algerian people to independence in the UNGA on December 13, 1958. Telegram from the Embassy in France to the Department of State, March 3, 1959, FRUS, 1958–1960, Western European Integration and Security, Canada, Volume VII, Part 1, ed. Glenn W. LaFantasie (Washington, DC: Government Printing Office, 2010), Document 192. See also Memorandum of Conversation, March 3, 1959, FRUS, 1958–1960, Western European Integration and Security, Canada, Volume VII, Part 1, ed. Glenn W. LaFantasie (Washington, DC: Government Printing Office, 2010), Document 192.

97. Memorandum of Conversation, March 3, 1959, FRUS, 1958–1960, Western European Integration and Security, Canada, Volume VII, Part 1, ed. Glenn W. LaFantasie (Washington: Government Printing Office, 2010), Document 192.

98. Editorial Note, FRUS, 1958–1960, Africa, Volume XIV, ed. Glenn W. LaFantasie (Washington, DC: Government Printing Office, 2010), Document 13.

99. Editorial Note, FRUS, 1958–1960, Western Europe, Volume VII, Part 2. ed. Glenn W. LaFantasie (Washington, DC: Government Printing Office, 2010), Document 107. Different aspects of Africa were discussed at the meeting, which had five sessions: Algeria, the French Community, the Maghreb, the Sahara, Guinea, arms, military strategy, and economic aid, all perceived and treated as linked to one another.

100. Memorandum of Conversation, Washington, March 31, 1959, FRUS, 1958–1960, Berlin Crisis, 1958–1959, Volume VIII, ed. Glenn W. LaFantasie (Washington, DC: Government Printing Office, 2010), Document 247.

101. Memorandum of Conversation, July 5, 1958, Department of State, Central Files, 611.51/7-558, FRUS, 1958–1960, Western Europe, Volume VII, Part 2, ed. Glenn W. LaFantasie (Washington, DC: Government Printing Office, 2010), Document 34.

102. Circular Telegram from the Delegation to the North Atlantic Council Ministerial Meeting to Certain Diplomatic Missions, April 4, 1959, FRUS, 1958–1960,

Berlin Crisis, 1958–1959, Volume VIII, ed. Glenn W. LaFantasie (Washington, DC: Government Printing Office, 2010), Document 252.

103. "The French Position on the Berlin Situation," Washington, April 7, 1959, FRUS, 1958– 1960, Berlin Crisis, 1958–1959, Volume VIII, ed. Glenn W. LaFantasie (Washington, DC: Government Printing Office, 2010), Document 256. During those same meetings in the spring, disagreements also emerged as to whether to link the issue of Berlin to that of disarmament, with the US in favor and French representatives against, "question[ing] the wisdom of linking general disarmament to German reunification and European security." Memorandum of Conversation, Washington, March 31, 1959, 4:45 p.m., FRUS, 1958–1960, Berlin Crisis, 1958–1959, Volume VIII, ed. Glenn W. LaFantasie (Washington, DC: Government Printing Office, 2010), Document 249.

104. Memorandum of Conversation, May 1, 1959, FRUS, 1958–1960, Western Europe, Volume VII, Part 2, ed. Glenn W. LaFantasie (Washington, DC: Government Printing Office, 2010), Document 109.

105. Memorandum of Conversation, July 5, 1958, Department of State, Central Files, 611.51/7-558, FRUS, 1958–1960, Western Europe, Volume VII, Part 2, ed. Glenn W. LaFantasie (Washington, DC: Government Printing Office, 2010), Document 34.

106. Institut de France (1959, 393).

107. Memorandum of Conversation, FRUS, 1958–1960, Western Europe, Volume VII, Part 2, Paris, September 2, 1959, ed. Glenn W. LaFantasie (Washington, DC: Government Printing Office, 2010), Document 129.

108. Institut de France (1959, 522, 525).

109. Letter from President Eisenhower to President de Gaulle, November 17, 1959, FRUS, 1958–1960, Western Europe, Volume VII, Part 2, ed. Glenn W. LaFantasie (Washington, DC: Government Printing Office, 2010), Document 146.

110. Letter from President Eisenhower to President de Gaulle, November 17, 1959, FRUS, 1958–1960, Western Europe, Volume VII, Part 2, ed. Glenn W. LaFantasie (Washington, DC: Government Printing Office, 2010), Document 146. In this personal letter to Eisenhower, De Gaulle combines somewhat inconsistently reassurances on the French position on the current US intentions but also casts doubt as to whether the present policy will be resilient to future unforeseen circumstances.

111. Institut de France (1959, 545).

112. Editorial Note, FRUS, 1958–1960, Western Europe, Volume VII, Part 2, ed. Glenn W. LaFantasie (Washington, DC: Government Printing Office, 2010), Document 156.

113. Sherman Kent, "The Summit Conference of 1960: An Intelligence Officer's View," declassified, https://webharvest.gov/peth04/20041021010531/http://www.cia.gov/csi/books/shermankent/8summit.html. Last accessed: July 13, 2022.

114. Letter from President Eisenhower to Prime Minister Macmillan, February 18, 1960, FRUS, 1958–1960, Western Europe, Volume VII, Part 2, ed. Glenn W. LaFantasie (Washington, DC: Government Printing Office, 2010), Document 158.

115. Institut de France (1962, 375). By January 1962, there was also a sense among US decision makers that France had "written Berlin off" and would not be willing to use

force on that issue. Source: Fax from Paris Embassy to Secretary of State, January 18, 1962, Papers of President Kennedy, NSF, Countries: France, Box 71, JFKPL.

116. Telegram from Paris Embassy to Secretary of State, February 14, 1962, Papers of President Kennedy, NSF, Countries: France, Box 71, JFKPL.

117. Institut de France (1962, 416).

118. Telegram from Paris to Secretary of State, May 28, 1962, Papers of President Kennedy, NSF, Countries: France, Box 71, JFKPL.

119. Memorandum of Conversation, President Kennedy and Couve de Murville, October 3, 1962, Papers of President Kennedy, NSF, Countries: France, Box 71A, JFKPL.

120. Political Consultation, President Kennedy and Couve de Murville, November 9, 1962, Papers of President Kennedy, NSF, Countries: France, Box 71A, JFKPL.

121. Institut de France (1963, 273).

122. Information Report, July 24, 1963, Papers of President Kennedy, NSF, Countries: France, Box 74, JFKPL.

123. "Radio and Television Address to the American People on the Nuclear Test Ban Treaty," July 26, 1963, JFKPL's website, https://www.JFKLibrary.org/archives/other-resources/john-f-kennedy-speeches/nuclear-test-ban-treaty-19630726. Last accessed October 13, 2021.

124. Institut de France (1963, 274).

125. Institut de France (1963, 283).

126. Institut de France (1963, 220–21).

127. Institut de France (1963, 237).

128. Institut de France (1963, 299).

129. Institut de France (1963, 248).

130. Institut de France (1963, 249).

131. Institut de France (1963, 257).

132. Institut de France (1964, 242–43).

133. Memcon, "Tripartite Discussion of Non-Dissemination," May 12, 1964, Secret, NSA Online Archive, https://nsarchive.gwu.edu/document/16321-document-26-memcon-tripartite-discussion-non. Last accessed October 13, 2021.

134. Institut de France (1964, 287).

135. Institut de France (1964, 298).

136. Institut de France (1965, 261).

137. Institut de France (1965, 285).

138. Institut de France (1965).

139. France also embraced a conflictual behavior toward the US on economic issues. At an International Monetary Fund (IMF) meeting in Tokyo, France accused the US of fostering inflation in other countries with their deficits, while rejecting the US request for greater monetary contributions from IMF members (Kolodziej, 1972, 119). In January 1965, France asked that the US convert $150 million of French withholdings into gold, even though the US had asked France not to do so. In a press conference the next month, De Gaulle accused the American ally of "shift[ing] the burden of its indebtedness to others," while "[i]ts behavior effectively defined the rules for the international system," whereas "sustained deficits [. . .]

[had] significant and adverse effects on the national economy of the European states (Kolodziej, 1972, 11–12). De Gaulle also proposed a return to the gold standard. In May of the same year, reports surfaced of an increased Anti-Americanism in French public opinion (Telegram from Embassy in Paris to Secretary of State, May 19, 1965, Papers of Lyndon B. Johnson President, NSF, Country File: France, Box Number 171, LBJPL). Disagreements and discussions on the monetary system between France and the US continued in 1965 (Memorandum of Conversation, July 8, 1965, FRUS, 1964–1968, Volume XII, Western Europe, ed. Glenn W. LaFantasie, Washington, DC: Government Printing Office, 2010, Document 50).

140. Institut de France (1962, 400).

141. Those talks had been interrupted on June 11 when the Soviets demanded to be treated as members of the Common Market. CIA Background Note, September 17, 1962, Papers of President Kennedy, NSF, Countries: France, Box 71A, JFKPL.

142. In October 1963, France voted with the US against giving China a permanent seat at the UN. In December, France stated to not want to recognize China but to welcome a distention of relations with the country (Institut de France, 1963, 328).

143. Martin (2008, 78). In January, for example, American documents reveal that Americans had only heard unconfirmed rumors about the impending recognition of China. Telegraph from the Embassy in Paris to the Department of State, January 9, 1964, Papers of Lyndon B. Johnson President, NSF, Country File: France, Box Number 169, LBJPL.

144. CIA Office of Research and Reports. "The Effect of French Recognition of Communist China on Sino-French Trade Prospects," February 1964, Papers of Lyndon B. Johnson President, NSF, Country File: France, Box Number 176, LBJPL.

145. "France Forces Taiwan to Break Diplomatic Ties; Taipei Acts after Being Told Paris Plans to Exchange Missions with Peking; De Gaulle Is Relieved; Embarrassing Two Chinas Situation Is Resolved Hands Freed in Asia," New York Times, February 11, 1964.

146. Telegram from the Embassy in France to the Department of State, February 12, 1964, FRUS, 1964–1968, Volume XII, Western Europe, ed. Glenn W. LaFantasie (Washington, DC: Government Printing Office, 2010), Document 25.

147. Institut de France (1965).

148. Institut de France (1964, Texts and Speeches).

149. "DeGaulle Proposes China Join a Plan to Neutralize Vietnam, Laos, Cambodia; Policy Defended; General Asserts Link with Peking Is Vital to Ease Tension," New York Times, February 1, 1964. See also Telegraph from Paris Embassy to Secretary of State, February 1, 1964, Papers of Lyndon B. Johnson President, NSF, Country File: France, Box Number 169, LBJPL.

150. Telegraph from the Embassy in Paris to the Department of State, January 10, 1964, Papers of Lyndon B. Johnson President, NSF, Country File: France, Box Number 169, LBJPL.

151. Institut de France (1965, 236).

152. Institut de France (1965, 242).

153. Institut de France (1965, 310).

154. Information Report, July 24, 1963, Papers of President Kennedy, NSF, Country: France, Box 74, JFKPL.

155. On the effects of nuclear weapons acquisition on countries' behaviors, including (but not limited to) conflictual behavior, see Bell (2015).

156. Institut de France (1962, 500). See also Telegram from Paris to Secretary of State, July 3, 1962, Papers of President Kennedy, NSF, Countries: France, Box 71A, JFKPL.

157. Institut de France (1964, 213).

158. Martin (2008, 56–57).

159. Martin (2008, 79).

160. Address to the Nation on the Nuclear Test Ban Treaty, July 26, 1963, JFKPL. Available at https://www.jfklibrary.org/learn/about-jfk/historic-speeches/televised-address-on-nuclear-test-ban-treaty#:~:text=In%20his%20speech%20the%20President,nati ons%20not%20currently%20possessing%20them. Last accessed: July 17, 2022.

161. Larkin (1997, 223).

162. Kahler (2014, 273–74).

163. Creswell (2006).

164. Hanrieder and Auton (1980, 123); Keeler (1990).

165. Menon (2000).

166. Creswell and Trachtenberg (2003).

167. Zelikow and May (2018, 179).

168. COPDAB codes interactions as happening in one of the following issue areas: symbolic, economic, military, cultural, natural resources, minority affairs, and diplomatic relations. A simple test of proportions between the two periods reveals that in five of these categories (symbolic, economic, military, cultural, natural resources), there is no statistically significant difference in the mean number of issues present in the interaction before and after 1962. Importantly, this is the case for traditionally salient issues such as those pertaining to the military and economic areas. For the diplomatic issue area and the minority affairs issue area, where there is a statistically significant difference, the incidence is slightly higher for the period post-1962 (p value < .001 in both cases), a finding that is not consistent with the hypothesis that volatility should derive from an increase in the frequency of issues present.

169. Memorandum for the President on Possible DeGaulle Visit, September 17, 1962, Papers of President Kennedy, NSF, Countries; France, Box 71A, JFKPL.

170. See, for example, Memorandum of Conversation, First Tripartite Talks on Africa, April 16, 1959, FRUS, 1958–1960, Africa, Volume XIV, p. 44. In 1956 in London, France explicitly connected the Suez crisis with Algeria, claiming events in both countries were intertwined into a North African crisis (Zelikow and May, 2018, 178, footnote 9). In July 1957, however, France protested against what it saw as American interferences on French domestic politics, as US decision makers made statements in support of Algerian rebels (Institut de France, 1957, 415).

171. Creswell and Trachtenberg (2003, 55)

172. See, for example, Institut de France (1963, 274).

173. Memorandum of Conversation, May 1, 1959, FRUS, 1958–1960, Western Europe, Volume VII, Part 2, ed. Glenn W. LaFantasie (Washington, DC: Government Printing Office, 2010), Document 109.

174. Memorandum of Conversation, May 1, 1959, FRUS, 1958–1960, Western Europe, Volume VII, Part 2, ed. Glenn W. LaFantasie (Washington, DC: Government Printing Office, 2010), Document 109.

175. Memorandum of Conversation, May 1, 1959, FRUS, 1958–1960, Western Europe, Volume VII, Part 2, ed. Glenn W. LaFantasie (Washington, DC: Government Printing Office, 2010), Document 109.

176. Horowitz, Ellis, and Stam (2015).

177. Right after assuming power, De Gaulle found numerous existing agreements linking France with the Atlantic Organization and the European community, which he maintained (Institut de France, 1964, 211). A similar continuity in the first years of De Gaulle's power could be found in his policies on the Common Market (Hanrieder and Auton, 1980, 124). American decision makers also noticed that De Gaulle "refused to integrate the air defense of France with NATO and refused to permit stockpiling of nuclear warheads within French territory unless under French control" but did so "as did earlier French governments" (National Security Council Report, Statement of US Policy on France, November 4, 1959, FRUS, 1958–1960, Western Europe, Volume VII, Part 2, ed. Glenn W. LaFantasie [Washington, DC: Government Printing Office, 2010], Document 145). Similarly, according to American officials, France's nuclear weapons plans had "begun long before de Gaulle returned to power in 1958" (Intelligence Report Prepared in the Bureau of Intelligence and Research, December 6, 1960, FRUS, 1958–1960, Western Europe, Volume VII, Part 2, ed. Glenn W. LaFantasie [Washington, DC: Government Printing Office, 2010], Document 201). In sum, American officials concluded that while they feared that De Gaulle would have acted "independently and perhaps against our interests [. . .] [s]ince his return to power he has not reverted to these tactics." Memorandum from the Assistant Secretary of State for European Affairs (Merchant) to Secretary of State Herter, May 5, 1959, FRUS, 1958–1960, Western Europe, Volume VII, Part 2, ed. Glenn W. LaFantasie (Washington, DC: Government Printing Office, 2010), Document 111.

178. Nicholas Wahl letter to Gavin, August 6, 1961, Papers of President Kennedy, NSF, Countries: France, Box 70A, JFKPL.

179. Change in Source of Leader Support (CHISOLS) dataset (Mattes, Leeds, and Matsumura, 2016). See in particular the dataset's Codebook, page 8. Available at http://www.chisols.org/users-manual.html. Last accessed: July 14, 2022.

180. In 1958 De Gaulle remarked on the power superiority of the two superpowers as well: "Each nation had its day. 'Yours is now—you and the Russians.'" Memorandum of Conversation, Paris, July 5, 1958, FRUS, 1958–1960, Western Europe, Volume VII, Part 2, ed. Glenn W. LaFantasie (Washington, DC: Government Printing Office, 2010), Document 34.

181. "France Will Take Full NATO Membership Again, with Greater Military Role," New York Times, March 11, 2009.

182. "Checklist of Factors and International Relationships involved in President De Gaulle's Impending Attack on NATO," March 4, 1966, Papers of Lyndon B. Johnson President, NSF, Country File: France, Box Number 177 [1 of 2], LBJPL.

183. Letter to De Gaulle, August 30, 1958, FRUS, 1958–1960, Western Europe, Volume VII, Part 2, Document 197.

184. France was extremely careful to keep the decision to recognize communist China secret from the United States (Martin, 2008, 70–71). As late as January 1965, Americans did not anticipate that France was going to take action on NATO. "Therefore, for the immediate future there is not much ground for anticipating any sudden French move in regard to NATO short of what De Gaulle would call a crisis or a drama. [. . .] Short of this he will undoubtedly wait until (A) the French nuclear force is really operational and (B) until close to 1969 North Atlantic Treaty date." Telegram from the Embassy in France to the Department of State, January 5, 1965. FRUS, 1964–1968, Volume XII, Western Europe, ed. Glenn W. LaFantasie (Washington, DC: Government Printing Office, 2010), Document 42.

185. Telegram from Paris to the Department of State, February 25, 1966, Papers of Lyndon B. Johnson President, NSF, Country File: France, Box Number 177 [1 of 2], LBJPL.

186. Telegram from Paris to Secretary of State, May 10, 1962, Papers of President Kennedy, NSF, Countries; France, Box 71, JFKPL.

187. "French Foreign Policy," National Intelligence Estimate Memo, June 2, 1965, Papers of Lyndon B. Johnson President, NSF, National Intelligence Estimates Box 5, LBJPL.

188. Telegraph from Secretary of State to Paris Embassy, March 12, 1964, Papers of Lyndon B. Johnson President, NSF, Country File: France, Box Number 169, LBJPL.

189. Memorandum for the Secretary of State from Ambassador Bohlen, March 19, 1964, Papers of Lyndon B. Johnson President, NSF, Country File: France, Box Number 169, LBJPL.

190. "All addressee agencies should take special measures to prevent U.S. activities in France which could needlessly embarrass United States relations with France. A study should be made to provide a complete catalogue of activities with respect to France being undertaken or planned to be undertaken by the United States, whether covert, clandestine, or overt, that could be regarded as illegal or that could cause embarrassment to the United States if the French decided to make an issue of them." National Security Action Memorandum No. 336, August 6, 1965, FRUS, 1964–1968, Volume XII, Western Europe, ed. Glenn W. LaFantasie (Washington, DC: Government Printing Office, 2010), Document 51.

191. "Initial Reactions to DeGaulle's Visit to Moscow," June 22, 1966, Papers of Lyndon B. Johnson President, Ex Co 81 France, 6/15/64, Box 30, LBJPL. Gallup Poll, July 8, 1966, "DeGaulle's Policies Seen Alienating Many Americans," Papers of Lyndon B. Johnson President, Ex Co 81 France, 6/15/64, Box 30, LBJPL.

192. Memorandum from the President's Special Assistant for National Security Affairs (Bundy) to Secretary of Defense McNamara, April 8, 1964, FRUS, 1964–1968, Volume XII, Western Europe, ed. Glenn W. LaFantasie (Washington, DC: Government Printing Office, 2010), Document 28.

193. Telegram from the Embassy in France to the Department of State, March 11, 1965, FRUS, 1964–1968, Volume XII, Western Europe, ed. Glenn W. LaFantasie (Washington, DC: Government Printing Office, 2010), Document 45.
194. Telegram from Paris Embassy to the Secretary of State, March 3, 1965, Papers of Lyndon B. Johnson President, NSF, Country File: France, Box Number 172, LBJPL.
195. Telegram from Paris Embassy to the Secretary of State, March 3, 1065, LBJ Library, Box 172.
196. Ellison (2007, 1).
197. "France Will Take Full NATO Membership Again, with Greater Military Role," *New York Times*, March 11, 2009.
198. The literature on alliance is rich and voluminous. See, for example, Snyder (1984); Walt (1990); Gowa (1994); Reed (1997); Leeds (2003); Leeds, Mattes, and Vogel (2009); Long and Leeds (2006); Mattes (2012); Fordham and Poast (2016).

Chapter 6

1. This phenomenon constitutes an example of nonlinearity: the consequences of actors' behaviors go beyond the linear sum of those behaviors, to include also the impressions and interpretations that those behaviors evoke (Jervis, 1998).
2. Jervis (1997, 586).
3. Jervis (1998, 165–76).
4. Betts (2000).
5. For a seminal work in political science on signal and noise and their impact on strategy, see Wohlstetter (1962).
6. Fitzsimmons (2006).
7. Betts (1982); Pillar (2004); Byman (2005).
8. See, for example, Fitzsimmons (2006) and McMaster (2015).
9. Friedman (2019).
10. Porter (2018).
11. Porter (2018, 11).
12. Indeed, arguably, habit represents the (artificial) taming of uncertainty: "Where the logic of habit predominates, international relations have less agency, less rationality, and less uncertainty than other logics would lead us to expect" (Hopf, 2010, 540).
13. McMaster (2015).
14. Hoffman (2002, 376).
15. Uslaner (2002).
16. Kydd (2000, 346).
17. Rathbun (2011, 25). Whether a state trusts another or not depends also on its internal configuration, and in particular on the presence of left-oriented groups, historically more prone to trusting (Rathbun, 2011, 7).
18. See, respectively, Hoffman (2006), Güvenç and Özel (2012), Wheeler (2009), Larson (1997), and Rathbun (2011).

19. Cooperation might matter greatly to stave off proliferation (Mattiacci, Mehta, and Whitlark, 2021), and states' domestic calculations matter to determine whether actors will indeed offer cooperation to proliferating countries (Mattiacci, 2021).

20. "How Months of Miscalculation Led the U.S. and Iran to the Brink of War," *New York Times*, February 27, 2020.

21. Escalation entails "an increase in the intensity or scope of conflict that crosses threshold(s) *considered significant* by one or more of the participants" (Morgan et al., 2008, 9). Emphasis added.

22. Smoke (1977, 268–89); Herz (1959, 249); Baker (2019).

23. Singer (1982), for instance, lists possible causes including capabilities, alliances, proximity, and systemic interdependence. Rasler and Thompson (2006) point instead to the presence of contested territory, while Colaresi and Thompson (2002) point to existing conflict, and Geller (1990) points to nuclear weapons possession.

24. For a review of the debate, see Simmons (1998).

25. See, for instance, Downs, Rocke, and Barsoom (1996) and Hathaway (2007).

26. Von Stein (2005).

27. See, for example, Bull (2012), Nelson (2010), and Avdeyeva (2012).

28. Among others, see Dixon (1993), Downs and Rocke (1995), Haftel and Thompson (2013), and Simmons (2002).

29. See, for example, Chiba, Johnson, and Leeds (2015).

30. Mercer (1996).

31. For a review of the research on reputation and its importance in world politics, see Dafoe, Renshon, and Huth (2014).

32. Jervis (1982); Huth (1997); Sartori (2013).

33. Weisiger and Yarhi-Milo (2015); Hopf (1994); Press (2005). Guisinger and Smith (2002), Lupton (2018), and Renshon, Dafoe, and Huth (2018), for example, compare leaders and states' reputation for resolve in crises. Tang (2005) argues that politicians display a cult of reputation, but reputation per se cannot matter due to the anarchical nature of the system.

34. Lupton (2018).

35. Respectively, Hopf (1994) demonstrates that Soviet leaders "did not infer from US actions in peripheral regions anything about likely behavior in Europe or East Asia." Weisiger and Yarhi-Milo (2015) show that the effects of past actions become weaker with time. And Mercer (1996) argues that countries assess other countries' reputations based on whether they are allies or rivals, not on their actions per se.

36. On mad man theory, see McManus (2019) and Sagan and Suri (2003).

37. Kertzer, Renshon, and Yarhi-Milo (2021).

38. Mercer (1996).

39. In commitment problems, "incentives ex ante to make promises about ex post behavior clash with the incentives ex post to act on promises made" (Gartzke and Gleditsch, 2004, 779–80).

40. Martin (2000) argues that legislatures' "interferences" with the foreign policy decision-making process add credibility to the commitments of the executive in democracies by constraining the executive. Lipson (2005) argues that democratic

institutions make democracies "reliable partners" because they inspire confidence that the agreements taken will stick. Leeds (1999) refers instead to democracies' need to be accountable to their domestic publics and the "lack of policymaking flexibility characteristic of democratic institutional structures." Leeds, Mattes, and Vogel (2009) also refer to greater "institutional constraints" that democracies face when changing policies. Chiba, Johnson, and Leeds (2015) argue that "leaders of democratic states experience high costs from violating past commitments."

41. Gartzke and Gleditsch (2004), for example, refer to the propensity of democratic regimes to policy cycling and to be captured by special interests to explain the commitment problems that they face. Still others argue that countries will likely be proactive and can decide to commit only to those agreements that they know either they can credibly commit to or that can truly work as commitment devices. See, for example, Chiba, Johnson, and Leeds (2015). Simmons and Danner (2010) argue instead that autocracies, precisely because they tend to be unaccountable, are more likely to be willing to commit to the International Criminal Court, so as to tie their hands in negotiations with domestic groups seeking to seize power.

42. It is also crucial to parse out, as this book has done, different institutional features of democracies to understand how each feature affects behavior. On the need to parse out institutional characteristics, see Weeks (2014). Mattes and Rodriguez (2014) dissect autocratic institutions and find variation in the way in which such institutions shape credible commitments.

43. Fearon (1994); Tomz (2007).

44. Kertzer and Brutger (2016), however, show that understanding audience cost components (the inconsistency costs and the belligerent costs) suggests that we might be overestimating how much domestic audiences actually worry about inconsistencies. Thomson (2016) also finds that inconsistencies are less likely to be punished when those inconsistencies take place during crises that do not threaten national security.

45. Schultz (2012); Gartzke and Lupu (2012).

46. Brutger and Kertzer (2018), for example, already find that hawks are more concerned about inconsistencies, while doves worry about belligerence and interventionism.

47. Potter and Baum (2013). Similarly, in the US, the institution of the presidency gives presidents a unique informational advantage and they can use it to manipulate the visibility of their behavior, at times aiding them in paying less of a price for inconsistencies (Levendusky and Horowitz, 2012). On the US presidents' ability to leverage new information, see also Levy et al. (2015). In the UK, by contrast, the prime minister seems to have less of an opportunity to do so (Davies and Johns, 2013).

48. Weeks (2008).

49. In particular, research shows that countries' actions, rooted in their domestic groups' preferences, shape the distribution of resources in the international system and that this distribution, in turn, shapes domestic interests (Braumoeller, 2012, 17).

50. For a review of the segregation model, see Schelling (2006).

51. Wendt (1999).

52. In particular, some have argued that in unipolar systems conflicts and wars between states are less likely because no state has the power to balance against the unipole and

therefore "the existing distribution of capabilities generates incentives for coopera-tion" (Wohlforth, 1999, 38).

53. Monteiro (2012a, 2014).

54. For a review, see Aronson and Huth (2017). On the role of relative capabilities in civil wars, see also Butler and Gates (2009).

55. Parkinson and Zaks (2018).

56. See, respectively, Mampilly (2012), Staniland (2014), Pearlman (2011), and Christia (2012).

57. Koubi et al. (2014).

58. Cunningham, Skrede Gleditsch, and Salehyan (2009).

59. Holtermann (2016).

60. Buhaug (2006).

61. Buhaug, Gates, and Lujala (2009).

62. Clayton (2013).

63. Weinstein (2006). Others have found instead that rebels with greater relative capabil-ities have also greater access to alternative strategies and might therefore be less likely to rely on this one strategy (Wood, 2010, 2014).

64. Mampilly (2012); Flynn and Stewart (2018). See also Stewart (2018) and Arjona (2016).

65. Sullivan and Karreth (2015); Jones (2017).

66. Salehyan, Gleditsch, and Cunningham (2011).

67. See, respectively, San-Akca (2016) and Toukan (2017).

68. For example, one way for rebels to ask for external support is to engage in rebel diplo-macy, either contacting countries' decision makers directly or using social media. See, in particular, Jones and Mattiacci (2019). Governments in civil wars too, however, can fight back, engaging in public diplomacy; see Mattiacci and Jones (2020).

69. See Szekely (2016), Popovic (2018) (who provides an example of an agenda that does not completely overlap), and Karlén (2019).

70. On rebels' defections vis-à-vis their state sponsor, see, for example, Popovic (2017).

71. Khong (2020). For a recent example, see Mario Del Pero, "Afghanistan and the Lessons That History Does Not Offer," The Hill, September 14, 2021.

72. See, among others, Bader (2016), Stenslie and Chen (2016), and Goldstein (2020). Jackobson (2016), however, notes how the increased influence of different domestic interests might be changing the ability of the Chinese leadership to pursue a stable foreign policy.

73. "The Elements of the China Challenge," Policy Planning Staff, Department of State, November 2020, 8–9.

74. Stein (2010, 14).

75. "How Americans View Trust, Facts, and Democracy Today," Pew Research Center, February 19, 2020.

Appendix

1. The WEIS data set goes to 1992, but for those dyads for which it is available, I use the Thompson data that employs the WEIS ontology up to 1998.
2. Inter-university Consortium for Political and Social Research (ICPSR) study 7767, Azar (1979).
3. ICPSR study 5211, McClelland (1978).
4. Brandt, Freeman, and Schrodt (2011, note 28).
5. See Box-Steffensmeier et al. (2014, Chapters 5 and 7).
6. Specifically, autoregressive processes indicate that a shock will die out exponentially at a rate equal to the estimated coefficient, while moving average processes indicate that the impact of a previous shock dies after a certain number of periods. Both processes can be present in one time series (Box-Steffensmeier et al., 2014, 129–30).
7. See Greene (2003, 609–24). For a description of the tests run, see the Appendix.
8. See, in particular, Box-Steffensmeier et al. (2014, Chapters 2, 5, and 7).
9. In particular, I compare the standard deviations of the whole series to the standard deviation of the residuals from a Box-Jenkins procedure applied to the series, once all the other forms of change have been removed. As I describe below, I propose this as a more reliable measure of volatility.
10. The residuals emerge from simulations of a correctly specified Box-Jenkins procedure on ARIMA time series, thus displaying mean equal to zero and constant variance.
11. See, for example, Freeman (1989) and Shellman (2004).
12. At times, the standard deviation of the time series of residuals from the Box-Jenkins procedure is not constant, and thus the series exhibits instead heteroskedasticity. I test for the presence of heterogeneity in the variance of the residuals using the Lagrange multiplier test for conditional heteroskedasticity. Generalized autoregressive conditional heteroskedasticity (GARCH) models allow scholars to further investigate variance in the residuals as an autoregressive moving average process, even adding covariates. GARCH models, however, do not make it possible to leverage cross-country variation. Moreover, most of the variables of interest in international politics vary meaningfully on an annual basis. Therefore, using those covariates as predictors of weekly or monthly series would not gain a lot of explanatory leverage, as these predictors do not vary much. Using panel data while employing a summary measure of volatility allows me instead to both leverage cross-country variation and limit the pitfalls of temporal aggregation in time series.

Bibliography

Achen, Christopher H. 2005. "Let's Put Garbage-Can Regressions and Garbage-Can Probits Where They Belong." *Conflict Management and Peace Science* 22 (4): 327–39.

Adcock, Robert. 2001. "Measurement Validity: A Shared Standard for Qualitative and Quantitative Research." *American Political Science Review* 95 (3): 529–46.

Adler, Emanuel. 1997. "Imagined (Security) Communities: Cognitive Regions in International Relations." *Millennium* 26 (2): 249–77.

Allison, Graham T. 1971. *Essence of Decision: Explaining the Cuban Missile Crisis.* New York: Pearson.

Arjona, Ana. 2016. *Rebelocracy: Social Order in the Colombian Civil War.* Cambridge: Cambridge University Press.

Aronson, Jacob, and Paul K. Huth. 2017. "The Size of Rebel and State Armed Forces in Internal Conflicts: Measurement and Implications." In *Peace and Conflict*, edited by D.A. Backer, R. Bhavnani, & Paul Huth, 46–57. New York: Routledge.

Arrow, Kenneth J. 1951. *Social Choice and Individual Values.* New Haven, CT: Yale University Press.

Art, Robert J. 2009. "The Fungibility of Force." In *The Use of Force: Military Power and International Politics*, edited by Robert J. Art and Kenneth N. Waltz, 3–20. Lanham, MD: Rowman & Littlefield.

Austin, John Langshaw. 1975. "How to Do Things with Words." *Oxford: Oxford University Press.*

Avdeyeva, Olga A. 2012. "Does Reputation Matter for States' Compliance with International Treaties? States Enforcement of Anti-Trafficking Norms." *International Journal of Human Rights* 16 (2): 298–320.

Azar, Edward. 1979. "Conflict and Peace Data Bank (COPDAB), 1948–78." *Interuniversity Consortium for Political and Social Research*, [distributor], June 3, 2009. https://doi.org/10.3886/ICPSR07767.v4.

Badel, Laurence. 2012. "France's Renewed Commitment to Commercial Diplomacy in the 1960s." *Contemporary European History* 21 (1): 61–78.

Bader, Jeffrey A. 2016. *How Xi Jinping Sees the World . . . and Why.* Washington, DC: Brookings Institution.

Baker, Joshua. 2019. "The Empathic Foundations of Security Dilemma De-Escalation." *Political Psychology* 40 (6): 1251–66.

Baldwin, David. 2002. "Power and International Relations." In *Handbook of International Relations*, edited by Walter Carlsnaes, Thomas Risse, and Beth A. Simmons, 273–98. Beverly Hills, CA: Sage.

Baldwin, David A. 2016. *Power and International Relations: A Conceptual Approach.* Princeton, NJ: Princeton University Press.

Barnett, Michael, and Raymond Duvall. 2005. "Power in International Politics." *International Organization* 59 (1): 39–75.

Bartolini, Stefano, and Paul Mair. 1990. *Identity, Competition, and Electoral Availability: The Stabilisation of European Electorates 1885–1985*. Cambridge: Cambridge University Press.

Bas, Muhammet A., and Robert Schub. 2017. "The Theoretical and Empirical Approaches to Uncertainty and Conflict in International Relations." In *Oxford Research Encyclopedia of Politics*. Oxford: Oxford University Press.

Bates, Genevieve, Ipek Cinar, and Monika Nalepa. 2019. "Accountability by Numbers: A New Global Transitional Justice Dataset (1946–2016)." *Perspectives on Politics* 18 (1): 1–24.

Bayer, Resat. 2006. "Diplomatic Exchange Data Set, V2006." *http://correlatesofwar.org*.

B.C. 1956. "The Waning Power of France in Vietnam." *World Today* 12 (2): 50–58.

Beardsley, Kyle, and Victor Asal. 2009. "Winning with the Bomb." *Journal of Conflict Resolution* 53 (2): 278–301.

Beasley, Ryan K., and Juliet Kaarbo. 2014. "Explaining Extremity in the Foreign Policies of Parliamentary Democracies." *International Studies Quarterly* 58 (4): 729–40.

Bell, Curtis. 2011. "Buying Support and Buying Time: The Effect of Regime Consolidation on Public Goods Provision." *International Studies Quarterly* 55 (3): 625–46.

Bell, Mark S. 2015. "Beyond Emboldenment: How Acquiring Nuclear Weapons Can Change Foreign Policy." *International Security* 40 (1): 87–119.

Bell, Mark S., and Nicholas L. Miller. 2015. "Questioning the Effect of Nuclear Weapons on Conflict." *Journal of Conflict Resolution* 59 (1): 74–92.

Bennett, D. Scott, and Timothy Nordstrom. 2000. "Foreign Policy Substitutability and Internal Economic Problems in Enduring Rivalries." *Journal of Conflict Resolution* 44 (1): 33–61.

Berry, William D., Matt Golder, and Daniel Milton. 2012. "Improving Tests of Theories Positing Interaction." *Journal of Politics* 74 (3): 653–71.

Betts, Richard. 1982. *Surprise Attack: Lessons for Defense Planning*. Washington, DC: Brookings Institution.

Betts, Richard K. 2000. "Is Strategy an Illusion?" *International Security* 25 (2): 5–50.

Birnir, Kristin. 2007. "Divergence in Diversity? The Dissimilar Effects of Cleavages on Electoral Politics in New Democracies." *American Journal of Political Science* 51 (3): 602–19.

Blainey, Geoffrey. 1988. *Causes of War*. New York: Simon and Schuster.

Blake, Daniel J. 2013. "Thinking Ahead: Government Time Horizons and the Legalization of International Investment Agreements." *International Organization* 67 (4): 827.

Boschee, Elizabeth, Jennifer Lautenschlager, Sean O'Brien, Steve Shellman, James Starz, and Michael Ward. 2015. "ICEWS Coded Event Data," Harvard Dataverse, V35, https://doi.org/10.7910/DVN/28075.

Box, George E. P., and Gwilym M. Jenkins. 1970. *Time Series Analysis: Forecasting and Control*. San Francisco: Holden-Day.

Box-Steffensmeier, Janet M., John R. Freeman, Matthew P. Hitt, and Jon C. W. Pevehouse. 2014. *Time Series Analysis for the Social Sciences*. Cambridge: Cambridge University Press.

Brambor, Thomas, William Roberts Clark, and Matt Golder. 2006. "Understanding Interaction Models: Improving Empirical Analyses." *Political Analysis* 14 (1): 63–82.

Brandt, Patrick, John Freeman, and Phillip Schrodt. 2011. "Real Time, Time Series Forecasting of Inter- and Intra-State Political Conflict." *Conflict Management and Peace Science* 28 (1): 41–64.

Braumoeller, Bear. 2012. *The Great Powers and the International System.* Cambridge: Cambridge University Press.

Braumoeller, Bear F. 2004. "Hypothesis Testing and Multiplicative Interaction Terms." *International Organization* 58 (4): 807–20.

Braumoeller, Bear F. 2006. "Explaining Variance; or, Stuck in a Moment We Can't Get Out Of." *Political Analysis* 14 (3): 268–90.

Braumoeller, Bear F., and Gary Goertz. 2000. "The Methodology of Necessary Conditions." *American Journal of Political Science* 44 (4): 844–58.

Brecher, Michael, Blema Steinberg, and Janice Stein. 1969. "A Framework for Research on Foreign Policy Behavior." *Journal of Conflict Resolution* 13 (1): 75–101.

Brecher, Michael, and Jonathan Wilkenfeld. 1997. *A Study of Crisis.* Ann Arbor: University of Michigan Press.

Brecher, Michael, Jonathan Wilkenfeld, Kyle Beardsley, Patrick James, and David Quinn. 2016. "International Crisis Behavior Data Codebook, Version 13." http://sites.duke. edu/icbdata/data-collections.

Brutger, Ryan, and Joshua D. Kertzer. 2018. "A Dispositional Theory of Reputation Costs." *International Organization* 72 (3): 693–724.

Bueno De Mesquita, Bruce, and Alastair Smith. 2005. *The Logic of Political Survival.* Cambridge, MA: MIT Press.

Bueno De Mesquita, Bruce, James D. Morrow Bruce, Randolph M. Siverson, and Alastair Smith. 1999. "An Institutional Explanation of the Democratic Peace." *American Political Science Review* 93 (4): 791–807.

Buhaug, Halvard. 2006. "Relative Capability and Rebel Objective in Civil War." *Journal of Peace Research* 43 (6): 691–708.

Buhaug, Halvard, Scott Gates, and Päivi Lujala. 2009. "Geography, Rebel Capability, and the Duration of Civil Conflict." *Journal of Conflict Resolution* 53 (4): 544–69.

Bull, Hedley. 2012. *The Anarchical Society: A Study of Order in World Politics.* London: Macmillan International Higher Education.

Bunge, Mario. 2004. "How Does It Work? The Search for Explanatory Mechanisms." *Philosophy of the Social Sciences* 34 (2): 182–210.

Burr, William, and Jeffrey T. Richelson. 2001. "Whether to 'Strangle the Baby in the Cradle': The United States and the Chinese Nuclear Program, 1960–64." *International Security* 25 (3): 54–99.

Butler, Christopher, and Scott Gates. 2009. "Asymmetry, Parity, and (Civil) War: Can International Theories of Power Help Us Understand Civil War?" *International Interactions* 35 (3): 330–40.

Byman, Daniel. 2005. "Strategic Surprise and the September 11 Attacks." *Annual Review of Political Science* 8: 145–70.

Campello, Daniela, and Cesar Zucco. 2020. *The Volatility Curse: Exogenous Shocks and Representation in Resource-Rich Democracies.* Cambridge: Cambridge University Press.

Carmines, Edward G., and James A. Woods. 2005. "Validity Assessment." In *Encyclopedia of Social Measurement,* edited by Kimberly Kempf-Leonard, 933–37. Amsterdam: Elsevier.

Carson, Austin. 2016. "Facing Off and Saving Face: Covert Intervention and Escalation Management in the Korean War." *International Organization* 70 (1): 103–31.

Carson, Austin, and Keren Yarhi-Milo. 2017. "Covert Communication: The Intelligibility and Credibility of Signaling in Secret." *Security Studies* 26 (1): 124–56.

Chapman, Terrence L., Johannes Urpelainen, and Scott Wolford. 2012. "International Bargaining, Endogenous Domestic Constraints, and Democratic Accountability." *Journal of Theoretical Politics* 25 (2): 1–24.

Cheng-Chwee, Kuik. 2008. "The Essence of Hedging: Malaysia and Singapore's Response to a Rising China." *Contemporary Southeast Asia: A Journal of International and Strategic Affairs* 30 (2): 159–85.

Chiba, Daina, Jesse C. Johnson, and Brett Ashley Leeds. 2015. "Careful Commitments: Democratic States and Alliance Design." *Journal of Politics* 77 (4): 968–82.

Chow, Clare, and Rakesh Sarin. 2001. "Comparative Ignorance and the Ellsberg Paradox." *Journal of Risk and Uncertainty* 22 (2): 129–39.

Chowdhury, Abdur R. 1993. "Does Exchange Rate Volatility Depress Trade Flows? Evidence from Error-Correction Models." *Review of Economics and Statistics* 75 (4): 700–706.

Christia, Fotini. 2012. *Alliance Formation in Civil Wars*. Cambridge: Cambridge University Press.

Cioffi-Revilla, Claudio. 1998. *Politics and Uncertainty: Theory, Models and Applications*. Cambridge: Cambridge University Press.

Citrin, Jack. 2001. "Conflict/Consensus." In *International Encyclopedia of the Social Behavioral Sciences*, edited by Neil J. Smelser and Paul B. Baltes, 2547–50. Amsterdam: Elsevier.

Clare, Joe. 2010. "Ideological Fractionalization and the International Conflict Behavior of Parliamentary Democracies." *International Studies Quarterly* 54 (4): 965–87.

Clark, David, Timothy Nordstrom, and William Reed. 2008. "Substitution Is in the Variance: Resources and Foreign Policy Choice." *American Journal of Political Science* 52 (4): 763–73.

Clarke, Kevin A., and Randall W. Stone. 2008. "Democracy and the Logic of Political Survival." *American Political Science Review* 102 (3): 387–92.

Clayton, Govinda. 2013. "Relative Rebel Strength and the Onset and Outcome of Civil War Mediation." *Journal of Peace Research* 50 (5): 609–22.

Colaresi, Michael. 2004. "When Doves Cry: International Rivalry, Unreciprocated Cooperation, and Leadership Turnover." *American Journal of Political Science* 48 (3): 557–70.

Colaresi, Michael. 2005. *Scare Tactics: The Politics of International Rivalry*. Syracuse, NY: Syracuse University Press.

Colaresi, Michael. 2012. "A Boom with Review: How Retrospective Oversight Increases the Foreign Policy Ability of Democracies." *American Journal of Political Science* 56 (3): 671–89.

Colaresi, Michael, Karen Rasler, and William Thompson. 2007. *Strategic Rivalries in World Politics: Position, Space and Conflict Escalation*. Cambridge: Cambridge University Press.

Colaresi, Michael, and William R. Thompson. 2002a. "Strategic Rivalries, Protracted Conflict, and Crisis Escalation." *Journal of Peace Research* 39 (3): 263–87.

Colaresi, Michael, and W. R. Thompson. 2002b. "Hot Spots or Hot Hands? Serial Crisis Behavior, Escalating Risks, and Rivalry." *Journal of Politics* 64 (4): 1175–98.

Copelovitch, Mark S. 2010. "Master or Servant? Common Agency and the Political Economy of IMF Lending." *International Studies Quarterly* 54 (1): 49–77.

Cranmer, Skylar, Bruce Desmarais, and Elizabeth J. Menninga. 2012. "Complex Dependencies in the Alliance Network." *Conflict Management and Peace Science* 29 (3): 279–313.

Creswell, Michael, and Marc Trachtenberg. 2003. "France and the German Question, 1945–1955." *Journal of Cold War Studies* 5 (3): 5–28.

Crombez, Christophe. 2000. "Spatial Models of Logrolling in the European Union." *European Journal of Political Economy* 16 (4): 707–37.

Cunningham, David E., Kristian Skrede Gleditsch, and Idean Salehyan. 2009. "It Takes Two: A Dyadic Analysis of Civil War Duration and Outcome." *Journal of Conflict Resolution* 53 (4): 570–97.

Dafoe, Allan, Jonathan Renshon, and Paul Huth. 2014. "Reputation and Status as Motives for War." *Annual Review of Political Science* 17: 371–93.

Dahl, Robert A. 1957. "The Concept of Power." *Systems Research and Behavioral Science* 2 (3): 201–15.

Dane, Erik. 2010. "Reconsidering the Trade-Off between Expertise and Flexibility: A Cognitive Entrenchment Perspective." *Academy of Management Review* 35 (4): 603.

Davenport, Christian, Erik Melander, and Patrick M. Regan. 2018. *The Peace Continuum: What It Is and How to Study It.* Oxford: Oxford University Press.

Davies, Graeme A. M., and Robert Johns. 2013. "Audience Costs among the British Public: The Impact of Escalation, Crisis Type, and Prime Ministerial Rhetoric." *International Studies Quarterly* 57 (4): 725–37.

Davis, Christina L. 2009. "Linkage Diplomacy: Economic and Security Bargaining in the Anglo-Japanese Alliance, 1902–23." *International Security* 33 (3): 143–79.

Demetriou, Chares. 2012. "Processual Comparative Sociology Building on the Approach of Charles Tilly." *Sociological Theory* 30 (1): 51–65.

DiCicco, Jonathan M. 2011. "Fear, Loathing, and Cracks in Reagan's Mirror Images." *Foreign Policy Analysis* 7 (3): 253–74.

Diehl, Paul Franc, and Gary Goertz. 2001. *War and Peace in International Rivalry.* Ann Arbor: University of Michigan Press.

Diehl, Paul Francis. 1998. *The Dynamics of Enduring Rivalries.* Champaign: University of Illinois Press.

Diehl, Paul Francis, and G. Goertz. 2001. *War and Peace in International Rivalry.* Ann Arbor: University of Michigan Press.

Dixon, William J. 1996. "Third-Party Techniques for Preventing Conflict Escalation and Promoting Peaceful Settlement." *International Organization* 50 (4): 653–81.

Down, Ian. 2007. "Trade Openness, Country Size and Economic Volatility: The Compensation Hypothesis Revisited." *Business and Politics* 9 (2).

Downs, George W., and David M. Rocke. 1995. *Optimal Imperfection?: Domestic Uncertainty and Institutions in International Relations.* Princeton, NJ: Princeton University Press.

Downs, George W., David M. Rocke, and Peter N. Barsoom. 1996. "Is the Good News about Compliance Good News about Cooperation?" *International Organization* 50 (3): 379–406.

Dreher, Axel, and Nathan M. Jensen. 2013. "Country or Leader? Political Change and UN General Assembly Voting." *European Journal of Political Economy* 29 (C) : 183–96.

Dreyer, David R. 2010. "Issue Conflict Accumulation and the Dynamics of Strategic Rivalry." *International Studies Quarterly* 54 (3): 779–95.

Drury, Cooper, and Yitan Li. 2006. "US Economic Sanction Threats against China: Failing to Leverage Better Human Rights." *Foreign Policy Analysis* 2 (4): 307–24.

Du, Ning, and David Budescu. 2005. "The Effects of Imprecise Probabilities and Outcomes in Evaluating Investment Options." *Management Science* 51 (12): 1791–803.

Duque, Marina G. 2018. "Recognizing International Status: A Relational Approach." *International Studies Quarterly* 62 (3): 577–92.

Easley, Leif-Eric. 2017. "How Proactive? How Pacifist? Charting Japan's Evolving Defense Posture." *Australian Journal of International Affairs* 71 (1): 63–87.

Edelman, Eric S., Andrew F. Krepinevich, and Evan Braden Montgomery. 2011. "The Dangers of a Nuclear Iran: The Limits of Containment." *Foreign Affairs* 90 (1): 66–81.

Ehrlich, Sean D. 2007. "Access to Protection: Domestic Institutions and Trade Policy in Democracies." *International Organization* 61 (3): 571–605.

Ellis, Cali Mortenson, Michael C. Horowitz, and Allan C. Stam. 2015. "Introducing the LEAD Data Set." *International Interactions* 41 (4): 718–41.

Ellison, James. 2007. *The United States, Britain and the Transatlantic Crisis: Rising to the Gaullist Challenge, 1963–68.* New York: Springer.

Ellsberg, Daniel. 1961. "Risk, Ambiguity, and the Savage Axioms." *Quarterly Journal of Economics* 75 (4): 643–69.

Elman, Miriam Fendius. 2000. "Unpacking Democracy: Presidentialism, Parliamentarism, and Theories of Democratic Peace." *Security Studies* 9 (4): 91–126.

Enders, Walter. 2008. *Applied Econometric Time Series.* Hoboken: John Wiley & Sons.

Evangelista, Matthew. 1989. "Issue-Area and Foreign Policy Revisited." *International Organization* 43 (1): 147–71.

Falleti, Tullia G., and Julia F. Lynch. 2009. "Context and Causal Mechanisms in Political Analysis." *Comparative Political Studies* 42 (9): 1143–66.

Fatas, Antonio, and Ilian Mihov. 2013. "Policy Volatility, Institutions and Economic Growth." *Review of Economics and Statistics* 95 (2): 362–76.

Fazal, Tanisha M. 2018. *Wars of Law: Unintended Consequences in the Regulation of Armed Conflict.* Ithaca, NY: Cornell University Press.

Fearon, James D. 1994. "Domestic Political Audiences and the Escalation of International Disputes." *American Political Science Review* 88 (3): 577–92.

Ferguson, Niall. 2015. *Kissinger: The Idealist.* London: Penguin Press.

FitzGerald, Thomas H. B., Raymond J. Dolan, and Karl J. Friston. 2014. "Model Averaging, Optimal Inference, and Habit Formation." *Frontiers in Human Neuroscience* 8, 457.

Fitzsimmons, Michael. 2006. "The Problem of Uncertainty in Strategic Planning." *Survival* 48 (4): 131–46.

Flynn, D. J., and Megan A. Stewart. 2018. "Secessionist Social Services Reduce the Public Costs of Civilian Killings: Experimental Evidence from the United States and the United Kingdom." *Research & Politics* 5 (4): 1–10.

Foot, Rosemary. 2006. "Chinese Strategies in a US-Hegemonic Global Order: Accommodating and Hedging." *International Affairs* 82 (1): 77–94.

Fordham, Benjamin. 1998. "The Politics of Threat Perception and the Use of Force: A Political Economy Model of US Uses of Force, 1949–1994." *International Studies Quarterly* 42 (3): 567–90.

Fordham, Benjamin O., and Katja B. Kleinberg. 2011. "International Trade and US Relations with China." *Foreign Policy Analysis* 7 (3): 217–36.

Fordham, Benjamin O., and Paul Poast. 2016. "All Alliances Are Multilateral: Rethinking Alliance Formation." *Journal of Conflict Resolution* 60 (5): 840–65.

France, Institut. 1954. *L'année Politique Économique Sociale et Diplomatique en France*. Paris: Presses Universitaires de France.

France, Institut. 1955. *L'année Politique Économique Sociale et Diplomatique en France*. Paris: Presses Universitaires de France.

France, Institut. 1956. *L'année Politique Économique Sociale et Diplomatique en France*. Paris: Presses Universitaires de France.

France, Institut. 1957. *L'année Politique Économique Sociale et Diplomatique en France*. Paris: Presses Universitaires de France.

France, Institut. 1958. *L'année Politique Économique Sociale et Diplomatique en France*. Paris: Presses Universitaires de France.

France, Institut. 1959. *L'année Politique Économique Sociale et Diplomatique en France*. Paris: Presses Universitaires de France.

France, Institut. 1961. *L'année Politique Économique Sociale et Diplomatique en France*. Paris: Presses Universitaires de France.

France, Institut. 1962. *L'année Politique Économique Sociale et Diplomatique en France*. Paris: Presses Universitaires de France.

France, Institut. 1963. *L'année Politique Économique Sociale et Diplomatique en France*. Paris: Presses Universitaires de France.

France, Institut. 1964. *L'année Politique Économique Sociale et Diplomatique en France*. Paris: Presses Universitaires de France.

France, Institut. 1965. *L'année Politique Économique Sociale et Diplomatique en France*. Paris: Presses Universitaires de France.

Freeman, John R. 1989. "Systematic Sampling, Temporal Aggregation, and the Study of Political Relationships." *Political Analysis* 1: 61–98.

Frieden, Jeff. 1988. "Sectoral Conflict and Foreign Economic Policy, 1914–1940." *International Organization* 42 (1): 59–90.

Friedman, Jeffrey A. 2019. *War and Chance: Assessing Uncertainty in International Politics*. Oxford: Oxford University Press.

Friman, H. Richard. 1993. "Side-Payments Versus Security Cards: Domestic Bargaining Tactics in International Economic Negotiations." *International Organization* 47 (3): 387–410.

Fuhrmann, Matthew. 2020. "When Do Leaders Free-Ride? Business Experience and Contributions to Collective Defense." *American Journal of Political Science* 64 (2): 416–31.

Fuhrmann, Matthew, and Michael C. Horowitz. 2015. "When Leaders Matter: Rebel Experience and Nuclear Proliferation." *Journal of Politics* 77 (1): 72–87.

Gaddis, John Lewis. 1986. "The Long Peace: Elements of Stability in the Postwar International System." *International Security* 10 (4): 99–142.

Galtung, Johan. 1969. "Violence, Peace, and Peace Research." *Journal of Peace Research* 6 (3): 167–91.

Gambetta, Diego. 1998. "Concatenations of Mechanisms." In *Social Mechanisms: An Analytical Approach to Social Theory*, edited by Peter Hedström and Richard Swedberg, 102–24. Cambridge: Cambridge University Press.

Ganguly, Sumit. 1995. "Indo–Pakistani Nuclear Issues and the Stability/Instability Paradox." *Studies in Conflict and Terrorism* 23 (4): 148–77.

Ganguly, Sumit, and William Thompson. 2011. *Asian Rivalries: Conflict, Escalation, and Limitations on Two-Level Games*. Redwood City, CA: Stanford University Press.

Garrison, Jean A. 2003. "Foreign Policy Analysis in 20/20: A Symposium." *International Studies Review* 5 (2): 155–202.

Garrison, Jean A. 2007. "Constructing the 'National Interest' in US–China Policy Making: How Foreign Policy Decision Groups Define and Signal Policy Choices." *Foreign Policy Analysis* 3(2): 105–26.

Gartzke, Erik, and Kristian Skrede Gleditsch. 2004. "Why Democracies May Actually Be Less Reliable Allies." *American Journal of Political Science* 48 (4): 775–95.

Gartzke, Erik, and Dong-Joon Jo. 2009. "Bargaining, Nuclear Proliferation, and Interstate Disputes." *Journal of Conflict Resolution* 53 (2): 209–33.

Gartzke, Erik, and Yonatan Lupu. 2012. "Still Looking for Audience Costs." *Security Studies* 21 (3): 391–97.

Geller, Daniel S. 1990. "Nuclear Weapons, Deterrence, and Crisis Escalation." *Journal of Conflict Resolution* 34 (2): 291–310.

Gelpern, Anna, Sebastian Horn, and Christoph Trebesch. 2021. *How China Lends: A Rare Look into 100 Debt Contracts with Foreign Governments*. Peterson Institute for International Economics Working Paper.

George, Alexander, and Andrew Bennett. 2005. *Case Studies and Theory Development in the Social Sciences*. Cambridge, MA: MIT Press.

Gerring, John. 2001. *Social Science Methodology: A Criterial Framework*. Cambridge: Cambridge University Press.

Gilli, Mario, Yuan Li, and Jiwei Qian. 2018. "Logrolling under Fragmented Authoritarianism: Theory and Evidence from China." *Public Choice* 175 (12): 197–214.

Gilpin, Robert. 1981. *War and Change in World Politics*. Cambridge: Cambridge University Press.

Glaser, Charles L., and Chaim Kaufmann. 1998. "What Is the Offense-Defense Balance and Can We Measure It?" *International Security* 22 (4): 44–82.

Goddard, Stacie E. 2009. *Indivisible Territory and the Politics of Legitimacy: Jerusalem and Northern Ireland*. Cambridge: Cambridge University Press.

Goertz, Gary. 2006. *Social Science Concepts*. Princeton, NJ: Princeton University Press.

Goertz, Gary, and Paul Francis Diehl. 1995. "Taking Enduring Out of Enduring Rivalry: The Rivalry Approach to War and Peace." *International Interactions* 21 (3): 291–308.

Goertz, Gary, Paul Francis Diehl, and Alexandru Balas. 2016. *The Puzzle of Peace: The Evolution of Peace in the International System*. Oxford: Oxford University Press.

Goffman, Erving. 1959. *The Presentation of Self in Everyday Life*. Garden City, NY: Doubleday Anchor Books.

Goh, Evelyn. 2005. "Meeting the China Challenge: The US in Southeast Asian Regional Security Strategies." *Policy Studies* 16 (1) : 1–82.

Goh, Evelyn. 2006. "Understanding Hedging in Asia-Pacific Security." *PacNet* 43 (31) :1–2.

Goldstein, Avery. 2020. "China's Grand Strategy under Xi Jinping: Reassurance, Reform, and Resistance." *International Security* 45 (1): 164–201.

Goldstein, Joshua S. 1992. "A Conflict-Cooperation Scale for Weis Events Data." *Journal of Conflict Resolution* 36 (2): 369–85.

Goldstein, Joshua S., and Jon C. Pevehouse. 1997. "Reciprocity, Bullying, and International Cooperation: Time-Series Analysis of the Bosnia Conflict." *American Political Science Review* 91 (3): 515–29.

Goldstein, Joshua S., Jon C. Pevehouse, Deborah J. Gerner, and Shibley Telhami. 2001. "Reciprocity, Triangularity, and Cooperation in the Middle East, 1979–97." *Journal of Conflict Resolution* 45 (5): 594–620.

Gordon, Sanford C., and Dimitri Landa. 2017. "Common Problems (or, What's Missing from the Conventional Wisdom on Polarization and Gridlock)." *Journal of Politics* 79 (4): 1433–37.

Gowa, Joanne. 1994. *Allies, Adversaries, and International Trade*. Princeton, NJ: Princeton University Press.

Gray, Julia. 2013. *The Company States Keep: International Economic Organizations and Investor Perceptions*. Cambridge: Cambridge University Press.

Gray, Julia, and Phillip Potter. 2012. "Trade and Volatility at the Core and Periphery of the Global Economy." *International Studies Quarterly* 56: 793–800.

Greene, William. 2003. *Econometric Analysis*. 5th ed. Hoboken, NJ: Prentice Hall.

Grynaviski, Eric. 2014. *Constructive Illusions: Misperceiving the Origins of International Cooperation*. Ithaca, NY: Cornell University Press.

Guisinger, Alexandra, and Alastair Smith. 2002. "Honest Threats: The Interaction of Reputation and Political Institutions in International Crises." *Journal of Conflict Resolution* 46 (2): 175–200.

Güvenç, Serhat, and Soli Özel. 2012. "NATO and Turkey in the Post-Cold War World: Between Abandonment and Entrapment." *Southeast European and Black Sea Studies* 12 (4): 533–53.

Haber, Stephen, and Victor Menaldo. 2011. "Do Natural Resources Fuel Authoritarianism? A Reappraisal of the Resource Curse." *American Political Science Review* 105 (1): 1–26.

Hafner-Burton, Emilie M. 2005. "Trading Human Rights: How Preferential Trade Agreements Influence Government Repression." *International Organization* 59 (3): 629.

Haftel, Yoram Z., and Alexander Thompson. 2013. "Delayed Ratification: The Domestic Fate of Bilateral Investment Treaties." *International Organization* 67 (2): 355–87.

Halperin, Morton H., and Priscilla Clapp. 2007. *Bureaucratic Politics and Foreign Policy*. Washington, DC: Brookings Institution Press.

Hanrieder, Wolfram F., and Graeme P. Auton. 1980. *The Foreign Policies of West Germany, France, and Britain*. Hoboken, NJ: Prentice Hall.

Hart, B. H. Liddell. 1960. *Deterrent or Defense: A Fresh Look at the West's Military Position*. New York: Praeger.

Hathaway, Oona A. 2007. "Why Do Countries Commit to Human Rights Treaties?" *Journal of Conflict Resolution* 51 (4): 588–621.

Hays, Jude, John Freeman, and Hans Nesseth. 2003. "Exchange Rate Volatility and Democratization in Emerging Market Countries." *International Studies Quarterly* 47 (2): 203–28.

Heath, Oliver. 2005. "Party Systems, Political Cleavages and Electoral Volatility in India: A State-Wise Analysis, 1998–1999." *Electoral Studies* 24 (2): 177–99.

Heginbotham, Eric. 2002. "The Fall and Rise of Navies in East Asia: Military Organizations, Domestic Politics, and Grand Strategy." *International Security* 27 (2): 125.

Henisz, Witold. 2004. "Political Institutions and Policy Volatility." *Economics & Politics* 16 (1): 1–27.

Henke, Marina E. 2017. "The Politics of Diplomacy: How the United States Builds Multilateral Military Coalitions." *International Studies Quarterly* 61 (2): 410–24.

Hensel, Paul R., and Sara McLaughlin Mitchell. 2007. *The Issue Correlates of War (ICOW) Project Issue Data Set: Territorial Claims Data.* Edited by Paul R. Hensel. Cambridge: Harvard Dataverse.

Hensel, Paul R., Sara McLaughlin Mitchell, Thomas E. Sowers, and Clayton L. Thyne. 2008. "Bones of Contention: Comparing Territorial, Maritime, and River Issues." *Journal of Conflict Resolution* 52 (1): 117–43.

Herz, John H. 1959. *International Politics in the Atomic Age.* Columbia Paperback 34. New York: Columbia University Press.

Hey, John, Gianna Lotito, and Anna Maffioletti. 2010. "The Descriptive and Predictive Adequacy of Theories of Decision Making under Uncertainty/Ambiguity." *Journal of Risk and Uncertainty* 41: 81–111.

Hobson, John M. 2000. *The State and International Relations.* Cambridge: Cambridge University Press.

Hoffman, Aaron M. 2002. "A Conceptualization of Trust in International Relations." *European Journal of International Relations* 83: 375–401.

Hoffman, Aaron M. 2006. *Building Trust: Overcoming Suspicion in International Conflict.* Albany: State University of New York Press.

Holmes, Jeremy, and Tobias Nolte. 2019. "'Surprise' and the Bayesian Brain: Implications for Psychotherapy Theory and Practice." *Frontiers in Psychology* 10: 592.

Holmes, Marcus. 2013. "The Force of Face-to-Face Diplomacy: Mirror Neurons and the Problem of Intentions." *International Organization* 67 (4): 829–61.

Holtermann, Helge. 2016. "Relative Capacity and the Spread of Rebellion: Insights from Nepal." *Journal of Conflict Resolution* 60 (3): 501–29.

Hopf, Ted. 1991. "Polarity, the Offense Defense Balance, and War." *American Political Science Review* 85 (2): 475–93.

Hopf, Ted. 1994. *Peripheral Visions: Deterrence Theory and American Foreign Policy in the Third World, 1965–1990.* Ann Arbor: University of Michigan Press.

Hopf, Ted. 2002. *Social Construction of International Politics: Identities & Foreign Policies, Moscow, 1955 and 1999.* Ithaca, NY: Cornell University Press.

Hopf, Ted. 2010. "The Logic of Habit in International Relations." *European Journal of International Relations* 16 (4): 539–61.

Horowitz, Donald L. 1985. *Ethnic Groups in Conflict, Updated Edition with a New Preface.* Oakland: University of California Press.

Horowitz, Michael C. 2009. "The Spread of Nuclear Weapons and International Conflict: Does Experience Matter?" *Journal of Conflict Resolution* 53 (2): 234–57.

Horowitz, Michael C. 2010. *The Diffusion of Military Power: Causes and Consequences for International Politics.* Princeton, NJ: Princeton University Press.

Horowitz, Michael C., Cali M. Ellis, and Allan C. Stam. 2015. "Replication Data for: Introducing the LEAD Data Set." Harvard Dataverse, V1, https://doi.org/10.7910/DVN/SYZZEY.

Horowitz, Michael C., Allan C. Stam, and Cali M. Ellis. 2015. *Why Leaders Fight.* Cambridge: Cambridge University Press.

Huelshoff, Michael G. 1994. "Domestic Politics and Dynamic Issue Linkage: A Reformulation of Integration Theory." *International Studies Quarterly* 38 (2): 255–79.

Huth, Paul K. 1988. "Extended Deterrence and the Outbreak of War." *American Political Science Review* 82 (2): 423–43.

Huth, Paul K. 1997. "Reputations and Deterrence: A Theoretical and Empirical Assessment." *Security Studies* 7 (1): 72–99.

Huth, Paul K. 1999. "Deterrence and International Conflict: Empirical Findings and Theoretical Debates." *Annual Review of Political Science* 2 (1): 25–48.

Hyde, Susan D., and Elizabeth N. Saunders. 2020. "Recapturing Regime Type in International Relations: Leaders, Institutions, and Agency Space." *International Organization* 74 (2): 363–95.

Irving, Ronald Eckford Mill. 1975. *The First Indochina War: French and American Policy, 1945–54.* Kent, UK: Croom Helm.

Jackman, Simon. 2008. "Measurement." In *The Oxford Handbook of Political Methodology*, edited by Janet M. Box-Steffensmeier, Henry E. Brady, and David Collier, 287–304. Oxford: Oxford University Press.

Jackobson, Linda. 2016. "Domestic Actors and the Fragmentation of China's Foreign Policy." In *China in the Era of Xi Jinping: Domestic and Foreign Policy Challenges*, edited by Robert S. Ross and Jo Inge Bekkevold, , Washington DC: Georgetown University Press. 137–64.

Jervis, Robert. 1976. *Perception and Misperception in International Politics.* Princeton, NJ: Princeton University Press.

Jervis, Robert. 1978. "Cooperation under the Security Dilemma." *World Politics* 30 (2): 167–214.

Jervis, Robert. 1982. "Deterrence and Perception." *International Security* 7 (3): 3–30.

Jervis, Robert. 1988. "War and Misperception." *Journal of Interdisciplinary History* 18 (4): 675–700.

Jervis, Robert. 1993. "Arms Control, Stability, and Causes of War." *Political Science Quarterly* 108 (2): 239–53.

Jervis, Robert. 1997. "Complexity and the Analysis of Political and Social Life." *Political Science Quarterly* 112 (4): 569–93.

Jervis, Robert. 1998. *System Effects: Complexity in Political and Social Life.* Princeton, NJ: Princeton University Press.

Jones, Benjamin T. 2017. "Altering Capabilities or Imposing Costs? Intervention Strategy and Civil War Outcomes." *International Studies Quarterly* 61 (1): 52–63.

Jones, Benjamin T., and Eleonora Mattiacci. 2019. "A Manifesto, in 140 Characters or Fewer: Social Media as a Tool of Rebel Diplomacy." *British Journal of Political Science* 49 (2): 739–61.

Jones, Benjamin T., Eleonora Mattiacci, and Bear F. Braumoeller. 2017. "Food Scarcity and State Vulnerability: Unpacking the Link between Climate Variability and Violent Unrest." *Journal of Peace Research* 54 (3): 335–50.

Jones, Daniel M., Stuart A. Bremer, and J. David Singer. 1996. "Militarized Interstate Disputes, 1816–1992: Rationale, Coding Rules, and Empirical Patterns." *Conflict Management and Peace Science* 15 (2): 163–213.

Jones, David Martin, Michael Smith, and Nicholas Khoo. 2013. *Asian Security and the Rise of China.* Northampton, MA: Edward Elgar Publishing.

Jones, Evan. 2017. "'Sellout' Ministries and Jingoes: China's Bureaucratic Institutions and the Evolution of Contested National Role Conceptions in the South China Sea." *Foreign Policy Analysis* 13 (2): 361–79.

Jones, Matthew. 2001. "'Groping Toward Coexistence': US China Policy during the Johnson Years." *Diplomacy and Statecraft* 12 (3): 175–90.

Jones-Rooy, Andrea, and Scott E. Page. 2012. "The Complexity of System Effects." *Critical Review* 24 (3): 313–42.

Kaarbo, Juliet. 2012. *Coalition Politics and Cabinet Decision Making: A Comparative Analysis of Foreign Policy Choices*. Ann Arbor: Michigan University Press.

Kaarbo, Juliet, and Ryan K. Beasley. 2008. "Taking It to the Extreme: The Effect of Coalition Cabinets on Foreign Policy." *Foreign Policy Analysis* 4 (1): 67–81.

Kadera, Kelly, and Gerald Sorokin. 2004. "Measuring National Power." *International Interactions* 30 (3): 211–30.

Kahler, Miles. 2014. *Decolonization in Britain and France: The Domestic Consequences of International Relations*. Princeton, NJ: Princeton University Press.

Kahn, Barbara, and Rakesh Sarin. 1988. "Modeling Ambiguity in Decisions under Uncertainty." *Journal of Consumer Research* 15 (2): 265–72.

Kapur, Ashok. 2000. *Pokhran and Beyond: India's Nuclear Weapons Capability*. Oxford: Oxford University Press.

Kapur, S. Paul. 2005. "India and Pakistan's Unstable Peace: Why Nuclear South Asia Is Not Like Cold War Europe." *International Security* 30 (2): 127–52.

Kapur, S. Paul. 2008. "Ten Years of Instability in a Nuclear South Asia." *International Security* 33 (2): 71–94.

Karlén, Niklas. 2019. "Turning Off the Taps: The Termination of State Sponsorship." *Terrorism and Political Violence* 31 (4): 733–58.

Keele, Luke, and Jennifer Wolak. 2006. "Value Conflict and Volatility in Party Identification." *British Journal of Political Science* 36 (4): 671–90.

Keeler, John T. S. 1990. "De Gaulle and Europe's Common Agricultural Policy: The Logic and Legacies of Nationalistic Integration." *French Politics and Society* 8 (4): 62–77.

Kemp, Tom. 1980. *Histoire Economique et Sociale de la France*. Tome IV. Paris: Presses Universitaires de France.

Kennedy, Ryan. 2009. "Survival and Accountability: An Analysis of the Empirical Support for 'Selectorate Theory.'" *International Studies Quarterly* 53 (3): 695–714.

Keohane, Robert O. 1984. *After Hegemony: Cooperation and Discord in the World Political Economy*. Princeton, NJ: Princeton University Press.

Kertzer, Joshua D. 2017. "Resolve, Time, and Risk." *International Organization* 71 (S1): S109–136.

Kertzer, Joshua D., and Ryan Brutger. 2016. "Decomposing Audience Costs: Bringing the Audience Back Into Audience Cost Theory." *American Journal of Political Science* 60 (1): 234–49.

Kertzer, Joshua D., Jonathan Renshon, and Keren Yarhi-Milo. 2021. "How Do Observers Assess Resolve?" *British Journal of Political Science* 51 (1): 308–30.

Khong, Yuen Foong. 1992. *Analogies at War: Korea, Munich, Dien Bien Phu, and the Vietnam Decisions of 1965*. Princeton, NJ: Princeton University Press.

Khong, Yuen Foong. 2020. *Analogies at War*. Princeton, NJ: Princeton University Press.

Kilcullen, David. 2020. *The Dragons and the Snakes: How the Rest Learned to Fight the West*. Oxford: Oxford University Press.

Kirby, William C., Gong Li, and Robert Ross. 2006. *The Normalization of US-China Relations: An International History*. Cambridge, MA: Harvard University Press.

Kleinberg, Katja B., and Benjamin O. Fordham. 2013. "The Domestic Politics of Trade and Conflict." *International Studies Quarterly* 57 (3): 605–19.

Klomp, Jeroen, and Jakob Haan. 2009. "Political Institutions and Economic Volatility." *European Journal of Political Economy* 25 (3): 311–26.

Knight, Frank. 1921. *Risk, Uncertainty and Profit*. Mineola, NY: Dover Publications.

Koch, Michael T., and Sarah A. Fulton. 2011. "In the Defense of Women: Gender, Office Holding, and National Security Policy in Established Democracies." *Journal of Politics* 73 (1): 1–16.

Koga, Kei. 2018. "The Concept of Hedging Revisited: The Case of Japan's Foreign Policy Strategy in East Asia's Power Shift." *International Studies Review* 20 (4): 663–60.

Kolodziej, Edward A. 1972. "French Monetary Diplomacy in the Sixties: Background Notes to the Current Monetary Crisis." *World Affairs* 135 (1): 5–39.

Koubi, Vally, Gabriele Spilker, Tobias Böhmelt, and Thomas Bernauer. 2014. "Do Natural Resources Matter for Interstate and Intrastate Armed Conflict?" *Journal of Peace Research* 51 (2): 227–43.

Krcmaric, Daniel, Stephen C. Nelson, and Andrew Roberts. 2020. "Studying Leaders and Elites: The Personal Biography Approach." *Annual Review of Political Science* 23: 133–51.

Kriner, Douglas, and Liam Schwartz. 2009. "Partisan Dynamics and the Volatility of Presidential Approval." *British Journal of Political Science* 39 (3): 609–31.

Kugler, Jacek, and William Domke. 1986. "Comparing the Strength of Nations." *Comparative Political Studies* 19 (1): 39–69.

Kuik, Cheng-Chwee. 2016. "How Do Weaker States Hedge? Unpacking ASEAN States? Alignment Behavior Towards China." *Journal of Contemporary China* 25 (100): 514.

Kydd, Andrew. 2000. "Trust, Reassurance, and Cooperation." *International Organization* 54 (2): 325–57.

Lake, David A. 2008. "The State and International Relations." In *The Oxford Handbook of International Relations*, edited by Christian Reus-Smit and Duncan Snidal, 40–61. Oxford: Oxford University Press.

Lane, Jan-Erik, and Svante O. Ersson. 1999. *Politics and Society in Western Europe*. Beverly Hills, CA: Sage.

Larkin, Maurice. 1997. *France Since the Popular Front: Government and People, 1936–1996*. Oxford: Oxford University Press.

Larson, Deborah Welch. 1997. "Trust and Missed Opportunities in International Relations." *Political Psychology* 18 (3): 701–34.

Leblang, David, and William Bernhard. 2006. "Parliamentary Politics and Foreign Exchange Markets: The World According to GARCH." *International Studies Quarterly* 50 (1): 69–92.

Leblang, David, and Steve Chan. 2003. "Explaining Wars Fought by Established Democracies: Do Institutional Constraints Matter?" *Political Research Quarterly* 56 (4): 385–400.

Leblang, David, and Bumba Mukherjee. 2004. "Presidential Elections and the Stock Market: Comparing Markov-Switching and Fractionally Integrated GARCH Models of Volatility." *Political Analysis* 12 (3): 296–322.

Leblang, David, and Bumba Mukherjee. 2005. "Government Partisanship, Elections, and the Stock Market: Examining American and British Stock Returns, 1930 to 2000." *American Journal of Political Science* 49 (4): 780–802.

Leeds, Brett Ashley. 1999. "Domestic Political Institutions, Credible Commitments, and International Cooperation." *American Journal of Political Science*, 43(4): 979–1002.

Leeds, Brett Ashley. 2003. "Alliance Reliability in Times of War: Explaining State Decisions to Violate Treaties." *International Organization* 57 (4): 801–27.

Leeds, Brett, Jeffrey Ritter, Sara Mitchell, and Andrew Long. 2002. "Alliance Treaty Obligations and Provisions, 1815–1944." *International Interactions* 28 (3): 237–60.

Leeds, Brett Ashley, Michaela Mattes, and Jeremy S. Vogel. 2009. "Interests, Institutions, and the Reliability of International Commitments." *American Journal of Political Science* 53 (2): 461–76.

Lektzian, David, and Dennis Patterson. 2015. "Political Cleavages and Economic Sanctions." *International Studies Quarterly* 59 (1): 46–58.

Leon, Pierre. 1976. *Histoire Économique et Sociale de la France: L'ère Industrielle et la Société D'ajourd'hui (Siècle 1880–1980). Panoramas de L'ère Industrielle (années 1880–Années 1970). Ambiguïtés des Débuts et Croissance Effective (années 1880–1914).* Paris: Presses Universitaires de France.

Lerner, Jennifer S., and Dacher Keltner. 2001. "Fear, Anger, and Risk." *Journal of Personality and Social Psychology* 81 (1): 146-59.

Levendusky, Matthew S., and Michael C. Horowitz. 2012. "When Backing Down Is the Right Decision: Partisanship, New Information, and Audience Costs." *Journal of Politics* 74 (2): 323–38.

Levis, Mario, Yaz Gülnur Muradoğlu, and Kristina Vasileva. 2016. "Home Bias Persistence in Foreign Direct Investments." *European Journal of Finance* 22 (8–9): 782–802.

Levy, Jack S. 1984. "The Offensive/Defensive Balance of Military Technology: A Theoretical and Historical Analysis." *International Studies Quarterly* 28 (2): 219–38.

Levy, Jack S., Michael K. McKoy, Paul Poast, and Geoffrey P. R. Wallace. 2015. "Backing Out or Backing In? Commitment and Consistency in Audience Costs Theory." *American Journal of Political Science* 59 (4): 988–1001.

Licht, Amanda A., and Susan Hannah Allen. 2018. "Repressing for Reputation: Leadership Transitions, Uncertainty, and the Repression of Domestic Populations." *Journal of Peace Research* 55 (5): 582–95.

Lim, Darren J., and Zack Cooper. 2015. "Reassessing Hedging: The Logic of Alignment in East Asia." *Security Studies* 24 (4): 696–727.

Lipset, Seimur Martin. 1963. *Political Man: The Social Bases of Politics.* Baltimore: Johns Hopkins University Press.

Lipset, Seimur Martinand Stein Rokkan. 1967. *Party Systems and Voter Alignments.* New York: Free Press.

Lipson, Charles. 2005. *Reliable Partners: How Democracies Have Made a Separate Peace.* Princeton, NJ: Princeton University Press.

Lobell, Steven E., Norrin M. Ripsman, and Jeffrey W. Taliaferro. 2009. *Neoclassical Realism, the State, and Foreign Policy.* Cambridge: Cambridge University Press.

Long, Andrew G., and Brett Ashley Leeds. 2006. "Trading for Security: Military Alliances and Economic Agreements." *Journal of Peace Research* 43 (4): 433–51.

Lupton, Danielle L. 2018. "Reexamining Reputation for Resolve: Leaders, States, and the Onset of International Crises." *Journal of Global Security Studies* 3 (2): 198–216.

Lupton, Danielle L. 2020. *Reputation for Resolve: How Leaders Signal Determination in International Politics.* Ithaca, NY: Cornell University Press.

Lüthi, Lorenz M. 2014. "Rearranging International Relations? How Mao's China and de Gaulle's France Recognized Each Other in 1963–1964." *Journal of Cold War Studies* 16 (1): 111–45.

Lynn-Jones, Sean M. 1995. "Offense-Defense Theory and Its Critics." *Security Studies* 4 (4): 660–91.

Mack, Andrew. 1975. "Why Big Nations Lose Small Wars: The Politics of Asymmetric Conflict." *World Politics* 27 (2): 175–200.

Madelin, Alain. 1997. *Aux Sources du Modèle Libéral Français*. Paris: Librairie Académique Perrin.

Madrid, Raul. 2005. "Ethnic Cleavages and Electoral Volatility in Latin America." *Comparative Politics* 38 (1): 1–20.

Magaloni, Beatriz. 2008. "Credible Power-Sharing and the Longevity of Authoritarian Rule." *Comparative Political Studies* 41 (4–5): 715–41.

Mahapatra, Chintamani. 1998. "Pokhran II and After: Dark Clouds over Indo-US Relations." *Strategic Analysis* 22 (5): 711–20.

Mainwaring, Scott, and Edurne Zoco. 2007. "Political Sequences and the Stabilization of Interparty Competition Electoral Volatility in Old and New Democracies." *Party Politics* 13 (2): 155–78.

Makino, Shige, and Eric W. K. Tsang. 2011. "Historical Ties and Foreign Direct Investment: An Exploratory Study." *Journal of International Business Studies* 42 (4): 557.

Mampilly, Zachariah Cherian. 2012. *Rebel Rulers: Insurgent Governance and Civilian Life during War*. Ithaca, NY: Cornell University Press.

Mansfield, Edward D., Helen V. Milner, and Jon C. Pevehouse. 2007. "Vetoing Cooperation: The Impact of Veto Players on Preferential Trading Arrangements." *British Journal of Political Science* 37 (3): 403–32.

Mansfield, Edward, and Eric Reinhardt. 2008. "International Institutions and the Volatility of International Trade." *International Organization* 62 (4): 621–52.

Maoz, Zeev, and Boaz Mor. 2002. *Bound by Struggle: The Strategic Evolution of Enduring International Rivalries*. Ann Arbor: University of Michigan Press.

Marshall, Monty G., and Keith Jaggers. 2002. *Polity IV Project: Political Regime Characteristics and Transitions, 1800–2002*. College Park: Center for International Development and Conflict Management, University of Maryland.

Martin, Garret. 2008. "Playing the China Card? Revisiting France's Recognition of Communist China, 1963–1964." *Journal of Cold War Studies* 10 (1): 52–80.

Martin, Lisa L. 2000. *Democratic Commitments: Legislatures and International Cooperation*. Princeton, NJ: Princeton University Press.

Mastanduno, Michael. 1997. "Preserving the Unipolar Moment: Realist Theories and U.S. Grand Strategy after the Cold War." *International Security* 21 (4): 49–88.

Mattes, Michaela. 2012. "Democratic Reliability, Precommitment of Successor Governments, and the Choice of Alliance Commitment." *International Organization* 66 (1): 153–72.

Mattes, Michaela, Brett Ashley Leeds, and Royce Carroll. 2015. "Leadership Turnover and Foreign Policy Change: Societal Interests, Domestic Institutions, and Voting in the United Nations." *International Studies Quarterly* 59 (2): 280–90.

Mattes, Michaela, Brett Ashley Leeds, and Naoko Matsumura. 2016. "Measuring Change in Source of Leader Support: The CHISOLS Dataset." *Journal of Peace Research* 53 (2): 259–67.

Mattes, Michaela, and Mariana Rodriguez. 2014. "Autocracies and International Cooperation." *International Studies Quarterly* 58 (3): 527–38.

Mattiacci, Eleonora. 2021. "How Nuclear Issue Salience Shapes Counterproliferation." *Global Studies Quarterly* 1 (3): 1–16.

Mattiacci, Eleonora, and Benjamin T. Jones. 2020. "Restoring Legitimacy: Public Diplomacy Campaigns during Civil Wars." *International Studies Quarterly* 64 (4): 867–78.

Mattiacci, Eleonora, Rupal N. Mehta, and Rachel Elizabeth Whitlark. 2021. "Atomic Ambiguity: Event Data Evidence on Nuclear Latency and International Cooperation." *Journal of Conflict Resolution* 66 (2): 272–96.

Mattson, Mark P. 2014. "Superior Pattern Processing Is the Essence of the Evolved Human Brain." *Frontiers in Neuroscience* 8: 265.

Mayer, Frederick W. 1992. "Managing Domestic Differences in International Negotiations: The Strategic Use of Internal Side-Payments." *International Organization* 46 (4): 793–818.

McClelland, Charles. 1978. "World Event/Interaction Survey (WEIS) Project, 1966–1978." Interuniversity Consortium for Political and Social Research (ICPSR).

McKelvey, Richard D. 1976. "Intransitivities in Multidimensional Voting Models and Some Implications for Agenda Control." *Journal of Economic Theory* 12 (3): 482.

McLaughlin Mitchell, Sara, and Will H. Moore. 2002. "Presidential Uses of Force during the Cold War: Aggregation, Truncation, and Temporal Dynamics." *American Journal of Political Science* 46 (2): 438–52.

McLaughlin Mitchell, Sara, and Brandon C. Prins. 2004. "Rivalry and Diversionary Uses of Force." *Journal of Conflict Resolution* 48 (6): 937–61.

McLaughlin Mitchell, Sara, and Cameron G. Thies. 2011. "Issue Rivalries." *Conflict Management and Peace Science* 28 (3): 230–60.

McMahon, Robert J. 1981. *Colonialism and Cold War: The United States and the Struggle for Indonesian Independence.* Ithaca, NY: Cornell University Press.

McManus, Roseanne W. 2019. "Revisiting the Madman Theory: Evaluating the Impact of Different Forms of Perceived Madness in Coercive Bargaining." *Security Studies* 28 (5): 976–1009.

McManus, Roseanne W., and Keren Yarhi-Milo. 2017. "The Logic of 'Offstage' Signaling: Domestic Politics, Regime Type, and Major Power-Protégé Relations." *International Organization* 71 (4): 701–33.

McMaster, H. R. 2015. "The Uncertainties of Strategy." *Survival* 57 (1): 197–208.

Medeiros, Evan S. 2005. "Strategic Hedging and the Future of Asia-Pacific Stability." *Washington Quarterly* 29 (1): 145–67.

Menon, Anand. 2000. "Domestic Constraints on French NATO Policy." *French Politics, Culture & Society* 18 (2): 49–68.

Mercer, Jonathan. 1996. *Reputation and International Politics.* Ithaca, NY: Cornell University Press.

Mettler, Simon A., and Dan Reiter. 2012. "Ballistic Missiles and International Conflict." *Journal of Conflict Resolution* 57 (5): 854–80.

Milner, Helen V., and Dustin H. Tingley. 2011. "Who Supports Global Economic Engagement? The Sources of Preferences in American Foreign Economic Policy." *International Organization* 65 (1): 37–68.

Monteiro, Nuno P. 2012a. "Unrest Assured: Why Unipolarity Is Not Peaceful." *International Security* 36 (3): 9–40.

Monteiro, Nuno P. 2012b. "We Can Never Study Merely One Thing: Reflections on Systems Thinking and IR." *Critical Review* 24 (3): 343–66.

Monteiro, Nuno P. 2014. *Theory of Unipolar Politics.* Cambridge: Cambridge University Press.

Moore, William, and Bumba Mukherjee. 2006. "Coalition Government Formation and Foreign Exchange Markets: Theory and Evidence from Europe." *International Studies Quarterly* 50 (1): 93–118.

Moravcsik, Andrew. 1997. "Taking Preferences Seriously: A Liberal Theory of International Politics." *International Organization* 51 (4): 513–53.

Morgan, Forrest E., Karl P. Mueller, Evan S. Medeiros, Kevin L. Pollpeter, and Roger Cliff. 2008. *Dangerous Thresholds: Managing Escalation in the 21st Century.* Santa Monica, CA: RAND Corporation.

Morgenthau, Hans Joachim. 1950. *Politics among Nations.* New York: Knopf.

Morrow, Daniel, and Michael Carriere. 1999. "The Economic Impacts of the 1998 Sanctions on India and Pakistan." *Nonproliferation Review* 6 (4): 1–16.

Morrow, James D., Bruce Bueno De Mesquita, Randolph M. Siverson, and Alastair Smith. 2008. "Retesting Selectorate Theory: Separating the Effects of W from Other Elements of Democracy." *American Political Science Review* 102 (3): 400.

Morse, Edward. 2015. *Foreign Policy and Interdependence in Gaullist France.* Princeton, NJ: Princeton University Press.

Morton, Rebecca B., and Kenneth C. Williams. 2010. *Experimental Political Science and the Study of Causality: From Nature to the Lab.* Cambridge: Cambridge University Press.

Most, B. A., and H. Starr. 1984. "International Relations Theory, Foreign Policy Substitutability, and 'Nice' Laws." *World Politics: A Quarterly Journal of International Relations* 36 (3): 383–406.

Narang, Vipin. 2010. "Posturing for Peace? Pakistan's Nuclear Postures and South Asian Stability." *International Security* 34 (3): 38–78.

Narang, Vipin, and Caitlin Talmadge. 2018. "Civil-Military Pathologies and Defeat in War: Tests Using New Data." *Journal of Conflict Resolution* 62 (7): 1379–405.

Narizny, Kevin. 2003. "Both Guns and Butter, or Neither: Class Interests in the Political Economy of Rearmament." *American Political Science Review* 97 (2): 220.

Narizny, Kevin. 2007. *The Political Economy of Grand Strategy.* Ithaca, NY: Cornell University Press.

Nelson, Stephen C. 2010. "Does Compliance Matter? Assessing the Relationship between Sovereign Risk and Compliance with International Monetary Law." *Review of International Organizations* 5 (2): 107–39.

Nelson, Stephen C., and Peter J. Katzenstein. 2014. "Uncertainty, Risk, and the Financial Crisis of 2008." *International Organization* 68 (2): 361–92.

Nieman, Mark David. 2011. "Shocks and Turbulence: Globalization and the Occurrence of Civil War." *International Interactions* 37 (3): 263–92.

Nincic, Miroslav. 1990. "US Soviet Policy and the Electoral Connection." *World Politics* 42 (3): 370–96.

Nincic, Miroslav. 2010. "Getting What You Want: Positive Inducements in International Relations." *International Security* 35 (1): 138–83.

Niou, Emerson M. S., Peter C. Ordeshook, and Gregory F. Rose. 2007. *The Balance of Power: Stability in International Systems.* Cambridge: Cambridge University Press.

Nooruddin, Irfan. 2011. *Coalition Politics and Economic Development: Credibility and the Strength of Weak Governments.* Cambridge: Cambridge University Press.

Organski, A. F. K. 1981. *The War Ledger.* Chicago: University of Chicago Press.

Palmer, Glenn, Tamar London, and Patrick Regan. 2004. "What's Stopping You?: The Sources of Political Constraints on International Conflict Behavior in Parliamentary Democracies." *International Interactions* 30 (1): 1–24.

Palmer, Glenn, and T. Clifton Morgan. 2011. *A Theory of Foreign Policy.* Princeton, NJ: Princeton University Press.

Park, Kyung-Ae. 1997. "Explaining North Korea's Negotiated Cooperation with the US." *Asian Survey* 37 (7): 623–36.

Parkinson, Sarah E., and Sherry Zaks. 2018. "Militant and Rebel Organizations." *Comparative Politics* 50 (2): 271–93.

Pearlman, Wendy. 2011. *Violence, Nonviolence, and the Palestinian National Movement.* Cambridge: Cambridge University Press.

Pedersen, Mogens. 1979. "The Dynamics of European Party Systems: Changing Patterns of Electoral Volatility." *European Journal of Political Research* 7 (1): 1–26.

Pevehouse, Jon C., and Joshua S. Goldstein. 2006. *International Cooperation and Regional Conflicts in the Post-Cold War World, 1987–1999.* Ann Arbor, MI: Inter-university Consortium for Political and Social Research.

Pillar, Paul R. 2004. "Intelligence." In *Attacking Terrorism: Elements of a Grand Strategy,* edited by Audrey Kurth Cronin and James M. Ludes. Washington, DC: Georgetown University Press, 115–140.

Piscopo, Jennifer M. 2020. "Women Leaders and Pandemic Performance: A Spurious Correlation." *Politics & Gender* 16 (4): 1–9.

Poast, Paul. 2012. "Does Issue Linkage Work? Evidence from European Alliance Negotiations, 1860 to 1945." *International Organization* 66 (2): 277–310.

Poast, Paul. 2013. "Issue Linkage and International Cooperation: An Empirical Investigation." *Conflict Management and Peace Science* 30 (3): 286–303.

Popovic, Milos. 2017. "Fragile Proxies: Explaining Rebel Defection against Their State Sponsors." *Terrorism and Political Violence* 29 (5): 922–42.

Popovic, Milos. 2018. "Inter-Rebel Alliances in the Shadow of Foreign Sponsors." *International Interactions* 44 (4): 749–76.

Porter, Patrick. 2018. "Why America's Grand Strategy Has Not Changed: Power, Habit, and the US Foreign Policy Establishment." *International Security* 42 (4): 46.

Post, Abigail S., and Paromita Sen. 2020. "Why Can't a Woman Be More Like a Man? Female Leaders in Crisis Bargaining." *International Interactions* 46 (1): 1–27.

Potrafke, Niklas. 2009. "Does Government Ideology Influence Political Alignment with the US? An Empirical Analysis of Voting in the UN General Assembly." *Review of International Organizations* 4 (3): 245–68.

Potter, Philip B. K., and Matthew A. Baum. 2013. "Looking for Audience Costs in All the Wrong Places: Electoral Institutions, Media Access, and Democratic Constraint." *Journal of Politics* 76 (1): 167–81.

Potter, William C. 1980. "Issue Area and Foreign Policy Analysis." *International Organization* 34 (3): 405–27.

Press, Daryl Grayson. 2005. *Calculating Credibility: How Leaders Assess Military Threats.* Ithaca, NY: Cornell University Press.

Pulford, Briony, and Andrew Colman. 2007. "Ambiguous Games: Evidence for Strategic Ambiguity Aversion." *Quarterly Journal of Experimental Psychology* 60 (8): 1083–100.

Putnam, Robert D. 1988. "Diplomacy and Domestic Politics: The Logic of Two-Level Games." *International Organization* 42 (3): 427–60.

Rana, Kishan S. 2015. "Prime Minister Narendra Modi's Visit to China, May 2015." *China Report* 51 (4): 327–38.

Rasler, Karen A., and William R. Thompson. 2006. "Contested Territory, Strategic Rivalries, and Conflict Escalation." *International Studies Quarterly* 50 (1): 145–67.

Rasler, Karen, William R. Thompson, and Sumit Ganguly. 2013. *How Rivalries End.* Philadelphia: University of Pennsylvania Press.

Rathbun, Brian C. 2007. "Uncertain About Uncertainty: Understanding the Multiple Meanings of a Crucial Concept in International Relations Theory." *International Studies Quarterly* 51 (3): 533–57.

Rathbun, Brian C. 2011. "Trust in International Cooperation: International Security Institutions, Domestic Politics and American Multilateralism." Cambridge: Cambridge University Press.

Rathbun, Brian C., Joshua D. Kertzer, and Mark Paradis. 2017. "Homo Diplomaticus: Mixed-Method Evidence of Variation in Strategic Rationality." *International Organization* 71 (S1): S33–60.

Reed, William. 1997. "Alliance Duration and Democracy: An Extension and Cross-Validation of 'Democratic States and Commitment in International Relations.'" *American Journal of Political Science* 41 (3): 1072–78.

Renshon, Jonathan, Allan Dafoe, and Paul Huth. 2018. "Leader Influence and Reputation Formation in World Politics." *American Journal of Political Science* 62 (2): 325–39.

Reuveny, R., and H. Kang. 1996. "International Conflict and Cooperation: Splicing COPDAB and WEIS Series." *International Studies Quarterly* 40 (2): 281–305.

Reynolds, Rosalind R. 1995. *Nuclear Proliferation: The Diplomatic Role of Non-Weaponized Programs*. Proliferation Series. Vol. 7. Chicago: International Studies Association.

Roberts, Kenneth, and Erik Wibbels. 1999. "Party Systems and Electoral Volatility in Latin America: A Test of Economic, Institutional, and Structural Explanations." *American Political Science Review* 93 (3): 575–90.

Roese, Neal J., and Kathleen D. Vohs. 2012. "Hindsight Bias." *Perspectives on Psychological Science* 7 (5): 411–26.

Rokkan, Stein. 1967. "Geography, Religion, and Social Class: Cross-Cutting Cleavages in Norwegian Politics." In *Party Systems and Voter Alignments. International Yearbook of Political Behaviour Research*, vol. 7, edited by Seymour M. Lipset and Stein Rokkan, 367–444. New York: Free Press.

Rose, Andrew. 2005. "Does the WTO Make Trade More Stable?" *Open Economies Review* 16 (1): 7–22.

Rose, Gideon. 1998. "Neoclassical Realism and Theories of Foreign Policy." *World Politics* 51 (1): 144–72.

Rosenau, James N. 1990. *Turbulence in World Politics: A Theory of Change and Continuity*. Princeton, NJ: Princeton University Press.

Ross, Jeffrey. 2012. *An Introduction to Political Crime*. Bristol: Policy Press.

Ross, Robert S., and Changbin Jiang. 2001. *Re-Examining the Cold War: US-China Diplomacy, 1954–1973*. Cambridge, MA: Harvard University Asia Center.

Sagan, Scott D., and Jeremi Suri. 2003. "The Madman Nuclear Alert: Secrecy, Signaling, and Safety in October 1969." *International Security* 27 (4): 150–83.

Salehyan, Idean, Kristian Skrede Gleditsch, and David E. Cunningham. 2011. "Explaining External Support for Insurgent Groups." *International Organization* 65 (4): 744.

Saltzman, Ilai Z. 2015. "Growing Pains: Neoclassical Realism and Japan's Security Policy Emancipation." *Contemporary Security Policy* 36 (3): 498–527.

San-Akca, Belgin. 2016. *States in Disguise: Causes of State Support for Rebel Groups*. Oxford: Oxford University Press.

Sartori, Anne E. 2013. *Deterrence by Diplomacy*. Princeton, NJ: Princeton University Press.

Sartori, Giovanni. 1970. "Concept Misformation in Comparative Politics." *American Political Science Review* 64 (4): 1033–53.

Saunders, Elizabeth N. 2011. *Leaders at War: How Presidents Shape Military Interventions.* Ithaca, NY: Cornell University Press.

Schedler, Andreas. 2012. "Judgment and Measurement in Political Science." *Perspectives on Politics* 10 (1): 21–36.

Schelling, Thomas C. 1980. *The Strategy of Conflict.* Cambridge, MA: Harvard University Press.

Schelling, Thomas C. 2006. *Micromotives and Macrobehavior.* New York: W. W. Norton & Company.

Schmidt, Cody J., Bomi K. Lee, and Sara McLaughlin Mitchell. 2021. "Climate Bones of Contention: How Climate Variability Influences Territorial, Maritime, and River Interstate Conflicts." *Journal of Peace Research* 58 (1): 132–50.

Schrodt, Philip. 2007. "Inductive Event Data Scaling Using Item Response Theory." Summer Meeting of the Society for Political Methodology. Pennsylvania State University, State College, PA.

Schultz, Kenneth A. 2012. "Why We Needed Audience Costs and What We Need Now." *Security Studies* 21 (3): 369–75.

Schwartenbeck, Philipp, Thomas H. B. FitzGerald, Christoph Mathys, Ray Dolan, Martin Kronbichler, and Karl Friston. 2015. "Evidence for Surprise Minimization over Value Maximization in Choice Behavior." *Nature Scientific Reports* 5: 16575).

Schweller, Randall L. 1994. "Bandwagoning for Profit: Bringing the Revisionist State Back In." *International Security* 19 (1): 72–107.

Schweller, Randall L. 2004. "Unanswered Threats: A Neoclassical Realist Theory of Underbalancing." *International Security* 29 (2): 159–201.

Selway, Joel Sawat. 2011. "The Measurement of Cross-Cutting Cleavages and Other Multidimensional Cleavage Structures." *Political Analysis* 19 (1): 48–65.

Shambaugh, David. 1996. "Containment or Engagement of China? Calculating Beijing's Responses." *International Security* 21 (2): 180–209.

Shannon, Claude E. 1948. "A Mathematical Theory of Communication." *Bell System Technical Journal* 27 (3): 379–423.

Shellman, S. M. 2004. "Time Series Intervals and Statistical Inference: The Effects of Temporal Aggregation on Event Data Analysis." *Political Analysis* 12 (1): 97–104.

Sikk, Allan. 2005. "How Unstable? Volatility and the Genuinely New Parties in Eastern Europe." *European Journal of Political Research* 44 (3): 391–412.

Simmons, Beth A. 1998. "Compliance with International Agreements." *Annual Review of Political Science* 1 (1): 75–93.

Simmons, Beth A. 2002. "Capacity, Commitment, and Compliance: International Institutions and Territorial Disputes." *Journal of Conflict Resolution* 46 (6): 829–56.

Simmons, Beth A., and Allison Danner. 2010. "Credible Commitments and the International Criminal Court." *International Organization* 64 (2): 225–56.

Singer, J. David. 1982. "Confrontational Behavior and Escalation to War 1816–1980: A Research Plan." *Journal of Peace Research* 19 (1): 37–48.

Singer, J. David. 1988. "Reconstructing the Correlates of War Dataset on Material Capabilities of States, 1816–1985." *International Interactions* 14 (2): 115–32.

Singer, J. David, Stuart Bremer, and John Stuckey. 1972. "Capability Distribution, Uncertainty, and Major Power War, 1820–1965." In *Peace, War, and Numbers*, edited by Bruce M. Russett, 19–48. Beverly Hills, CA: Sage.

Singh, Sonali, and Christopher R. Way. 2004. "The Correlates of Nuclear Proliferation: A Quantitative Test." *Journal of Conflict Resolution* 48 (6): 859–85.

Slantchev, Branislav L. 2006. "Politicians, the Media, and Domestic Audience Costs." *International Studies Quarterly* 50 (2): 445–77.

Smith, Sheila A. 2015. *Intimate Rivals: Japanese Domestic Politics and a Rising China*. New York: Columbia University Press.

Smoke, Richard. 1977. *Controlling Escalation*. Cambridge, MA: Harvard University Press.

Snyder, Glenn. 1965. "The Balance of Power and the Balance of Terror." In *The Balance of Power*, edited by Paul Seabury, 114–26. San Francisco: Chandler.

Snyder, Glenn H. 1984. "The Security Dilemma in Alliance Politics." *World Politics* 36 (4): 461–95.

Snyder, Jack L. 1991. *Myths of Empire: Domestic Politics and International Ambition*. Ithaca, NY: Cornell University Press.

Solingen, Etel. 1994. "The Political Economy of Nuclear Restraint." *International Security* 19 (2): 126–69.

Solingen, Etel. 2007. "Pax Asiatica Versus Bella Levantina: The Foundations of War and Peace in East Asia and the Middle East." *American Political Science Review* 101 (4): 757–80.

Staniland, Paul. 2014. *Networks of Rebellion: Explaining Insurgent Cohesion and Collapse*. Ithaca, NY: Cornell University Press.

Stein, Janice Gross. 2010. "Crisis Behavior: Miscalculation, Escalation, and Inadvertent War." In *The International Studies Encyclopedia*, edited by Robert A. Denemark and Renée Marlin-Bennett, Vol. III, 1320–27. London: International Studies Association/ Wiley-Blackwell.

Stenslie, Stig, and Gang Chen. 2016. "Xi Jinping's Grand Strategy: From Vision to Implementation." In *China in the Era of Xi Jinping: Domestic and Foreign Policy Challenges*, edited by Robert S. Ross and Jo Inge Bekkevold, 117–36. Washington DC: Georgetown University Press..

Sterling-Folker, Jennifer. 2009. "Neoclassical Realism and Identity: Peril Despite Profit across the Taiwan Strait." In *Neoclassical Realism, the State, and Foreign Policy*, edited by Steven E. Lobell, Norrin M. Ripsman, and Jeffrey W. Taliaferro, 91–138. Cambridge: Cambridge University Press.

Stewart, Megan A. 2018. "Civil War as State-Making: Strategic Governance in Civil War." *International Organization* 72 (1): 205–26.

Stoll, Richard J. 1984. "The Guns of November Presidential Reelections and the Use of Force, 1947–1982." *Journal of Conflict Resolution* 28 (2): 231–46.

Stratmann, Thomas. 1992. "The Effects of Logrolling on Congressional Voting." *American Economic Review* 82 (5): 1162–76.

Sullivan, Patricia L., and Johannes Karreth. 2015. "The Conditional Impact of Military Intervention on Internal Armed Conflict Outcomes." *Conflict Management and Peace Science* 32 (3): 269–88.

Szekely, Ora. 2016. "A Friend in Need: The Impact of the Syrian Civil War on Syria's Clients (A Principal–Agent Approach)." *Foreign Policy Analysis* 12 (3): 450–68.

Tang, Shiping. 2005. "Reputation, Cult of Reputation, and International Conflict." *Security Studies* 14 (1): 34–62.

Tang, Shiping. 2008. "Fear in International Politics: Two Positions." *International Studies Review* 10 (3): 451–71.

Tellis, Ashley J., Janice Bially, Christopher Layne, and Melissa McPherson. 2000. *Measuring National Power in the Postindustrial Age*. Santa Monica, CA: RAND Corporation.

Tessman, Brock F. 2012. "System Structure and State Strategy: Adding Hedging to the Menu." *Security Studies* 21 (2): 192–231.

Thompson, William R. 1999. *Great Power Rivalries*. Columbia: University of South Carolina Press.

Thompson, William R. 2001. "Identifying Rivals and Rivalries in World Politics." *International Studies Quarterly* 45 (4): 557–86.

Thompson, William R. 2003. "A Streetcar Named Sarajevo: Catalysts, Multiple Causation Chains, and Rivalry Structures." *International Studies Quarterly* 47 (3): 474.

Thomson, Catarina P. 2016. "Public Support for Economic and Military Coercion and Audience Costs." *British Journal of Politics and International Relations* 18 (2): 407–21.

Thyne, Clayton L. 2009. *How International Relations Affect Civil Conflict: Cheap Signals, Costly Consequences*. Washington, DC: Rowman & Littlefield.

Tilly, Charles. 2001. "Mechanisms in Political Processes." *Annual Review of Political Science* 4 (1): 21–41.

Tilly, Charles, and Robert E. Goodin. 2006. "It Depends." In *The Oxford Handbook of Contextual Political Analysis*, edited by E. Robert, 3–32. Oxford: Oxford University Press.

Tollison, Robert D., and Thomas D. Willett. 1979. "An Economic Theory of Mutually Advantageous Issue Linkages in International Negotiations." *International Organization* 33 (4): 425–49.

Tomz, Michael. 2007. "Domestic Audience Costs in International Relations: An Experimental Approach." *International Organization* 61 (4): 821–40.

Toukan, Mark. 2017. *International Politics by Other Means: Interstate Rivalries and the Escalation of Civil Conflicts*. Madison: University of Wisconsin.

Trubowitz, Peter. 1992. "Sectionalism and American Foreign Policy: The Political Geography of Consensus and Conflict." *International Studies Quarterly* 36 (2): 173–90.

Trubowitz, Peter. 1998. *Defining the National Interest: Conflict and Change in American Foreign Policy*. Chicago: University of Chicago Press.

Tsebelis, George. 2011. *Veto Players: How Political Institutions Work*. Princeton, NJ: Princeton University Press.

Tunsjø, Øystein. 2013. *Security and Profit in China's Energy Policy: Hedging against Risk*. New York: Columbia University Press.

Uslaner, Eric M. 2002. *The Moral Foundations of Trust*. Cambridge: Cambridge University Press.

Viscusi, Kip, and Harrell Chesson. 1999. "Hopes and Fears: The Conflicting Effects of Risk and Ambiguity." *Theory and Decision* 47 (2): 157–84.

Von Stein, Jana. 2005. "Do Treaties Constrain or Screen? Selection Bias and Treaty Compliance." *American Political Science Review* 99 (4): 611–22.

Walt, Stephen M. 1990. *The Origins of Alliance*. Ithaca, NY: Cornell University Press.

Waltz, Kenneth N. 1959. *Man, the State and War*. New York: Columbia University Press.

Waltz, Kenneth N. 1979. *Theory of International Politics*. New York: McGraw-Hill.

Ward, Michael. 1981. "Seasonality, Reaction, Expectation, Adaptation, and Memory in Cooperative and Conflictual Foreign Policy Behavior." *International Interactions* 8 (3): 229–45.

Warner, Jeroen Frank. 2016. "Of River Linkage and Issue Linkage: Transboundary Conflict and Cooperation on the River Meuse." *Globalizations* 13 (6): 741–66.

Weeks, Jessica L. 2008. "Autocratic Audience Costs: Regime Type and Signaling Resolve." *International Organization* 62 (1): 35–64.

Weeks, Jessica L. 2012. "Strongmen and Straw Men: Authoritarian Regimes and the Initiation of International Conflict." *American Political Science Review* 1 (1): 1–22.

Weeks, Jessica L. 2014. *Dictators at War and Peace*. Ithaca, NY: Cornell University Press.

Weinstein, Jeremy M. 2006. *Inside Rebellion: The Politics of Insurgent Violence*. Cambridge: Cambridge University Press.

Weisiger, Alex, and Keren Yarhi-Milo. 2015. "Revisiting Reputation: How Past Actions Matter in International Politics." *International Organization* 69 (2): 473–95.

Weiss, Jessica Chen. 2013. "Authoritarian Signaling, Mass Audiences, and Nationalist Protest in China." *International Organization* 67 (1): 1–35.

Wendt, Alexander. 1999. *Social Theory of International Politics*. Cambridge: Cambridge University Press.

Whaley, Robert E. 2000. "The Investor Fear Gauge." *Journal of Portfolio Management* 26 (3): 12–17.

Wheeler, Nicholas J. 2009. "Beyond Waltz's Nuclear World: More Trust May Be Better." *International Relations* 23 (3): 428–45.

Williams, Philip Maynard. 1958. *Politics in Post-War France: Parties and the Constitution in the Fourth Republic*. London: Longmans, Green and Company.

Windrow, Martin. 2013. *The French Indochina War 1946–54*. London: Bloomsbury Publishing.

Wohlforth, William C. 1999. "The Stability of a Unipolar World." *International Security* 24 (1): 5–41.

Wohlstetter, Roberta. 1962. *Pearl Harbor: Warning and Decision*. Redwood City, CA: Stanford University Press.

Wood, Reed M. 2010. "Capability and Strategic Violence against Civilians." *Journal of Peace Research* 47 (5): 601–14.

Wood, Reed M. 2014. "Opportunities to Kill or Incentives for Restraint? Rebel Capabilities, the Origins of Support, and Civilian Victimization in Civil War." *Conflict Management and Peace Science* 31 (5): 461–80.

Yarhi-Milo, Keren, Joshua D. Kertzer, and Jonathan Renshon. 2018. "Tying Hands, Sinking Costs, and Leader Attributes." *Journal of Conflict Resolution* 62 (10): 2150–79.

Zelikow, Philip, and Ernest May. 2018. *Suez Deconstructed: An Interactive Study in Crisis, War, and Peacemaking*. Washington, DC: Brookings Institution Press.

Index

For the benefit of digital users, indexed terms that span two pages (e.g., 52–53) may, on occasion, appear on only one of those pages.

Tables and figures are indicated by *t* and *f* following the page number

Printed in the USA/Agawam, MA
February 16, 2023

805901.032